Pondering the Word...

THE ANAWIM WAY

Daily Liturgical Meditations

Ash Wednesday to Holy Thursday

February 22 to April 6, 2023
Cycle A - Year 1

D1500685

CONTENTS

What is the Anawim Spirituality?

Our spirituality has three essential characteristics:

Liturgical

The Liturgy is the source of our formation. Daily, we draw inspiration from the readings and prayers of the Liturgy, which we understand to be the ponderings of Mary's heart. For this reason, we honor Mary under the title of Our Lady of the Liturgical Life.

Eucharistic

Jesus in the Eucharist is the center of our spirituality. By faithful participation in Holy Mass and frequent Eucharistic Adoration, we are empowered by the Presence of Jesus to go forth to serve the people of God in all the circumstances of life.

Marian

We entrust ourselves to Mary, the mother and model of every Christian. She continually forms us in her spirit of humility, compassion and reconciling love, transforming us into the likeness of Jesus. She shares with us her spiritual motherhood as we are called to bring forth the life of Jesus in others.

If you would like to explore the Anawim Community further, we invite you to contact us.

SEASONAL INTRODUCTION TO LENT

The liturgy has brought us through Advent, Christmas, and Ordinary Time before Lent, always guiding us to a fuller life in Christ. As we pondered words of wisdom for the formation of our minds and hearts, we were brought to experience the power of the real presence of "God with us." We are called to be "one holy people," a "light to the nations." Now the liturgy guides us through the Season of Lent, a period of "forty days" which represents our ascetical journey of life.

The Lenten Season is a pilgrimage of faith into our interior life where we meet the Lord and open our hearts to his transforming love. Made aware of the universal affliction of sin in the past few weeks, Lent gives us the grace to deal with the terrible hold it has on our flesh and prescribes the practical asceticism of prayer, fasting, and almsgiving.

When we give alms in love, we strip ourselves of our selfish attachment to physical possessions. In this way we open our hearts, freeing ourselves to receive the gifts of the Spirit. By fasting our senses, we empty ourselves more deeply, leaving us with a sense of privation – a sort of death to the flesh – allowing us to be lifted up by the Spirit to God. When we open our hearts in prayer, the word of God cuts as a two-edged sword, separating our flesh and spirit. The Spirit shows us how we are following the will of the Lord in our lives and how we are not. The Spirit gives us the strength to make the necessary changes in our lives.

Mary guides us in our journey. As we strive for purity of conscience, she walks with us, encouraging us to remain in the crosses of our life, that we may be washed by the Blood of the Lamb and emerge as a new creation.

From the writings of Fr. Francis J. Marino, S.M.
Founder of the Anawim Community

Ash Wednesday

"Take care not to perform righteous deeds in order that people may see them; otherwise, you will have no recompense from your heavenly Father."

Mathew 6:1

Theme for the Week

We begin the Holy Season of Lent with a day of prayer and fasting. The whole Season is an interior pilgrimage of faith, a grace-filled time to deepen our relationship with the Lord through prayer and the Sacraments, through self-denial and sacrifice, through selfless love and acts of charity. Let us open our hearts during our Lenten journey to the transforming power of the grace the Lord offers us.

The Pope's Message for Lent for 2023 had not been released as of printing of this issue. We have included here his Message from last year.

MESSAGE OF HIS HOLINESS POPE FRANCIS FOR LENT 2022

**"Let us not grow tired of doing good,
for in due time we shall reap our harvest if we do not give up.
So then, while we have the opportunity, let us do good to all"
(Gal 6:9-10)**

Dear Brothers and Sisters,

Lent is a favorable time for personal and community renewal, as it leads us to the Paschal Mystery of the Death and Resurrection of Jesus Christ. For our Lenten journey in 2022, we will do well to reflect on Saint Paul's exhortation to the Galatians: "Let us not grow tired of doing good, for in due time we shall reap our harvest, if we do not give up. So then, while we have the opportunity (*kairós*), let us do good to all" (Gal 6:9-10).

1. Sowing and reaping

In these words, the Apostle evokes the image of sowing and reaping, so dear to Jesus (cf. Mt 13). Saint Paul speaks to us of a *kairós*: an opportune time for sowing goodness in view of a future harvest. What is this "opportune time" for us? Lent is certainly such an opportune time, but so is our entire existence, of which Lent is in some way an image.[1] All too often in our lives, greed, pride and the desire to possess, accumulate and consume have the upper hand, as we see from the story of the foolish man in the Gospel parable, who thought his life was safe and secure because of the abundant grain and goods he had stored in his barns (cf. Lk 12:16-21). Lent invites us to conversion, to a change in mindset, so that life's truth and beauty may be found not so much in possessing as in giving, not so much in accumulating as in sowing and sharing goodness.

The first to sow is God himself, who with great generosity "continues to sow abundant seeds of goodness in our human family" (*Fratelli Tutti*, 54). During Lent we are called to respond to God's gift

---

[1] Cf. St. Augustine, *Serm.* 243, 9,8; 270, 3; *En. in Ps.* 110, 1.

by accepting his word, which is "living and active" (Heb 4:12). Regular listening to the word of God makes us open and docile to his working (cf. Jas 1:21) and bears fruit in our lives. This brings us great joy, yet even more, it summons us to become God's co-workers (cf. 1 Cor 3:9). By making good use of the present time (cf. Eph 5:16), we too can sow seeds of goodness. This call to sow goodness should not be seen as a burden but a grace, whereby the Creator wishes us to be actively united with his own bountiful goodness.

What about the harvest? Do we not sow seeds in order to reap a harvest? Of course! Saint Paul points to the close relationship between sowing and reaping when he says: "Anyone who sows sparsely will reap sparsely as well, and anyone who sows generously will reap generously as well" (2 Cor 9:6). But what kind of harvest are we talking about? A first fruit of the goodness we sow appears in ourselves and our daily lives, even in our little acts of kindness. In God, no act of love, no matter how small, and no "generous effort" will ever be lost (cf. *Evangelii Gaudium*, 279). Just as we recognize a tree by its fruits (cf. Mt 7:16, 20), so a life full of good deeds radiates light (cf. Mt 5:14-16) and carries the fragrance of Christ to the world (cf. 2 Cor 2:15). Serving God in freedom from sin brings forth fruits of sanctification for the salvation of all (cf. Rom 6:22).

In truth, we see only a small portion of the fruits of what we sow, since, according to the Gospel proverb, "one sows, while another reaps" (Jn 4:37). When we sow for the benefit of others, we share in God's own benevolent love: "it is truly noble to place our hope in the hidden power of the seeds of goodness we sow, and thus to initiate processes whose fruits will be reaped by others" (*Fratelli Tutti*, 196). Sowing goodness for the benefit of others frees us from narrow self-interest, infuses our actions with gratuitousness, and makes us part of the magnificent horizon of God's benevolent plan.

The word of God broadens and elevates our vision: it tells us that the real harvest is eschatological, the harvest of the last, undying day. The mature fruit of our lives and actions is "fruit for eternal life" (Jn 4:36), our "treasure in Heaven" (Lk 12:33; 18:22). Jesus himself uses the image of the seed that dies in the ground in order to bear fruit as a symbol of the mystery of his Death and Resurrection (cf. Jn 12:24); while Saint Paul uses the same image to speak of the resurrection of our bodies: "What is sown is perishable, but what is raised is imperishable; what is sown is contemptible, but what is raised is glorious; what is sown is weak, but what is raised is powerful; what is sown is a natural body, and what is raised is a spiritual body" (1 Cor 15:42-44). The hope of resurrection is the great light that the risen Christ brings to the world, for "if our hope in Christ has been for this life only, we are of all people the most pitiable. In fact, however, Christ has been raised from the dead, as the first-fruits of all who have fallen asleep" (1 Cor 15:19-20). Those who are intimately united to him in love "by dying a death like his" (Rom 6:5) will also be united to his Resurrection for eternal life (cf. Jn 5:29). "Then the upright will shine like the sun in the Kingdom of their Father" (Mt 13:43).

2. "Let us not grow tired of doing good"

Christ's Resurrection enlivens earthly hopes with the "great hope" of eternal life, planting the seed of salvation in our present time (cf. Benedict XVI, *Spe Salvi*, 3; 7). Bitter disappointment at shattered dreams, deep concern for the challenges ahead and discouragement at the poverty of our resources, can make us tempted to seek refuge in self-centeredness and indifference to the suffering of others. Indeed, even our best resources have their limitations: "Youths grow tired and weary, the young stumble and fall" (Is 40:30). Yet God "gives strength to the weary, he strengthens the powerless... Those who hope in the Lord will regain their strength, they will soar on wings like eagles; though they run they will not grow weary, though they walk they will never tire" (Is 40:29, 31). The Lenten season calls us to place our faith and hope in the Lord (cf. 1 Pet 1:21), since only if we fix our gaze on the risen Christ (cf. Heb 12:2) will we be able to respond to the Apostle's appeal, "Let us never grow tired of doing good" (Gal 6:9).

Let us not grow tired of praying. Jesus taught us to "pray always without becoming weary" (Lk 18:1). We need to pray because we need God. Thinking that we need nothing other than ourselves is a dangerous illusion. If the pandemic has heightened the awareness of our own personal and social fragility, may this Lent allow us to experience the consolation provided by faith in God, without whom we cannot stand firm (cf. Is 7:9). No one attains salvation alone, since we are all in the same boat, amid the storms of history;[2] and certainly no one reaches salvation without God, for only the Paschal Mystery of Jesus Christ triumphs over the dark waters of death. Faith does not spare us life's burdens and tribulations, but it does allow us to face them in union with God in Christ, with the great hope that does not disappoint, whose pledge is the love that God has poured into our hearts through the Holy Spirit (cf. Rom 5:1-5).

Let us not grow tired of uprooting evil from our lives. May the corporal fasting to which Lent calls us fortify our spirit for the battle against sin. *Let us not grow tired of asking for forgiveness in the Sacrament of Penance and Reconciliation,* knowing that God never tires of forgiving.[3] *Let us not grow tired of fighting against concupiscence,* that weakness which induces to selfishness and all evil, and finds in the course of history a variety of ways to lure men and women into sin (cf. *Fratelli Tutti,* 166). One of these is addiction to the digital media, which impoverishes human relationships. Lent is a propitious time to resist these temptations and to cultivate instead a more integral form of human communication (ibid., 43) made up of "authentic encounters" (ibid., 50), face-to-face and in person.

Let us not grow tired of doing good in active charity towards our neighbors. During this Lent, may we practice almsgiving by giving joyfully (cf. 2 Cor 9:7). God who "supplies seed to the sower and bread for food" (2 Cor 9:10) enables each of us not only to have food to eat, but also to be generous in doing good to others. While it is true that we have our entire life to sow goodness, let us take special advantage of this Lenten season to care for those close to us and to reach out to our brothers and sisters who lie wounded along the path of life (cf. Lk 10:25-37). Lent is a favorable time to seek out – and not to avoid – those in need; to reach out – and not to ignore – those who need a sympathetic ear and a good word; to visit – and not to abandon – those who are lonely. Let us put into practice our call to do good to all, and take time to love the poor and needy, those abandoned and rejected, those discriminated against and marginalized (cf. *Fratelli Tutti,* 193).

---

[2] Cf. *Extraordinary Moment of Prayer presided over by Pope Francis* (27 March 2020).
[3] Cf. *Angelus,* 17 March 2013.

3. "If we do not give up, we shall reap our harvest in due time"

Each year during Lent we are reminded that "goodness, together with love, justice and solidarity, are not achieved once and for all; they have to be realized each day" (ibid., 11). Let us ask God to give us the patient perseverance of the farmer (cf. Jas 5:7), and persevere in doing good, one step at a time. If we fall, let us stretch out our hand to the Father, who always lifts us up. If we are lost, if we are misled by the enticements of the evil one, let us not hesitate to return to God, who "is generous in forgiving" (Is 55:7). In this season of conversion, sustained by God's grace and by the communion of the Church, let us not grow tired of doing good. The soil is prepared by fasting, watered by prayer, and enriched by charity. Let us believe firmly that "if we do not give up, we shall reap our harvest in due time" and that, with the gift of perseverance, we shall obtain what was promised (cf. Heb 10:36), for our salvation and the salvation of others (cf. 1 Tim 4:16). By cultivating fraternal love towards everyone, we are united to Christ, who gave his life for our sake (cf. 2 Cor 5:14-15), and we are granted a foretaste of the joy of the Kingdom of Heaven, when God will be "all in all" (1 Cor 15:28).

May the Virgin Mary, who bore the Savior in her womb and "pondered all these things in her heart" (Lk 2:19), obtain for us the gift of patience. May she accompany us with her maternal presence, so that this season of conversion may bring forth fruits of eternal salvation.

Pope Francis, November 11, 2021
© Copyright 2021 - Libreria Editrice Vaticana

First Reading: Joel 2:12-18

Even now, says the LORD,
   return to me with your whole heart,
     with fasting, and weeping, and mourning;
Rend your hearts, not your garments,
   and return to the LORD, your God.
For gracious and merciful is he,
   slow to anger, rich in kindness,
   and relenting in punishment.
Perhaps he will again relent
   and leave behind him a blessing,
Offerings and libations
   for the LORD, your God.

Blow the trumpet in Zion!
   proclaim a fast,
   call an assembly;
Gather the people,
   notify the congregation;
Assemble the elders,
   gather the children
   and the infants at the breast;
Let the bridegroom quit his room
   and the bride her chamber.
Between the porch and the altar
   let the priests, the ministers of the LORD, weep,
And say, "Spare, O LORD, your people,
   and make not your heritage a reproach,
   with the nations ruling over them!
Why should they say among the peoples,
   'Where is their God?'"

Then the LORD was stirred to concern for his land
   and took pity on his people.

Responsorial Psalm: Psalm 51:3-4, 5-6ab, 12-13, 14 and 17
Be merciful, O Lord, for we have sinned.

Have mercy on me, O God, in your goodness;
 in the greatness of your compassion wipe out my offense.
Thoroughly wash me from my guilt
 and of my sin cleanse me.
R. Be merciful, O Lord, for we have sinned.
For I acknowledge my offense,
 and my sin is before me always:
"Against you only have I sinned,
 and done what is evil in your sight."
R. Be merciful, O Lord, for we have sinned.
A clean heart create for me, O God,
 and a steadfast spirit renew within me.
Cast me not out from your presence,
 and your Holy Spirit take not from me.
R. Be merciful, O Lord, for we have sinned.
Give me back the joy of your salvation,
 and a willing spirit sustain in me.
O Lord, open my lips,
 and my mouth shall proclaim your praise.
R. Be merciful, O Lord, for we have sinned.

Second Reading: 2 Corinthians 5:20-6:2
 Brothers and sisters: We are ambassadors for Christ, as if God were appealing through us. We implore you on behalf of Christ, be reconciled to God. For our sake he made him to be sin who did not know sin, so that we might become the righteousness of God in him.

 `Working together, then, we appeal to you not to receive the grace of God in vain. For he says:
  In an acceptable time I heard you,
   and on the day of salvation I helped you.
Behold, now is a very acceptable time; behold, now is the day of salvation.

Gospel Acclamation: see Psalm 95:8
If today you hear his voice, harden not your hearts.

Gospel: Matthew 6:1-6, 16-18
 Jesus said to his disciples: "Take care not to perform righteous deeds in order that people may see them; otherwise, you will have no recompense from your heavenly Father. When you give alms, do not

blow a trumpet before you, as the hypocrites do in the synagogues and in the streets to win the praise of others. Amen, I say to you, they have received their reward. But when you give alms, do not let your left hand know what your right is doing, so that your almsgiving may be secret. And your Father who sees in secret will repay you.

"When you pray, do not be like the hypocrites, who love to stand and pray in the synagogues and on street corners so that others may see them. Amen, I say to you, they have received their reward. But when you pray, go to your inner room, close the door, and pray to your Father in secret. And your Father who sees in secret will repay you.

"When you fast, do not look gloomy like the hypocrites. They neglect their appearance, so that they may appear to others to be fasting. Amen, I say to you, they have received their reward. But when you fast, anoint your head and wash your face, so that you may not appear to be fasting, except to your Father who is hidden. And your Father who sees what is hidden will repay you."

Meditation:

God created us so that we may enjoy his presence for all eternity in Heaven. It is for this reason that Jesus came into this world, so that by the merits of his Passion and Death we may share in the glory of Heaven. And it is for this reason that the Church, through this Season of Lent, invites us to reflect deeply on the goal of our existence here on earth and on how to attain eternal life. Lent can be said to be a Holy Season during which we look forward to the joy of Heaven, the Eternal Easter, and prepare for it with a greater intensity and fervor.

The Liturgy of Ash Wednesday that solemnly begins the Season of Lent very keenly reminds us of our human mortality. With the imposition of the ashes on our head, we are instructed: *remember that you are dust, and to dust you shall return.* This instruction is a sharp reminder that we will die and our bodies will decay. It carries an implied lesson as well: that we are made for an infinitely greater life on the other side of death, and so we need to prepare for it.

The readings of today show us how to prepare not only for the celebration of Easter at the end of this season but also to prepare for the Eternal Easter that is meant to follow our "return to dust." Since it is through the merits of Christ's Passion and Death that we reach the joy of Easter and the Easter of eternal life, our best and most fruitful preparation is to enter into the mystery of his Passion, meditating on it and imitating it in view of the joy of Heaven. Through this prism of the Lord's Passion, we can profitably read, ponder, and interpret the Scripture passages given to us as we solemnly begin this Holy Season.

In today's second reading, St. Paul, keeping our Lord's Passion in mind, as well as our fitting response, makes a heartfelt appeal: "We implore you on behalf of Christ, to be reconciled to God. For our sake he made him to be sin who did not know sin, so that we might become the righteousness of God in him." God willed in his infinite mercy that Christ his Son would suffer and die for our sins so that we may be justified and go to Heaven. So Paul tells us that it is now the "acceptable time" to avail of the merits of the Lord's Passion and to accept the reconciliation that God offers us through him.

To help us embrace God's gift of reconciliation, the Church in her wisdom offers us a most apt first reading today. God, through his prophet Joel, describes to us a path of penance and reconciliation. He says through the prophet: "Return to me with your whole heart, / with fasting, and weeping, and mourning; / Rend your hearts, not your garments, / and return to the LORD, your God." It is an invitation to "return," to accept what he has done for us through his Son Jesus Christ. God wishes to reconcile us to himself, motivated purely by mercy: "For gracious and merciful is he, / slow to anger, rich in kindness, / and relenting in punishment."

In today's Gospel, Jesus teaches us three effective means of returning to the Lord and accepting his reconciliation during this Holy Season: *almsgiving*, *prayer*, and *fasting*. These personal and communal disciplines are not an end in themselves; they are means of combatting our sinful inclinations so that we will more readily turn to God and be reconciled. The traditional practices of *almsgiving*, *prayer*, and *fasting* are our ways of participating in the life of Christ who served us, prayed for us, and suffered and died for us. Now we are privileged to be able to share more deeply in his Passion and Death so that we may share in his glorious Resurrection, the Easter of eternal life.

How am I preparing spiritually to enter the Holy Season of Lent? As the priest marks my forehead with ashes, what is my inner response to my human mortality? How does prayer, almsgiving and fasting deepen my spiritual life?

Mary, guide me on my Lenten journey to the Resurrection.

Introduction to the "Ashen Triduum"

Lent begins with Ash Wednesday, but the First Week of Lent begins with the First Sunday. This leaves the three days between Ash Wednesday and the First Sunday in an unusual liturgical interval; they are part of Lent, but not part of the weeks of Lent. Their official names are simply the Thursday, Friday, and Saturday "after Ash Wednesday."

Fr. Francis, the Founder of the Anawim Community, noting the special character of this liturgical period and its connection to Ash Wednesday, coined a term to describe these days: the "Ashen Triduum." In describing the Ashen Triduum he wrote:

"It is a time after the gathering of Ash Wednesday to come aside and withdraw for three days, to interpret how we are going to proceed for the journey ahead. The focus of these three days is essentially that of a retreat, a time to be alone with oneself before God, to be silent from within, and to take time for prayer and serious reflection."

During this short preparation retreat, we may reflect on the way Jesus prepared for his own "forty days" in the wilderness. His immediate preparation for this period of fasting was his baptism in the Jordan. The Spirit who descended on him was the one who led him into the wilderness to do battle with the Devil. Let us use this triduum, then, as a time to recall the grace of our own Baptism and be strengthened by the Spirit for the demanding forty-day journey ahead.

February 23, Thursday after Ash Wednesday
Saint Polycarp, Bishop and Martyr

 First Reading: Deuteronomy 30:15-20
Moses said to the people: "Today I have set before you life and prosperity, death and doom. If you obey the commandments of the LORD, your God, which I enjoin on you today, loving him, and walking in his ways, and keeping his commandments, statutes and decrees, you will live and grow numerous, and the LORD, your God, will bless you in the land you are entering to occupy. If, however, you turn away your hearts and will not listen, but are led astray and adore and serve other gods, I tell you now that you will certainly perish; you will not have a long life on the land that you are crossing the Jordan to enter and occupy. I call heaven and earth today to witness against you: I have set before you life and death, the blessing and the curse. Choose life, then, that you and your descendants may live, by loving the LORD, your God, heeding his voice, and holding fast to him. For that will mean life for you, a long life for you to live on the land that the LORD swore he would give to your fathers Abraham, Isaac and Jacob."

Responsorial Psalm: Psalm 1:1-2, 3, 4 and 6
Blessed are they who hope in the Lord.
Blessed the man who follows not
    the counsel of the wicked
Nor walks in the way of sinners,
    nor sits in the company of the insolent,
But delights in the law of the LORD
    and meditates on his law day and night.
R. Blessed are they who hope in the Lord.
He is like a tree
    planted near running water,
That yields its fruit in due season,
    and whose leaves never fade.
    Whatever he does, prospers.
R. Blessed are they who hope in the Lord.
Not so the wicked, not so;
    they are like chaff which the wind drives away.
For the LORD watches over the way of the just,
    but the way of the wicked vanishes.
R. Blessed are they who hope in the Lord.

Gospel Acclamation: Matthew 4:17
Repent, says the Lord; the Kingdom of heaven is at hand.

✝ Gospel: Luke 9:22-25

Jesus said to his disciples: "The Son of Man must suffer greatly and be rejected by the elders, the chief priests, and the scribes, and be killed and on the third day be raised."

Then he said to all, "If anyone wishes to come after me, he must deny himself and take up his cross daily and follow me. For whoever wishes to save his life will lose it, but whoever loses his life for my sake will save it. What profit is there for one to gain the whole world yet lose or forfeit himself?"

Meditation:

We have entered into the beautiful and profound Season of Lent, a time of grace and conversion. These first days of Lent present us with an opportunity to reflect on our Lenten journey and orient it in the direction in which God is calling us. Yesterday we were given the fundamental disciplines of prayer, fasting, and almsgiving. We were reminded that we will all return to dust; we will all die someday. Today Jesus speaks to us about a different kind of "death," a death that we are to embrace daily, what he calls *losing our life for his sake.*

Since our time here on earth is limited, not infinite, we have to face questions involving life and death. We ask: "What should I do with this life? How can I best save my life?" As followers of Jesus Christ we ask another question: "What does *God* want me to do with his gift of life?" We must make a fundamental decision: *Am I going to live for God or against him?*

In today's first reading, Moses makes clear the implications of this most basic choice – *for* God or *against* him. He explains that being for God means obeying him, loving him, and walking in his ways, as we keep his commandments. It is not simply a matter of putting on a show of religiosity; it is a choice that involves our whole being, our whole life. The choice for God is the choice for life itself.

When we make choices that are not in agreement with God's will – that is, when we sin – we are actually choosing death. Moses' words give a sense of urgency to our Lenten journey. "*Today* I have set before you life and prosperity, death and doom." We must make a decision *today*: life or death, blessing or curse. Now is the time to change our path; now is the time to decide for God. "Choose life, then, that you and your descendants may live, by loving the LORD, your God, heeding his voice, and holding fast to him."

The Gospel deepens our understanding of what this choice for God means. It is a choice to follow Jesus, the Way, the Truth, and the Life. When we follow the One who suffered, died, and rose again, we are making the decision to lose our lives for his sake. Therefore, the choice for life is paradoxically also a choice for death. It is a choice to deny ourselves, take up our cross daily, and follow in the Lord's steps. The choice for life – real life, eternal life with God – means denying ourselves anything that threatens that life.

We are naturally intimidated by any mention of suffering or death, which never seem to be a way to life. To overcome this natural fear, we can find support in the lives and prayers of the Saints. Today's example is that of the great martyr of the early Church, St. Polycarp. In the lives of the Saints we see the very pattern that Jesus sets forth for us – self-denial, carrying the cross, losing of life for his sake. But we also see the conclusion to which this process leads: not death but eternal life in glory! The cross of suffering is not an end in itself but a means to a much greater goal. Lent gives us the opportunity to sharpen our spiritual perspective on where we are really going and how to get there. It is important for us to know from the start the true meaning of making the choice for God and for life.

> *In what spirit am I carrying my cross and accepting life's burdens? What can I do to overcome my fear of death? How does the Cross of Jesus become my identity or mark as a Christian?*

Mary, help me to always choose to follow Jesus.
St. Polycarp, pray for us.

Polycarp was born around 69. He was baptized by the Apostle John and became one of his disciples. Later, as Bishop of Smyrna (in present-day western Turkey), he was a revered leader who fought the heresy of Gnosticism (a belief system that considered the material world evil). Only one of the many letters he wrote has survived, the one to the Church of Philippi, Macedonia. In 155, at age 86, during the Roman persecution of Christians in Smyrna, Polycarp was burned alive in the local stadium, but the flames did not harm him. He was finally killed by a dagger and his body burned. St. Ignatius of Antioch, one of his friends, said of him, "His mind is grounded in God as on an immovable rock."

First Reading: Isaiah 58:1-9a

Thus says the Lord GOD:
    Cry out full-throated and unsparingly,
      lift up your voice like a trumpet blast;
Tell my people their wickedness,
      and the house of Jacob their sins.
They seek me day after day,
      and desire to know my ways,
Like a nation that has done what is just
      and not abandoned the law of their God;
They ask me to declare what is due them,
      pleased to gain access to God.
"Why do we fast, and you do not see it?
      afflict ourselves, and you take no note of it?"

Lo, on your fast day you carry out your own pursuits,
      and drive all your laborers.
Yes, your fast ends in quarreling and fighting,
      striking with wicked claw.
Would that today you might fast
      so as to make your voice heard on high!
Is this the manner of fasting I wish,
      of keeping a day of penance:
That a man bow his head like a reed
      and lie in sackcloth and ashes?
Do you call this a fast,
      a day acceptable to the LORD?
This, rather, is the fasting that I wish:
      releasing those bound unjustly,
      untying the thongs of the yoke;
Setting free the oppressed,
      breaking every yoke;
Sharing your bread with the hungry,
      sheltering the oppressed and the homeless;
Clothing the naked when you see them,
      and not turning your back on your own.
Then your light shall break forth like the dawn,
      and your wound shall quickly be healed;

Your vindication shall go before you,
and the glory of the LORD shall be your rear guard.
Then you shall call, and the LORD will answer,
you shall cry for help, and he will say: Here I am!

Responsorial Psalm: Psalm 51:3-4, 5-6ab, 18-19
A heart contrite and humbled, O God, you will not spurn.

Have mercy on me, O God, in your goodness;
in the greatness of your compassion wipe out my offense.
Thoroughly wash me from my guilt
and of my sin cleanse me.

R. A heart contrite and humbled, O God, you will not spurn.

For I acknowledge my offense,
and my sin is before me always:
"Against you only have I sinned,
and done what is evil in your sight."

R. A heart contrite and humbled, O God, you will not spurn.

For you are not pleased with sacrifices;
should I offer a burnt offering, you would not accept it.
My sacrifice, O God, is a contrite spirit;
a heart contrite and humbled, O God, you will not spurn.

R. A heart contrite and humbled, O God, you will not spurn.

Gospel Acclamation: see Amos 5:14
Seek good and not evil so that you may live, and the Lord will be with you.

Gospel: Matthew 9:14-15
The disciples of John approached Jesus and said, "Why do we and the Pharisees fast much, but your disciples do not fast?" Jesus answered them, "Can the wedding guests mourn as long as the bridegroom is with them? The days will come when the bridegroom is taken away from them, and then they will fast."

Meditation:
We learned on Ash Wednesday that we must take on three basic Lenten disciplines: prayer, fasting, and almsgiving (or mercy). St. Peter Chrysologus teaches that these three cannot be separated. "If you have only one of them or not all together, you have nothing. So if you pray, fast; if you fast, show mercy" (*Sermon* 43; cf. *Liturgy of the Hours*, Office of Rdgs.,Tues., 3rd Week of Lent). With this awareness, today we focus on one of the three disciplines: *fasting*. This is fitting,

for on Fridays of Lent we traditionally practice a particular form of fasting, abstinence from meat. In order to practice fasting properly, we need an appreciation of its meaning and value.

The Gospel tells us that the disciples of John the Baptist had a question for Jesus about this very topic: "Why do we and the Pharisees fast much, but your disciples do not fast?" Their puzzlement was based on their customary understanding of the practices of self-denial. It seemed to them that Jesus' disciples were not very serious about their discipleship, that they were taking an easy, comfortable route. Little did they realize that the self-denial Jesus calls for is much more challenging than what they were practicing. It is never easy to fast from food, but it is much harder to take up one's cross and deny one's very self.

Jesus' reply to the questioners shows that, in focusing on the disciples, they were missing the most important factor of all: the arrival of the Master. With the coming of Jesus, an entirely new situation has come about, one that changes everything. The fasting of the past was appropriate for the past, in the time of waiting and preparing for the arrival of the Groom, but now that the Groom has arrived – that is, Jesus himself – it is inappropriate to fast. It would even be insulting: "Can the wedding guests mourn as long as the Bridegroom is with them?"

Jesus does not say that we should not fast at all. He indicates that there will be a time for fasting – when the Groom is taken away. He is referring to the approaching days of his Passion and Death. The strict fast we practice on Good Friday is in part inspired by these words of Jesus.

But now that Jesus is risen, he will never again be "taken away" from us. He himself said, "Behold, I am with you always, until the end of the age" (Mt 28:20). Then, we may well ask, why should we fast anymore? The answer lies in the fact that although Jesus is always with us, we are not always with him. We are easily distracted. Our hearts turn to various created things, to which we become attached. We have our prejudices and preferences, our habits and our vices. We need to fast because we need to be set free from the incessant demands of the flesh in order to follow the Lord, in order to enter into the joy of being with the Groom.

The first reading identifies for us very clearly the sort of fasting that we must still practice. Isaiah explains that fasting is not simply a matter of denying ourselves food; it is not mere external observance. In those days, the people *were* fasting – but they were also quarreling and fighting and oppressing their employees. They were fulfilling their religious obligations, but they were not changing their hearts. That sort of fasting is of no value at all! The Lord proposes an alternative: "This is the fasting that I wish…." Then he lists a number of works of mercy. Fasting, then, is not only about food, but about being obedient to God and being compassionate to our neighbor, especially those most in need. This kind of fasting never goes out of season!

During this Season of Lent, as we take on the practice of personal sacrifices and self-denial, let us at the same time translate these disciplines into acts of kindness toward others. The time we save by giving up some of our daily pastimes can become more time with our family. The money we save by denying ourselves some food can be shared with the poor. The material things that we really do not need are meant to benefit others who do need them. Our fasting should never diminish our love for our neighbor; it should enrich it. Let us deny ourselves in ways that God desires in order to be united more deeply with him and more dedicated to what is truly good for our brothers and sisters.

> *What do I need to fast from this Lenten season? How has fasting deepened my relationship with God? When do I find it difficult to be compassionate towards others?*

Mary, teach me how I can take on and practice the Lenten disciplines of fasting and mercy.

Notes

First Reading: Isaiah 58:9b-14

Thus says the LORD:
If you remove from your midst oppression,
false accusation and malicious speech;
If you bestow your bread on the hungry
and satisfy the afflicted;
Then light shall rise for you in the darkness,
and the gloom shall become for you like midday;
Then the LORD will guide you always
and give you plenty even on the parched land.
He will renew your strength,
and you shall be like a watered garden,
like a spring whose water never fails.
The ancient ruins shall be rebuilt for your sake,
and the foundations from ages past you shall raise up;
"Repairer of the breach," they shall call you,
"Restorer of ruined homesteads."

If you hold back your foot on the sabbath
from following your own pursuits on my holy day;
If you call the sabbath a delight,
and the LORD's holy day honorable;
If you honor it by not following your ways,
seeking your own interests, or speaking with malice –
Then you shall delight in the LORD,
and I will make you ride on the heights of the earth;
I will nourish you with the heritage of Jacob, your father,
for the mouth of the LORD has spoken.

Responsorial Psalm: Psalm 86:1-2, 3-4, 5-6
Teach me your way, O Lord, that I may walk in your truth.

Incline your ear, O LORD; answer me,
for I am afflicted and poor.
Keep my life, for I am devoted to you;
save your servant who trusts in you.
You are my God.

R. Teach me your way, O Lord, that I may walk in your truth.

27

Have mercy on me, O Lord,
      for to you I call all the day.
Gladden the soul of your servant,
      for to you, O Lord, I lift up my soul.
R. Teach me your way, O Lord, that I may walk in your truth.
For you, O Lord, are good and forgiving,
      abounding in kindness to all who call upon you.
Hearken, O LORD, to my prayer
      and attend to the sound of my pleading.
R. Teach me your way, O Lord, that I may walk in your truth.

Gospel Acclamation: Ezekiel 33:11
I take no pleasure in the death of the wicked man, says the Lord, but rather in his conversion, that he may live.

Gospel: Luke 5:27-32
Jesus saw a tax collector named Levi sitting at the customs post. He said to him, "Follow me." And leaving everything behind, he got up and followed him. Then Levi gave a great banquet for him in his house, and a large crowd of tax collectors and others were at table with them. The Pharisees and their scribes complained to his disciples, saying, "Why do you eat and drink with tax collectors and sinners?" Jesus said to them in reply, "Those who are healthy do not need a physician, but the sick do. I have not come to call the righteous to repentance but sinners."

Meditation:
"Teach me your way, O Lord...." This Psalm response expresses the cry of our hearts as we enter into the great Season of Lent. As we come to the third day of the preparatory "Lenten Triduum," we realize that we have very much to learn about the Lord's way. So we beg the Lord to teach us his way, and we pray: "Incline your ear, O LORD; answer me, / for I am afflicted and poor." One of the ways the Lord answers our longing for his guidance is through the daily Liturgy. If we can attend daily Mass during Lent, we can receive abundant grace and instruction. If we cannot, we can still ponder the readings of each day, and these will guide us throughout the Lenten journey.

In Lent the Lord calls us to repentance, to a radical change of heart, a radical change in the way we live. In the first reading, Isaiah gives us wisdom about how this change can actually take place. The power to change comes from God, but we must open the door to him. If we repent of our sin, then the Lord will bless us abundantly. His mercy is "like a spring whose water never fails." If we turn away from violating the Lord's law, then he will make us "repairers of the breach," "restorers of ruined homesteads." A *breach* is a gap, an opening in the wall of defense; it allows the enemy to enter. The breach that must be repaired is the breach in our hearts, through which sin has entered. The *ruined homestead* is a description of our own interior life, the dwelling place of God which has been ruined by sin. Our inner homestead is restored by way of repentance; the breach is repaired by our decision to trust in God and change our lives. Then he does the rest, through the power of his mercy.

Levi, also known as Matthew, is a model of someone who discovers the way of restoration and becomes a joyous follower of Jesus. Today's Gospel tells the beautiful story of his conversion. Levi is a tax collector, a profession notorious for dishonest practices, known to attract thieves. His conversion from tax collector to disciple can be seen in three simple stages. First we see Levi in his natural condition, *sitting*: sitting in worldliness and greed, stuck in sin, in the darkness of his ignorance. The empty promises and false security that come with the allure of money have a firm hold upon him. Next Jesus comes and says, "*Follow me.*" He breaks through the darkness and summons Levi to freedom, to a whole new way of life. The third stage depends on Levi's decision to answer the call. He *got up* – "leaving everything behind, he got up and followed him."

Levi's conversion reveals a pattern for us to follow throughout the whole Lenten journey. Ash Wednesday found us sitting, stuck in sin. We heard the voice of the Lord calling us to follow him: "Turn away from sin and be faithful to the Gospel." Now we are to get up and become Jesus' follower – a basic, simple idea, but not so easy to do. In our fallen condition, we have a strange capacity to move quickly from condemning ourselves to canonizing ourselves. When we are in sin, we may be tempted by despair, thinking we can never get better, and that no one can help us. That is why we cling to sin, even though it makes us miserable. When we forget our sin condition, we think we are already fine, often secretly judging that we are better than others. So, instead of going from sinner to disciple, we go from tax collector to Pharisee.

If we are standing in judgment of the sins of others, believing that the problem is in them but not in us, then we are really Pharisees. Full of self-righteousness, we look down at the "terrible sinners" we see around us. It is easy to fall into this sin because we like to look good in our own eyes. But self-righteousness is a sure sign of pride, the deadliest sin of all. It leaves us sick yet unwilling to admit our need for a doctor.

Jesus prods our pharisaical hearts with this statement: "I have not come to call the righteous to repentance but sinners." In other words, if we want to respond to his invitation to follow him, we must admit that we are sinners. Refusal to acknowledge our sin condition leaves us unable to receive the mercy Jesus offers us. As a result, nothing happens – no progress, no healing. All our pious Lenten practices are fruitless if we do not admit we are sinners in need of the mercy of Jesus Christ.

Levi shows us that the right way to relate to our fellow sinners, our brothers and sisters, is not to judge them but to befriend them, and invite them to join us in the company of Jesus. Jesus does not exclude anyone who wants to join his "great banquet," so we should not exclude them either.

We need the grace of Lent because our journey of conversion is not yet finished. The Lord calls us – today and every day – to turn away from sin and embrace the Good News, letting his grace penetrate more deeply into our hearts. As we hear Jesus saying to us today, "Follow me," let us get up, leave our sin behind and follow him.

How does pondering the readings of each day guide me spiritually throughout my Lenten journey? What is the radical change in my life that I am asking the Lord for guidance during this Lent? How does my self-righteousness hinder me from true repentance?

Mary, grant me the grace this Lent to ask forgiveness my sins and to forgive those who have wronged me.

First Week of Lent

A clean heart create for me, O God,
and a steadfast spirit renew within me.

Psalm 51:10

Theme for the Week

We begin the first week of the grace-filled Season of Lent full of hope for a glorious outcome of our difficult desert journey, a journey of penance and conversion. In the trials and temptations we will face, we rely on the power of Jesus' victory over Satan, sin, and death. With confidence we pray, "A clean heart create for me, O God, and a steadfast spirit renew within me."

THE WORD OF GOD IS MORE POWERFUL
THAN THE DEVIL
A Spiritual Reflection by Pope Francis

On this first Sunday of Lent, the Gospel (cf. Mt 4:1-11) narrates that, after being baptized in the River Jordan, Jesus "was led up by the Spirit into the wilderness to be tempted by the devil" (v. 1). Jesus prepares himself to begin his mission as proclaimer of the Kingdom of Heaven and, just as Moses and Elijah (cf. Ex 24:18; 1 Kings 19:8) had done in the Old Testament, he does so by fasting for 40 days. He enters into "Lent."

At the end of this period of fasting, the tempter, the devil, breaks in and tries to put Jesus to the test three times. The first temptation arises when Jesus is hungry. The devil suggests, "If you are the Son of God, command these stones to become loaves of bread" (v. 3). A challenge. But Jesus' response is clear: "Man shall not live by bread alone, but by every word that proceeds from the mouth of God" (v. 4). He refers to when Moses reminded the people of their long journey in the desert, through which they learned that their lives depended on the Word of God (cf. Dt 8:3).

The devil then makes a second attempt (vv. 5-6). He becomes more astute, and he too, quotes the Sacred Scripture. The strategy is clear: if you are so confident in God's power, then experience it. For Scripture itself affirms that you will be aided by the angels (v. 6). But also in this case, Jesus does not allow himself to be confounded, because those who believe do not put God to the test, but rather they entrust themselves to God's goodness. Thus, to the words of the Bible that Satan interpreted for his own purposes, Jesus responds with another quotation: "Again it is written; 'You shall not tempt the Lord your God'" (v. 7).

Lastly, the third attempt (vv. 8-9) reveals the devil's true reasoning: since the coming of the Kingdom of Heaven marks the beginning of his own defeat, the evil one wants to distract Jesus from accomplishing his mission by offering him a perspective of political messianism. But Jesus rejects the idolatry of power and human glory and, in the end, drives the tempter away, and says "Begone, Satan! For it is written, 'You shall worship the Lord your God and him only shall you serve'" (v. 10). At this point, the angels draw near to serve Jesus, who is faithful in handing himself over to the Father (cf. v. 11).

This teaches us one thing: Jesus does *not dialogue* with the devil. Jesus responds to the devil *with the Word of God,* not with his own words. In temptation, we often begin to dialogue with temptation, to dialogue with the devil: "yes, I may do this..., then I will go to confession, then this, then that...." We must *never* dialogue with the devil. Jesus does two things with the devil: he either sends him away or, like in this case, he responds with the Word of God. Be attentive to this: *never* dialogue with temptation, *never* dialogue with the devil.

Today too, Satan breaks into people's lives to tempt them with his enticing proposals. He mixes his own voice to the many other voices that try to tame our conscience. Messages come to us from many places, inviting us to "allow ourselves to be tempted," to experience the intoxication of transgression. Jesus' experience teaches us that temptation is an attempt to walk paths that are alternative to those of God. "Do this, there's no problem, then God forgives! One day of joy for yourself ...." "But it is a sin! – No, it is nothing." Alternative paths, paths that give us the impression of self-sufficiency, of enjoying life as an end in itself. However, all this is illusory. We soon realize that the more we distance ourselves from God, the more defenseless and helpless we feel when facing life's big problems.

May the Virgin Mary, the Mother of he who crushed the head of the serpent, help us during this Lenten period to be vigilant when confronted with temptation, not to submit ourselves to any idol of this world, and to follow Jesus in the struggle against evil. Thus we too will be victorious as Jesus.

Pope Francis, Angelus Message, March 1, 2020
© Copyright 2020 - Libreria Editrice Vaticana

First Reading: Genesis 2:7-9; 3:1-7

The LORD God formed man out of the clay of the ground and blew into his nostrils the breath of life, and so man became a living being.

Then the LORD God planted a garden in Eden, in the east, and placed there the man whom he had formed. Out of the ground the LORD God made various trees grow that were delightful to look at and good for food, with the tree of life in the middle of the garden and the tree of the knowledge of good and evil.

Now the serpent was the most cunning of all the animals that the LORD God had made. The serpent asked the woman, "Did God really tell you not to eat from any of the trees in the garden?" The woman answered the serpent: "We may eat of the fruit of the trees in the garden; it is only about the fruit of the tree in the middle of the garden that God said, 'You shall not eat it or even touch it, lest you die.'" But the serpent said to the woman: "You certainly will not die! No, God knows well that the moment you eat of it your eyes will be opened and you will be like gods who know what is good and what is evil." The woman saw that the tree was good for food, pleasing to the eyes, and desirable for gaining wisdom. So she took some of its fruit and ate it; and she also gave some to her husband, who was with her, and he ate it. Then the eyes of both of them were opened, and they realized that they were naked; so they sewed fig leaves together and made loincloths for themselves.

Responsorial Psalm: Psalm 51:3-4, 5-6, 12- 3, 17
Be merciful, O Lord, for we have sinned.

Have mercy on me, O God, in your goodness;
    in the greatness of your compassion wipe out my offense.
Thoroughly wash me from my guilt
    and of my sin cleanse me.
R. Be merciful, O Lord, for we have sinned.
For I acknowledge my offense,
    and my sin is before me always:
"Against you only have I sinned,
    and done what is evil in your sight."
R. Be merciful, O Lord, for we have sinned.

A clean heart create for me, O God,
  and a steadfast spirit renew within me.
Cast me not out from your presence,
  and your Holy Spirit take not from me.
R. Be merciful, O Lord, for we have sinned.
Give me back the joy of your salvation,
  and a willing spirit sustain in me.
O Lord, open my lips,
  and my mouth shall proclaim your praise.
R. Be merciful, O Lord, for we have sinned.

Second Reading: Romans 5:12-19
(Short Form: Romans 5:12, 17-19)

Brothers and sisters: Through one man sin entered the world, and through sin, death, and thus death came to all men, inasmuch as all sinned— for up to the time of the law, sin was in the world, though sin is not accounted when there is no law. But death reigned from Adam to Moses, even over those who did not sin after the pattern of the trespass of Adam, who is the type of the one who was to come.

But the gift is not like the transgression. For if by the transgression of the one, the many died, how much more did the grace of God and the gracious gift of the one man Jesus Christ overflow for the many. And the gift is not like the result of the one who sinned. For after one sin there was the judgment that brought condemnation; but the gift, after many transgressions, brought acquittal. For if, by the transgression of the one, death came to reign through that one, how much more will those who receive the abundance of grace and of the gift of justification come to reign in life through the one Jesus Christ. In conclusion, just as through one transgression condemnation came upon all, so, through one righteous act, acquittal and life came to all. For just as through the disobedience of the one man the many were made sinners, so, through the obedience of the one, the many will be made righteous.

Gospel Acclamation: Matthew 4:4b

One does not live on bread alone, but on every word that comes forth from the mouth of God.

Gospel: Matthew 4:1-11

At that time Jesus was led by the Spirit into the desert to be tempted by the devil. He fasted for forty days and forty nights, and afterwards he was hungry. The tempter approached and said to him, "If you are the Son of God, command that these stones become loaves of bread." He said in reply, "It is written:

> One does not live on bread alone,
> but on every word that comes forth
> from the mouth of God."

Then the devil took him to the holy city, and made him stand on the parapet of the temple, and said to him, "If you are the Son of God, throw yourself down. For it is written:

> He will command his angels concerning you
> and with their hands they will support you,
> lest you dash your foot against a stone."

Jesus answered him, "Again it is written,

> You shall not put the Lord, your God, to the test."

Then the devil took him up to a very high mountain, and showed him all the kingdoms of the world in their magnificence, and he said to him, "All these I shall give to you, if you will prostrate yourself and worship me." At this, Jesus said to him, "Get away, Satan! It is written:

> The Lord, your God, shall you worship
> and him alone shall you serve."

Then the devil left him and, behold, angels came and ministered to him.

Meditation:

On the first Sunday of Lent we turn to the account of Jesus' temptations in the desert. The first line of the Gospel says, "At that time Jesus was led by the Spirit into the desert to be tempted by the devil. He fasted for forty days and forty nights and afterwards he was hungry." We read this passage at the beginning of Lent because the forty days of Jesus in the desert are the reason why Lent lasts for forty days. As he fasted, we fast. The symbolism here goes deeper. The "forty days" are not just forty days; they represent the whole span of our life in this world. The "desert" is not only a desert; it is also a symbol of the world itself as a place of temptation. In the desert, there is the tempter, Satan, who is not a symbol. He is a real angel, a fallen angel, who actively and persistently opposes Jesus and all his followers.

Why did the Spirit lead Jesus into the desert? "To be tempted by the devil." He was in the desert for this very reason, to be tempted and to overcome temptation – and to show us how to overcome temptation. Jesus went there to gain victory over Satan, and to show us how to share in his victory. Everyone is tempted, including Jesus, but not everyone is victorious over temptation. Temptation, we must recall, is not sin; it is an invitation to sin. It is an invitation to consider what appears to us to be a better option. At the core of every temptation is a lie because Satan is a liar. He even lies to Jesus!

The reading from Genesis gives us precious insight into the pattern of temptation. It is the story of the first temptation, experienced by the first man and woman in the garden of Eden. The tempter, symbolized by a serpent, begins by asking the woman a question: "Did God really tell you not to eat from any of the trees in the garden?" It is not an outright lie but a suggestion, a clever way of planting doubt in the mind of the woman. He is trying to make it look like God is withholding something good, and that he is therefore not trustworthy. Once the tempter draws the woman into conversation, then he proposes his lie: "You certainly will not die! No, God knows well that the moment you eat of it your eyes will be opened and you will be like gods who know what is good and what is evil." Here is the temptation: this action will be good for you, even though God said otherwise.

Satan does this to us all the time, and we often fall for it. He invites us to doubt God's goodness and truth. He suggests to us that what is evil is, in fact, good. He presents himself as the one telling the truth. This is the devil's unchanging *modus operandi*. He presents something evil, but makes it look good. Reflection on our own experience of sin exposes the lie. We need only ask ourselves, "Was that sin good for me? Did it make me happy?" If we are honest, we know that sin never fulfills the promise that Satan attaches to it. Perhaps for a moment we have enjoyment, but it is short lived, and in the end we are worse off than before we believed the lie.

In the Gospel, Jesus shows us that we do not have to fall for temptation; we do not have to sin. He shows us how to overcome temptation and win in the contest against Satan. The first step is not to welcome Satan's lies, so that they cannot enter our imagination. Jesus does not accept the lies; he immediately counters them with the truth of God's word. In this week's Spiritual Reflection, Pope Francis explains this: "We must *never* dialogue with the devil. Jesus does two things with the devil: he either sends him away or, like in this case, he responds with the Word of God. Be attentive to this: *never* dialogue with temptation, *never* dialogue with the devil."

To each of the temptations, Jesus responds with a Scripture passage. First, to the suggestion that he should command stones to become loaves of bread, he says, *"One does not live on bread alone, but on every word that comes forth from the mouth of God."* This is a powerful truth for us to hold on to, especially when we feel tempted by materialism, or by cravings to satisfy a physical appetite. When we are longing for physical things, it is often a sign that we are spiritually hungry, starving for the word of God. Lent is a good time to feed daily from the Scriptures. The daily Mass readings during Lent are rich food for our spiritual life. By filling ourselves with the truth of God's word, we gain strength to overcome our cravings for material things.

The second Scripture Jesus quotes to Satan is, *"You shall not put the Lord, your God, to the test."* With this answer he is saying that he is not going to give the devil's suggestion another thought. This is the proper way to respond when we are tempted: a firm decision not even to consider what is wrong. Why should we turn away from what we know is true about God and step onto a path that is false? Temptation is an invitation, and the correct answer to this invitation is "No!"

The third response of Jesus is, *"The Lord, your God, shall you worship and him alone shall you serve."* This answer defeats the devil's invitation to worship him. This must be our answer as well. We belong to God; we worship and serve him alone. The door is shut on all false gods and all their empty works and all their empty promises. When we call upon the Name of Jesus and hold firmly on to the truth, the devil finds himself powerless; he must simply leave empty-handed. Satan can enter only when we open the door, when we begin to dialogue with him.

In the second reading, St. Paul expands on the topic of victory over sin and death. Death reigned over the human family because of the transgression of one man, Adam. But by "the grace of God and the gracious gift of one man" – Jesus Christ, the New Adam – we received acquittal and life. Jesus overcame disobedience, the weapon of the devil, by a much greater obedience. He overcame death by the power of his own death on the Cross. And in the abundance of his gift, he enables us to reign with him forever! "For if, by the transgression of the one, death came to reign through that one, how much more will those who receive the abundance of grace and of the gift of justification come to reign in life through the one Jesus Christ."

In Jesus, who overcame the enemy, we have victory! Jesus has entered the desert of our sin condition and engaged Satan in battle, easily overcoming him. Jesus is with us throughout the "forty days" of our lives. In the power of his Spirit, he enables us to overcome every temptation, every time, on every level. If we trust in him, hold on to his word, and rely on his power, he will bring about his victory in us. This is the Church's message for us as we begin the Holy Season of Lent.

> *How can I follow Jesus' example of fasting in the desert? When was I trapped by the lies of the devil and felt worse off than before? In what ways will I implore the Spirit to guide me through the desert of life this Lent?*

Mary, take my hand and lead me to overcome the desert in my life.

Notes

First Reading: Leviticus 19:1-2, 11-18

The LORD said to Moses, "Speak to the whole assembly of the children of Israel and tell them: Be holy, for I, the LORD, your God, am holy.

"You shall not steal. You shall not lie or speak falsely to one another. You shall not swear falsely by my name, thus profaning the name of your God. I am the LORD.

"You shall not defraud or rob your neighbor. You shall not withhold overnight the wages of your day laborer. You shall not curse the deaf, or put a stumbling block in front of the blind, but you shall fear your God. I am the LORD.

"You shall not act dishonestly in rendering judgment. Show neither partiality to the weak nor deference to the mighty, but judge your fellow men justly. You shall not go about spreading slander among your kin; nor shall you stand by idly when your neighbor's life is at stake. I am the LORD.

"You shall not bear hatred for your brother in your heart. Though you may have to reprove him, do not incur sin because of him. Take no revenge and cherish no grudge against your fellow countrymen. You shall love your neighbor as yourself. I am the LORD."

Responsorial Psalm: Psalm 19:8, 9, 10, 15
Your words, Lord, are Spirit and life.

The law of the LORD is perfect,
  refreshing the soul.
The decree of the LORD is trustworthy,
  giving wisdom to the simple.
R. Your words, Lord, are Spirit and life.
The precepts of the LORD are right,
  rejoicing the heart.
The command of the LORD is clear,
  enlightening the eye.
R. Your words, Lord, are Spirit and life.
The fear of the LORD is pure,
  enduring forever;
The ordinances of the LORD are true,
  all of them just.
R. Your words, Lord, are Spirit and life.

Let the words of my mouth and the thought of my heart
    find favor before you,
    O LORD, my rock and my redeemer.
R. Your words, Lord, are Spirit and life.

Gospel Acclamation: 2 Corinthians 6:2b

Behold, now is a very acceptable time; behold, now is the day of salvation.

Gospel: Matthew 25:31-46

Jesus said to his disciples: "When the Son of Man comes in his glory, and all the angels with him, he will sit upon his glorious throne, and all the nations will be assembled before him. And he will separate them one from another, as a shepherd separates the sheep from the goats. He will place the sheep on his right and the goats on his left. Then the king will say to those on his right, 'Come, you who are blessed by my Father. Inherit the kingdom prepared for you from the foundation of the world. For I was hungry and you gave me food, I was thirsty and you gave me drink, a stranger and you welcomed me, naked and you clothed me, ill and you cared for me, in prison and you visited me.' Then the righteous will answer him and say, 'Lord, when did we see you hungry and feed you, or thirsty and give you drink? When did we see you a stranger and welcome you, or naked and clothe you? When did we see you ill or in prison, and visit you?' And the king will say to them in reply, 'Amen, I say to you, whatever you did for one of these least brothers of mine, you did for me.' Then he will say to those on his left, 'Depart from me, you accursed, into the eternal fire prepared for the Devil and his angels. For I was hungry and you gave me no food, I was thirsty and you gave me no drink, a stranger and you gave me no welcome, naked and you gave me no clothing, ill and in prison, and you did not care for me.' Then they will answer and say, 'Lord, when did we see you hungry or thirsty or a stranger or naked or ill or in prison, and not minister to your needs?' He will answer them, 'Amen, I say to you, what you did not do for one of these least ones, you did not do for me.' And these will go off to eternal punishment, but the righteous to eternal life."

Meditation:

Yesterday we learned that the word of God strengthens us to overcome temptation. So far in Lent the divine word has already introduced us to the three traditional disciplines: prayer, fasting, and almsgiving. Today the readings focus on the third one, *almsgiving* or *charity*. The Lord is inviting us to reflect on and grow in our *love for our neighbor*. It is not simply a matter of being humanly better; it is a call to a divine way of life. God loves our neighbor as he loves us, and he calls us to be like him.

The reading from the Book of Leviticus gives us a list of what not to do, a sort of catalog of sins against our neighbor which we must avoid: do not lie, steal, cheat, slander, and do not bear grudges or hatred. The Pharisees followed these rules well, and thought that this proved their holiness. They were only partly right. They were indeed correct to avoid the sins on the list, but they missed the deeper instruction found in this reading: "Be holy, for I, the LORD, your God, am holy." The foundation of all the specific rules is the universal rule, the call to holiness. To be holy as God is holy means choosing what God chooses, loving as he loves.

The reading closes with: "You shall love your neighbor as yourself. I am the LORD." This reveals to us that it is not *rules* that are the basis for right living, but *love*. This verse was cited by Our Lord as the second of the two greatest commandments (cf. Mk 12:31). In the parable of the Good Samaritan, he clarified who is the "neighbor" whom we must love. Our neighbor is not only our fellow countrymen, but all men, even our enemies (cf. Lk 10:29-37).

Today's Gospel presents us with another challenging instruction on the demands of love of neighbor. The parable of the Last Judgment shows that in the end we will not be judged on what rules we have followed or what sins we have avoided, but on whether or not we have loved our neighbor – which is the same as loving Jesus Christ in and through our neighbor. Jesus mentions six of the traditional seven corporal works of mercy (omitting only the counsel to bury the dead). Before the throne of God we will have to face the truth about our charity – about how we have served our neighbor in need or neglected to serve him. As often as we neglect to do it for one of the least of our brothers or sisters, we neglect to do for Jesus Christ himself. And on this we will be judged.

This parable poses a question to our conscience: how well *have* we loved our neighbor? If we are wise, we will constantly reflect on this question and not simply wait until we are surprised at the Last

Judgment. When we look at ourselves honestly, we must admit that we often fall into the category of the goats. This does not mean, however, that we should despair of being saved. The wonder of God's mercy is that he can transform us into sheep. But to be faithful sheep, we must strive to follow the Shepherd! As we ponder his words, which are for us "Spirit and life," we find the path of love revealed to us, so that we can become ever more holy as he is holy.

> *How am I striving to be more holy? How do I manifest my love for my neighbor as God loves me? During this Lent, what will help me to see the face of Jesus in everyone I meet?*

Mary, help me to open my eyes to the needs of my neighbors and my hands to help them.
St. Gregory of Narek, pray for us.

Gregory of Narek, priest, monk, mystic, philosopher, writer, composer, poet, and theologian, was born in Narek, Armenia in 950. He came from a line of scholars and churchmen. At the death of his mother, his father sent him and his two brothers to a monastery where he lived most of his life. As an Armenian monk, he lived humbly and taught at the monastic school. At that time Armenia was experiencing a literature, painting, architecture, and theology renaissance in which Gregory was a leading figure. His greatest mystical writing, *The Book of Lamentations*, is a long mystic poem in 95 sections with the theme of man's separation from God and his quest to reunite with him. This Armenian classic has been translated into thirty languages. The Russian text was set to music in 1985. Gregory called it his last testament. The *Catechism* notes that while Western Medieval piety developed the Rosary as a lay substitute for praying the Psalms, the Armenian tradition developed hymns and songs to Mary as the primary expression of popular piety, as seen in the works of St. Gregory of Narek (cf. *CCC* 2678). Pope John Paul II also refers to St. Gregory in his encyclical on Mary, *Redemptoris Mater*: "with powerful poetic inspiration [St. Gregory] ponders the different aspects of the mystery of the Incarnation, and each of them is for him an occasion to sing and extol the extraordinary dignity and magnificent beauty of the Virgin Mary, Mother of the Word made flesh" (31). In 2015, as the world observed the 100th anniversary of the Armenian genocide by the Ottoman Empire, Pope Francis concelebrated a Mass at the Vatican with Patriarch Nerses Bedros XIX and declared Gregory the 36th Doctor of the Church. In 2021, by the decision of Pope Francis, the Vatican Congregation of Divine Worship declared February 27 as an optional memorial of Gregory, who died in 1005.

First Reading: Isaiah 55:10-11
Thus says the LORD:
Just as from the heavens
the rain and snow come down
And do not return there
till they have watered the earth,
making it fertile and fruitful,
Giving seed to the one who sows
and bread to the one who eats,
So shall my word be
that goes forth from my mouth;
It shall not return to me void,
but shall do my will,
achieving the end for which I sent it.

Responsorial Psalm: Psalm 34:4-5, 6-7, 16-17, 18-19
From all their distress God rescues the just.
Glorify the LORD with me,
let us together extol his name.
I sought the LORD, and he answered me
and delivered me from all my fears.
R. From all their distress God rescues the just.
Look to him that you may be radiant with joy,
and your faces may not blush with shame.
When the poor one called out, the LORD heard,
and from all his distress he saved him.
R. From all their distress God rescues the just.
The LORD has eyes for the just,
and ears for their cry.
The LORD confronts the evildoers,
to destroy remembrance of them from the earth.
R. From all their distress God rescues the just.
When the just cry out, the LORD hears them,
and from all their distress he rescues them.
The LORD is close to the brokenhearted;
and those who are crushed in spirit he saves.
R. From all their distress God rescues the just.

Gospel Acclamation: Matthew 4:4b
One does not live on bread alone, but on every word that comes forth
from the mouth of God.

✝ *Gospel: Matthew 6:7-15*

Jesus said to his disciples: "In praying, do not babble like the pagans, who think that they will be heard because of their many words. Do not be like them. Your Father knows what you need before you ask him.

"This is how you are to pray:
Our Father who art in heaven,
   hallowed be thy name,
   thy Kingdom come,
thy will be done,
   on earth as it is in heaven.
Give us this day our daily bread;
and forgive us our trespasses,
   as we forgive those who trespass against us;
and lead us not into temptation,
   but deliver us from evil.

"If you forgive men their transgressions, your heavenly Father will forgive you. But if you do not forgive men, neither will your Father forgive your transgressions."

Meditation:

Prayer, fasting, almsgiving: this is our Lenten program. We already know what we need to do, but we need encouragement and inspiration to put it into practice. The Church gives us guidance and support through the Sacraments, the daily readings from the word of God, and the constant support of the communion of saints. Today's lesson focuses on *prayer*, particularly on the power of the divine word and on the power of the divinely inspired prayer, the *Our Father*.

Jesus teaches us two essential truths concerning prayer when he says, "Your Father knows what you need before you ask him." First, that God is our Father, and second, that he already knows everything we need. This means that when we pray, we speak as children who know God as our Father and who put all our trust in him. Our prayer is based much more on our relationship with him than on our desire to receive anything from him. Thus, before we say, "give us this day our daily bread," we honor his Name, welcome his Kingdom, and open our hearts to his will, "on earth as it is in Heaven."

Although our Father knows what we need before we ask him, Jesus still tells us that we should ask; "Ask and you shall receive" (Mt 7:7). He even tells us what sort of things we should ask for: for our daily

45

needs, for forgiveness, for protection. The Lord's Prayer is structured on its seven petitions. The wisdom behind all these petitions is that asking puts us in the right disposition before God. In prayer we are not to "babble like the pagans." Rather, we come humbly before the Giver of all gifts. As we open our hearts to our Father, we are not informing him of anything, but we are communicating to him our desire to be united with his will. "Thy will be done" is the core of every prayer made from humble hearts.

In the final part of the Church's *Catechism*, there is a long and enlightening section (over one hundred paragraphs) specifically devoted to the Lord's Prayer (cf. 2759-2865). We read there that the Lord's Prayer "is truly the summary of the whole Gospel" (2761). It is "the most perfect of prayers.... In it we ask, not only for all the things we can rightly desire, but also in the sequence that they should be desired" (2763).

The Lord's Prayer is both God's word to us and our words to him. We can appreciate the value of this marvelous prayer if we reflect further on the gift of the divine word, which is beautifully described in today's first reading. The divine word, the prophet Isaiah says, is like life-giving rain and snow. It has intrinsic power to accomplish the end for which God speaks it. Thus, he says, "it shall not return to me void, but shall do my will."

The word is to our hearts what water is to the earth. It is life-giving, life-bearing, life-changing and life-saving. It makes us "fertile and fruitful." In Sunday's Gospel, Jesus used the word of God to defeat Satan, and he referred to the word as being more sustaining than food: "Man does not live on bread alone, but on every word that comes forth from the mouth of God." This is why in our prayer we not only speak to God but also listen intently to him, pondering his word, for the divine word is vital, and its power at work in us transforms our hearts. As we pray to our Father in Heaven, we open our hearts to his word which is intent on fulfilling his will, that it may find a home in us.

> *Knowing that my Heavenly Father is so near to me, why do I hesitate to call upon him? How do I avoid rambling in prayer? In what way has the word of God changed my life?*

Mary, when I pray to the Father, help me to acknowledge my fragility and mortality.

First Reading: Jonah 3:1-10

The word of the LORD came to Jonah a second time: "Set out for the great city of Nineveh, and announce to it the message that I will tell you." So Jonah made ready and went to Nineveh, according to the LORD's bidding. Now Nineveh was an enormously large city; it took three days to go through it. Jonah began his journey through the city, and had gone but a single day's walk announcing, "Forty days more and Nineveh shall be destroyed," when the people of Nineveh believed God; they proclaimed a fast and all of them, great and small, put on sackcloth.

When the news reached the king of Nineveh, he rose from his throne, laid aside his robe, covered himself with sackcloth, and sat in the ashes. Then he had this proclaimed throughout Nineveh, by decree of the king and his nobles: "Neither man nor beast, neither cattle nor sheep, shall taste anything; they shall not eat, nor shall they drink water. Man and beast shall be covered with sackcloth and call loudly to God; every man shall turn from his evil way and from the violence he has in hand. Who knows, God may relent and forgive, and withhold his blazing wrath, so that we shall not perish." When God saw by their actions how they turned from their evil way, he repented of the evil that he had threatened to do to them; he did not carry it out.

Responsorial Psalm: Psalm 51:3-4, 12-13, 18-19

A heart contrite and humbled, O God, you will not spurn.

Have mercy on me, O God, in your goodness;
    in the greatness of your compassion wipe out my offense.
Thoroughly wash me from my guilt
    and of my sin cleanse me.

R. A heart contrite and humbled, O God, you will not spurn.

A clean heart create for me, O God,
    and a steadfast spirit renew within me.
Cast me not out from your presence,
    and your Holy Spirit take not from me.

R. A heart contrite and humbled, O God, you will not spurn.

For you are not pleased with sacrifices;
    should I offer a burnt offering, you would not accept it.
My sacrifice, O God, is a contrite spirit;
    a heart contrite and humbled, O God, you will not spurn.

R. A heart contrite and humbled, O God, you will not spurn.

Gospel Acclamation: Joel 2:12-13

Even now, says the LORD, return to me with your whole heart for I am gracious and merciful.

✝ Gospel: Luke 11:29-32

While still more people gathered in the crowd, Jesus said to them, "This generation is an evil generation; it seeks a sign, but no sign will be given it, except the sign of Jonah. Just as Jonah became a sign to the Ninevites, so will the Son of Man be to this generation. At the judgment the queen of the south will rise with the men of this generation and she will condemn them, because she came from the ends of the earth to hear the wisdom of Solomon, and there is something greater than Solomon here. At the judgment the men of Nineveh will arise with this generation and condemn it, because at the preaching of Jonah they repented, and there is something greater than Jonah here."

Meditation:

One week into Lent, we come to the annual "Jonah Mass." Jesus himself points out the importance of Jonah when he tells the crowds that the only sign that will be given is "the sign of Jonah." In saying this, he invites us to reflect on who this prophet is and what he represents.

Today's first reading takes us to what may be called the central event of the whole Book of Jonah, the dramatic conversion of the Ninevites. Although Jonah was a reluctant and even disobedient messenger, when he finally submitted to the will of God, he was an amazingly effective instrument. Just one day of his preaching moved the entire city to repentance. This is truly something to ponder: one day of minimal effort by an unenthusiastic prophet, speaking to a city notorious for its sin and cruelty, resulted in a sudden and total conversion! Jonah did not perform any miraculous signs. He said only one sentence, a dire warning: "Forty days more and Nineveh shall be destroyed." The people, despite their evil ways and bad reputation, must have had good hearts, interiorly disposed to respond to the word of God. They immediately repented and began to fast in sackcloth and ashes.

The Ninevites repented without a sign; Jonah himself, unworthy as he was, was the sign. Likewise, those who heard the preaching of John the Baptist repented without a sign; John himself was the sign. We should not delay our repentance waiting for miraculous signs. The word of God, proclaimed by a messenger sent by God, is enough. Jesus tells us that Jonah is actually a sign for every generation. We are to look beyond Jonah and see what God is doing through him.

The "sign of Jonah" raises a question: if Jonah was the instrument of an enormous miracle of repentance, what would happen if someone greater than Jonah came along? Should we not expect an even more widespread and wholehearted wave of conversion? That is what *should* have happened when Jesus came. He is far greater than Jonah and far wiser than Solomon. But he was met with hardness of heart, refusal to change, and a demand for signs. No wonder he exclaimed, "This generation is an evil generation!"

We still live in an evil generation, for the tendency to seek signs is as strong as ever. This tendency is built on the empty hope that something other than what God offers us will satisfy our hungry hearts. In our desire for "signs," we look for answers from people and things that can never satisfy us. Some expect political figures to cure the ills of society. Others depend on money or on physical force. Some put their hope in technological progress, thinking that a better phone or computer or whatever is the latest gadget will save us from our problems. Young people often look to celebrities as their role models. Again and again modern culture looks around for another messiah, seeking any sign, any message, any hope of salvation other than the One who has been given us, the One *greater than all others*, the true Messiah, Jesus Christ.

Lent, then, points our hearts back to Jesus, our only Savior, the center of our hope, our faith, and our love. As we pray, fast, and give alms, we strive to gain insight and some measure of control over the preoccupations that distract us. The interior struggle that usually arises during our attempts to fast reveals that we are still clinging to comfort and natural satisfactions. In our effort to be more charitable to others, we discover that we are often looking for something *from* them rather than making a gift of ourselves *to* them. Our anxiety over empty concerns indicates that our nature is still looking for something other than Jesus Christ. We can only find inner peace if we turn to Jesus, the Son of Man, who comes to us today as a sign "to this generation" and for all ages to come. The Ninevites show us how we should respond to him, with rapid and deep repentance.

> *How is my heart open to the word of God spoken daily to me? What are the anxieties that distract me in my pursuit of holiness? Why do I look for signs from people or things and not trust in the providence of God?*

Mary, may the mercy and love of God touch my heart.

First Reading: Esther C:12, 14-16, 23-25

Queen Esther, seized with mortal anguish, had recourse to the LORD. She lay prostrate upon the ground, together with her handmaids, from morning until evening, and said: "God of Abraham, God of Isaac, and God of Jacob, blessed are you. Help me, who am alone and have no help but you, for I am taking my life in my hand. As a child I used to hear from the books of my forefathers that you, O LORD, always free those who are pleasing to you. Now help me, who am alone and have no one but you, O LORD, my God.

"And now, come to help me, an orphan. Put in my mouth persuasive words in the presence of the lion and turn his heart to hatred for our enemy, so that he and those who are in league with him may perish. Save us from the hand of our enemies; turn our mourning into gladness and our sorrows into wholeness."

Responsorial Psalm: Psalm 138:1-2ab, 2cde-3, 7c-8
Lord, on the day I called for help, you answered me.

I will give thanks to you, O LORD, with all my heart,
    for you have heard the words of my mouth;
    in the presence of the angels I will sing your praise;
I will worship at your holy temple
    and give thanks to your name.
R. *Lord, on the day I called for help, you answered me.*

Because of your kindness and your truth;
    for you have made great above all things
    your name and your promise.
When I called, you answered me;
    you built up strength within me.
R. *Lord, on the day I called for help, you answered me.*

Your right hand saves me.
The LORD will complete what he has done for me;
    your kindness, O LORD, endures forever;
    forsake not the work of your hands.
R. *Lord, on the day I called for help, you answered me.*

Gospel Acclamation: Psalm 51:12a, 14a
A clean heart create for me, God; give me back the joy of your salvation.

✠ *Gospel: Matthew 7:7-12*

Jesus said to his disciples: "Ask and it will be given to you; seek and you will find; knock and the door will be opened to you. For everyone who asks, receives; and the one who seeks, finds; and to the one who knocks, the door will be opened. Which one of you would hand his son a stone when he asked for a loaf of bread, or a snake when he asked for a fish? If you then, who are wicked, know how to give good gifts to your children, how much more will your heavenly Father give good things to those who ask him.

"Do to others whatever you would have them do to you. This is the law and the prophets."

Meditation:

Today's readings invite us to ponder once again the topic of *prayer*. This is such a vital topic! A Christian cannot survive without prayer any more than a person can live without breathing. We need to pray, yet we do not know how to pray as we ought! (cf. Rm 8:26). In the Gospel Jesus teaches us some of the fundamental principles behind the practice of prayer, and in the first reading Queen Esther is set before us as a model of how to pray with humility and confidence.

Jesus gives us very strong encouragement to pray. The verbs he uses are key: *ask* and *receive, seek* and *find, knock* and the door *will be opened.* There is a remarkable confidence in the Lord's understanding of prayer and its effects: *do this and it will work!* A superficial reading of these lines may distort what he really means. He is not saying that we have absolute power over God or that some magical formula is guaranteed to produce the effect we desire. He is saying that we should pray with what the *Catechism* calls *"filial boldness"* (*CCC* 2610), the great confidence of children who know the goodness of their Father.

A central aspect of the mystery of prayer, as Jesus presents it, is our relationship with the Father. When we ask the Lord for things, the basis of all our asking is our relationship with him, the relationship of a child with a loving Father. Our natural family relationships, then, teach us much about prayer. Most fathers love their children and will do anything they can for their good. However, no human father is a perfect example of love. Many people have been hurt, neglected, or rejected by their fathers. This can make it hard for them to trust in God the Father. When we cling to harmful or imperfect images of God, we obscure the truth about him.

Jesus reveals the fullness of the truth about the Father, that his love is perfect, sacrificial, and unconditional. Jesus is explicit in comparing human fathers to God the Father: "If you then, who are wicked, know how to give good gifts to your children, how much more will your heavenly Father give good things to those who ask him." We are not sheep without a shepherd, nor are we orphans without a father. This is why we can be so confident in asking, seeking, and knocking in prayer.

In our prayer, we do much more than ask God our Father for things we want. We come to him with whatever hopes, dreams, and burdens we hold in our hearts. He knows the jumble of thoughts, feelings, and memories that we carry. As we share all that is in our hearts with our Father, that is already prayer. This is what we are made for, to be in an intimate relationship with God.

The first reading gives us an example of a master of prayer, Queen Esther. She is "seized with mortal anguish" because she must approach King Ahasuerus of Persia to ask for mercy for her people – yet to enter his presence without being given prior permission was an offense punishable by death. Without friend or ally, Esther experiences her total dependence on God alone. "I am alone and have no one but you, O LORD, my God." Her humanly desperate situation does not lead to despair but to stronger faith. She appeals to an even greater King, the Lord, the "King of gods and Ruler of every power" (Est C:23). Her prayer is full of both humility and hope – humility because she can do nothing on her own, hope because she trusts in God who can do everything. The Responsorial Psalm echoes Esther's prayer: "Lord, on the day I called for help, you answered me."

These readings are meant to move us to more fervent and confident prayer. It is God himself, our Father who wants us to pray to him, to lift up our hearts to him, to humbly present to him our every need. Turning to him, we pray, *Here I am, Lord; help me! There is no one else who really knows me and loves me as you do. I trust in you!*

> *How does the humble and confident prayer of Queen Esther strengthen my faith? With confidence in God's goodness, do I humbly present to him my every need? When I pray, am I open to what God's will is for me or do I demand that he must answer my prayer?*

Mary, grant me the grace to fully trust in God's fatherly love and care for me.

First Reading: Ezekiel 18:21-28

Thus says the Lord GOD: If the wicked man turns away from all the sins he committed, if he keeps all my statutes and does what is right and just, he shall surely live, he shall not die. None of the crimes he committed shall be remembered against him; he shall live because of the virtue he has practiced. Do I indeed derive any pleasure from the death of the wicked? says the Lord GOD. Do I not rather rejoice when he turns from his evil way that he may live?

And if the virtuous man turns from the path of virtue to do evil, the same kind of abominable things that the wicked man does, can he do this and still live? None of his virtuous deeds shall be remembered, because he has broken faith and committed sin; because of this, he shall die. You say, "The LORD's way is not fair!" Hear now, house of Israel: Is it my way that is unfair, or rather, are not your ways unfair? When someone virtuous turns away from virtue to commit iniquity, and dies, it is because of the iniquity he committed that he must die. But if the wicked, turning from the wickedness he has committed, does what is right and just, he shall preserve his life; since he has turned away from all the sins that he committed, he shall surely live, he shall not die.

Responsorial Psalm: Psalm 130:1-2, 3-4, 5-7a, 7bc-8
If you, O Lord, mark iniquities, who can stand?

Out of the depths I cry to you, O LORD;
    LORD, hear my voice!
Let your ears be attentive
    to my voice in supplication.

R. *If you, O Lord, mark iniquities, who can stand?*

If you, O LORD, mark iniquities,
    LORD, who can stand?
But with you is forgiveness,
    that you may be revered.

R. *If you, O Lord, mark iniquities, who can stand?*

I trust in the LORD;
    my soul trusts in his word.
My soul waits for the LORD
    more than sentinels wait for the dawn.
    Let Israel wait for the LORD.

R. *If you, O Lord, mark iniquities, who can stand?*

For with the LORD is kindness
   and with him is plenteous redemption;
And he will redeem Israel
   from all their iniquities.
R. If you, O Lord, mark iniquities, who can stand?

Gospel Acclamation: Ezekiel 18:31
Cast away from you all the crimes you have committed, says the Lord,
and make for yourselves a new heart and a new spirit.

Gospel: Matthew 5:20-26
   Jesus said to his disciples: "I tell you, unless your righteousness
surpasses that of the scribes and Pharisees, you will not enter into the
Kingdom of heaven.
   "You have heard that it was said to your ancestors, *You shall not
kill; and whoever kills will be liable to judgment.* But I say to you,
whoever is angry with his brother will be liable to judgment, and
whoever says to his brother, *Raqa*, will be answerable to the Sanhedrin,
and whoever says, 'You fool,' will be liable to fiery Gehenna. Therefore,
if you bring your gift to the altar, and there recall that your brother has
anything against you, leave your gift there at the altar, go first and be
reconciled with your brother, and then come and offer your gift. Settle
with your opponent quickly while on the way to court. Otherwise your
opponent will hand you over to the judge, and the judge will hand you
over to the guard, and you will be thrown into prison. Amen, I say to
you, you will not be released until you have paid the last penny."

Meditation:
   In the Season of Lent, the Lord calls us all to repentance because
   he calls us all to *holiness.* Today's readings instruct us further
on what holiness really means. Most of us think that we are already holy,
at least to some degree. We were baptized as infants and perhaps grew
up in a Catholic family. Even better, we ponder the Scriptures almost
every day, and sometimes attend daily Mass. We have devotion to the
Sacred Heart or to the Blessed Mother or to one of the Saints. We pray
the Rosary and participate in other religious activities. We tend to think
that this is all good evidence that we are holy – not saints, perhaps, but
fairly holy.

   This is how the scribes and Pharisees thought about their own
holiness. They followed all the rules, attended temple services, said
many prayers, and even clothed themselves with all the proper religious

apparel. By their own standards, they were the holy ones. Others who did not follow all their rules were obviously less holy than they – including Jesus, who scandalously "worked" on the Sabbath.

Jesus, however, did not agree. He did not consider the Pharisees particularly holy, and his evaluation of our holiness is quite different from ours as well. He proclaimed an altogether different standard by which holiness is to be measured. In his Sermon on the Mount, he said something quite shocking about the true measure of holiness: *"Unless your righteousness surpasses that of the scribes and Pharisees, you will not enter into the Kingdom of Heaven."* In other words, the Pharisees were at risk of not even entering the Kingdom of God because their righteousness was not true holiness at all. It was merely religiosity, a superficial show of piety. Jesus' statement is meant to shake us out of our complacency. We may look just as holy as the scribes and Pharisees did, but in reality we may be just as empty.

The prophet Ezekiel gives us a similar message. He teaches us that we cannot rest on our laurels or past accomplishments for the Lord. Virtue is not record-keeping but an ongoing pursuit of God's will. We are to be continually seeking his will and following his call for us. If we are secretly harboring the attitude that "the LORD's way is not fair!", that is a sure sign that there is something wrong with us.

This brings us to the true work of Lent: we need a change of heart, which is a much deeper, more challenging work than simply looking holy, or claiming that we are holy because of what we did in the past. Our prayer must come more from the heart than from the mouth; our self-denial must cut more deeply into our flesh; our love of our neighbor must be more selfless and genuine.

The focus of today's Gospel is especially on love of neighbor, and in particular on anger and the work of reconciliation. Jesus tells us to look behind the sin of murder to its emotional prelude, which is anger. Anger is a natural human reaction to injustice, but when we misuse our anger against another, it is sin. Jesus mentions three dimensions of anger: growing angry with our brother, using abusive language, like *"Raqa"* ("good-for-nothing"), and holding another in utter contempt, considering him a fool. The third case, looking down on a neighbor as a fool, results in the worst consequence, "fiery Gehenna." In other words, there is a kind of anger that goes beyond a momentary outburst of angry or abusive words. It is an attitude of contempt, an inner judgment, a silent disdain of another. It is a refusal to reconcile, a decision to completely exclude the other from our lives. Jesus says that if we hold the poison of contempt in our hearts, we are putting our eternal life at risk.

Jesus tells us further that if we are not reconciled with a brother, the effectiveness of our prayer is greatly diminished. We are better off leaving the altar to reconcile; then we can go back and worship with a pure heart. This is another reminder that holiness is not sitting in church or doing holy-looking things. Holiness is true love of God and love of our neighbor.

The call to holiness, that is, to love, is urgent. The Gospel says, "Settle with your opponent quickly…" We are not guaranteed a certain amount of time, so we must not act as if we have all the time in the world. Our life on earth is represented by the Forty Days; at the end, the journey is over and we will be judged. So let us work for true reconciliation this Lent, and for the true holiness to which the Lord calls us.

> *How am I responding to God's call to holiness? How similar or different am I from the Pharisees? When I have something against another, what enables me to seek reconciliation with him?*

Mary, strengthen me as I struggle to love others as God loves me. St. Katharine Drexel, pray for us.

Katharine Drexel was born to a wealthy American family in 1858. Her mother died when she was a month old. Her father soon remarried. Both parents instilled in her that their wealth was simply on loan to them and was to be shared with others. Early in life she became aware of the material and spiritual plight of the Blacks and Native Americans. During an audience with Pope Leo XIII in 1887, she asked him for more missionaries to help these people. The pope replied, "Why don't you become a missionary?" In 1891, with a few companions, she founded the Sisters of the Blessed Sacrament for Indians and Blacks. The name of the community summed up the two great driving forces in her life – devotion to the Blessed Sacrament and love for the most deprived people in America. From age of 33 until her death in 1955, she dedicated her life and fortune of $20 million to this work.

March 4, Saturday, 1st Week of Lent
Saint Casimir

 First Reading: Deuteronomy 26:16-19
Moses spoke to the people, saying: "This day the LORD, your God, commands you to observe these statutes and decrees. Be careful, then, to observe them with all your heart and with all your soul. Today you are making this agreement with the LORD: he is to be your God and you are to walk in his ways and observe his statutes, commandments and decrees, and to hearken to his voice. And today the LORD is making this agreement with you: you are to be a people peculiarly his own, as he promised you; and provided you keep all his commandments, he will then raise you high in praise and renown and glory above all other nations he has made, and you will be a people sacred to the LORD, your God, as he promised."

Responsorial Psalm: Psalm 119:1-2, 4-5, 7-8
Blessed are they who follow the law of the Lord!
Blessed are they whose way is blameless,
 who walk in the law of the LORD.
Blessed are they who observe his decrees,
 who seek him with all their heart.
R. Blessed are they who follow the law of the Lord!
You have commanded that your precepts
 be diligently kept.
Oh, that I might be firm in the ways
 of keeping your statutes!
R. Blessed are they who follow the law of the Lord!
I will give you thanks with an upright heart,
 when I have learned your just ordinances.
I will keep your statutes;
 do not utterly forsake me.
R. Blessed are they who follow the law of the Lord!

Gospel Acclamation: 2 Corinthians 6:2b
Behold, now is a very acceptable time; behold, now is the day of salvation.

Gospel: Matthew 5:43-48
Jesus said to his disciples: "You have heard that it was said, *You shall love your neighbor and hate your enemy.* But I say to you, love your enemies, and pray for those who persecute you, that you may be

children of your heavenly Father, for he makes his sun rise on the bad and the good, and causes rain to fall on the just and the unjust. For if you love those who love you, what recompense will you have? Do not the tax collectors do the same? And if you greet your brothers and sisters only, what is unusual about that? Do not the pagans do the same? So be perfect, just as your heavenly Father is perfect."

Meditation:

In Sunday's Gospel Jesus taught us that we do not live on bread alone but on every word that comes from the mouth of God. The power of the word is a crucial element for gaining victory over temptation and over Satan. In the Season of Lent, the word of God in the daily Liturgy is particularly incisive. The word probes our hearts more deeply than ever, moving us to make a fuller response to God.

Today's reading from Deuteronomy reminds us that this response must be made *now, today*. Just as Jesus said in yesterday's Gospel, "Settle with your opponent *quickly*," today Moses stresses the importance of responding to God in the present moment: "*This day* the LORD, your God, commands you…." "*Today* you are making this agreement with the LORD…." "*Today* the LORD is making this agreement with you…." The Gospel Acclamation speaks to us with the same emphasis on the present moment: "Behold, *now* is a very acceptable time; behold, *now* is the day of salvation."

With our conscience awakened to the grace of this "now moment," we face the question: will we choose *today* to turn away from sin, from selfishness, from earthly pride, from our independent spirit, and turn humbly to the Lord for his forgiveness and healing, and follow his ways? Or will we procrastinate, pushing his word away from our consciousness for another day and continuing in our old ways? This is the choice before us.

If we choose the Lord's way in obedient faith and love, we need to make some practical changes; we need to turn our decision into a way of life. In yesterday's Gospel, the change Jesus spoke about was our need to overcome sins of anger. He told us that our righteousness must surpass that of the scribes and Pharisees. Today, in a later section from the great Sermon on the Mount, he teaches us that our righteousness must also surpass that of tax collectors and pagans. After all, even non-believers and public sinners love those who love them. Why then do we feel so self-righteous when we merely do the same? God is calling us to something much greater than this. He calls us into his own way of love, a love which pours itself out even towards those who offend us, who persecute us, those who are our enemies.

The Old Testament commandment was *"You shall love your neighbor."* Jesus extends the category of "neighbor" to include even our enemies. This is the revolutionary challenge that today's Gospel presents to us. In considering this challenge, we realize almost instinctively that such a way of life is impossible for us, based on our human strength alone. It does not even make sense to us. The question is whether or not we will open ourselves to God's word and allow his radical idea about love to enter our hearts. Only with his power can we love those whom we cannot love and do not even want to love. If we are striving to love those who hate us, it is a clear sign that God is at work in us, transforming our hearts. He will reward all who choose to love with an increase of his own divine love. Our heavenly Father is the One who makes it possible for us to "be perfect" as he is perfect. This perfection can be understood in terms of *mercy*, as Jesus himself says in a parallel Gospel passage, "Be merciful, just as your Father is merciful" (Lk 6:36).

Now is the time for us to make the faith-decision to love our enemies. We can put this decision into practice by praying earnestly for our persecutors. We do this in obedience to the Lord, not because we like those who hate us, and certainly not because we like their wrongdoing. The way of love will always seem absurd to our flesh and to the world. It is *peculiar*! But as Moses says, the Lord calls us "to be a people *peculiarly* his own." The Lord wants us, his people, to know the joy of loving as he loves. This is the purpose of the commandments. "Blessed are they who follow the law of the Lord... who seek him with all their heart!"

> *As I progress on my journey in Lent, how is the word probing my heart to respond to God more fully? How do I take seriously the command of Jesus, "...behold, now is the day of salvation."? What is my struggle as I strive to love even those who offend and persecute me?*

Mary, grant me a loving heart to understand those who may hurt me in any way.

St. Casimir, pray for us.

Casimir, a Polish prince, was born in Krakow in 1458. He received a good religious formation from his mother and from a very holy priest, Fr. Dlugosz. His father, King Casimir IV, educated him well concerning public affairs, and made him Grand Duke of Lithuania at 13 and King of Hungary at 15. He obeyed and took the Crown but would not exercise his military power. He returned home as a conscientious objector to war. He lived a highly disciplined, even severe, life – sleeping on the ground, spending many hours a night in prayer – and dedicated himself to lifelong celibacy, even under pressure to marry the emperor's daughter. He had a great devotion to Mary, supported the poor, and lived a virtuous life amid the dissolute court. He developed severe lung problems which led to his early death at age 26. He is the patron of Poland and Lithuania. In 1948 Pope Pius XII named him the special patron of all youth.

Notes

Second Week of Lent

*"This is my beloved Son,
with whom I am well pleased;
listen to him."*

Matthew 17:5

Theme for the Week

Our Father reveals to us the glory of Jesus his Beloved Son and calls us to "listen to him!" Let us put our trust in him and follow as he leads us. In every moment and through all circumstances he is our Source of light and strength. Listening to the Lord is our daily guide throughout our journey of Lent and of life.

WE HAVE BEEN MADE WITNESSES OF CHRIST JESUS BY THE GIFT OF THE SPIRIT
A Spiritual Reflection by Pope Francis

...The Gospel of this Second Sunday of Lent (cf. Mt 17:1-9), presents to us the account of the Transfiguration of Jesus. He takes Peter, James, and John with him up a high mountain, symbol of closeness to God, to open them to a fuller understanding of the mystery of his Person, that must suffer, die, and then rise again. Indeed, Jesus had begun to speak to them of the suffering, death and Resurrection that awaited him, but they were unable to accept this prospect. Therefore, once they reached the summit of the mountain, Jesus immersed himself in prayer and was transfigured before the three disciples: "his face," says the Gospel, "shone like the sun, and his clothes became white as light" (v. 2).

Through the wondrous event of the Transfiguration, the three disciples are called to recognize in Jesus the Son of God shining with glory. Thus, they advance in their knowledge of their Master, realizing that the human aspect does not express all his reality; in their eyes the otherworldly and divine dimension of Jesus is revealed. And from on High there resounds a voice that says: "This is my beloved Son.... Listen to him" (v. 5). It is the heavenly Father who confirms the "investiture" — let us call it that — that Jesus already received on the day of his Baptism in the Jordan and invites the disciples to listen to him and to follow him.

It must be emphasized that, from among the group of the Twelve, Jesus chose to take James, John, and Peter with him up the mountain. He reserved for them the privilege of witnessing the Transfiguration. But why did he select these three? Because they are the holiest? No. Yet, at the hour of trial, Peter will deny him; and the two brothers James and John will ask for the foremost places in his Kingdom (cf. Mt 20:20-23). However, Jesus does not choose according to our criteria, but according to his plan of love. Jesus' love is without measure: it is love, and he chooses with that plan of love. It is a free, unconditional choice, a free initiative, a divine friendship that asks for nothing in return. And just as he called those three disciples, so today too he calls some to be close to him, to be able to bear witness. To be witnesses to Jesus is a gift we have not deserved; we may feel inadequate but we cannot back out with the excuse of our incapacity.

We have not been on Mount Tabor; we have not seen with our own eyes the face of Jesus shining like the sun. However, we too were given the Word of Salvation, faith was given to us, and we have experienced the joy of meeting Jesus in different ways. Jesus also says to us: "Rise, and have no fear" (Mt 17:7). In this world, marked by selfishness and greed, the light of God is obscured by the worries of everyday life. We often say: I do not have time to pray, I am unable to carry out a service in the parish, to respond to the requests of others.... But we must not forget that the Baptism and Confirmation we have received have made us witnesses, not because of our ability, but as a result of the gift of the Spirit.

In the favorable time of Lent, may the Virgin Mary obtain for us that docility to the Spirit which is indispensable for setting out resolutely on the path of conversion.

Pope Francis, Angelus Message, March 8, 2020
© Copyright 2020 – Libreria Editrice Vaticana

First Reading: Genesis 12:1-4a

The LORD said to Abram: "Go forth from the land of your kinsfolk and from your father's house to a land that I will show you.

"I will make of you a great nation,
and I will bless you;
I will make your name great,
so that you will be a blessing.
I will bless those who bless you
and curse those who curse you.
All the communities of the earth
shall find blessing in you."
Abram went as the LORD directed him.

Responsorial Psalm: Psalm 33:4-5, 18-19, 20, 22

Lord, let your mercy be on us, as we place our trust in you.

Upright is the word of the LORD,
and all his works are trustworthy.
He loves justice and right;
of the kindness of the LORD the earth is full.

R. Lord, let your mercy be on us, as we place our trust in you.

See, the eyes of the LORD are upon those who fear him,
upon those who hope for his kindness,
to deliver them from death
and preserve them in spite of famine.

R. Lord, let your mercy be on us, as we place our trust in you.

Our soul waits for the LORD,
who is our help and our shield.
May your kindness, O LORD, be upon us
who have put our hope in you.

R. Lord, let your mercy be on us, as we place our trust in you.

Second Reading: 2 Timothy 1:8b-10

Beloved: Bear your share of hardship for the gospel with the strength that comes from God.

He saved us and called us to a holy life, not according to our works but according to his own design and the grace bestowed on us in Christ Jesus before time began, but now made manifest through the appearance of our savior Christ Jesus, who destroyed death and brought life and immortality to light through the gospel.

From the shining cloud the Father's voice is heard: This is my beloved Son, hear him.

Gospel: Matthew 17:1-9

Jesus took Peter, James, and John his brother, and led them up a high mountain by themselves. And he was transfigured before them; his face shone like the sun and his clothes became white as light. And behold, Moses and Elijah appeared to them, conversing with him. Then Peter said to Jesus in reply, "Lord, it is good that we are here. If you wish, I will make three tents here, one for you, one for Moses, and one for Elijah." While he was still speaking, behold, a bright cloud cast a shadow over them, then from the cloud came a voice that said, "This is my beloved Son, with whom I am well pleased; listen to him." When the disciples heard this, they fell prostrate and were very much afraid. But Jesus came and touched them, saying, "Rise, and do not be afraid." And when the disciples raised their eyes, they saw no one else but Jesus alone.

As they were coming down from the mountain, Jesus charged them, "Do not tell the vision to anyone until the Son of Man has been raised from the dead."

Meditation:

Pope Francis, in this week's Spiritual Reflection, tells us that Jesus chose Peter, James, and John "according to his plan of love," to accompany him up the high mountain. There, above the noise of the villages below, Jesus is transfigured. He appears with Moses and Elijah. Moses, who led the Chosen People out of Egypt, that place of slavery, represents the Law. Elijah, who proclaimed and prepared for the coming of the Messiah, and who was taken aloft in a whirlwind, represents all the prophets. Now, here before the eyes of the three astonished disciples, Jesus is revealed as a New Moses who will lead us out of slavery to sin, and as the very Messiah long awaited by the prophets. His divinity is revealed on his face which "shone like the sun" and through his clothes which "became white as light."

Peter, despite his awe at the glorious vision of Jesus transfigured, is still able to converse with him, saying, "Lord, it is good that we are here. If you wish, I will make three tents here, one for you, one for Moses, and one for Elijah." His suggestion to erect tents is rooted in the traditions of the Old Testament, especially the days when the Ark of the

Covenant was kept in a tent or "tabernacle." The voice of the Father reveals to them that something new has arrived, the very Presence of God, not under a tent but in Jesus himself: "This is my beloved Son, with whom I am well pleased; listen to him."

Peter, James, and John have begun to realize that they have been brought deeper into the reality of who Jesus is and they are "very much afraid." Jesus urges them not to be afraid – not to be afraid of who he has revealed himself to be, and not to be afraid of the voice of the Father, confirming his identity. Instead they should "rise," rise to a new level of understanding and a new way of living as disciples. It is time for them to allow the divine light of Christ and the voice of God to penetrate them more deeply. The old covenant is past, the new is before them. It is time to grow in faith in the One they have seen with their eyes, Jesus Christ the Son of God.

As they come down the mountain Jesus tells them not to tell anyone about this until his Resurrection. In obedience they wait while they ponder the mysterious vision in their hearts. But it will not be long before they will deny him and abandon him during his Passion. This is a sobering Lenten lesson – no matter how beautifully, deeply, or clearly Jesus has revealed himself to us, while we live here below, we are still capable of denying him and abandoning him in a moment of doubt and fear.

In reflecting on the Transfiguration, the Church invites us to learn from Abraham, our father in faith, who in the first reading is addressed by the Lord as Abram. He hears the Lord tell him to "go forth from the land of [his] kinsfolk." He listens, trusts, and obeys. Everything the Lord tells him is to take place in an unknown future, in an unknown place, in an unknown way: "I *will* show you…. I *will* make of you… I *will* bless you…." His prompt response to these vast yet imprecise promises of the Lord is described very simply: "Abram went as the LORD directed him." He walked by faith and not by sight (cf. 2 Cor 5:7) – a beautiful example and Lenten instruction on prompt obedience of faith.

The second reading gives us our marching orders: "Bear your share of hardship for the Gospel with the strength that comes from God." Walking by faith is not a matter of making progress by our own strength, "according to our works." Rather it is to live by God's plan of love, "according to his own design." He gives us the grace we need to persevere in our journey "down from the mountain" of the Transfiguration and up Mount Calvary with Jesus. The "strength that comes from God" is what makes it possible for us to take our rightful place in his beautiful plan of love. We journey with our eyes of faith fixed on the promise of a glorious future, eternal life with the Blessed Trinity, where we will see God face to face, shining like the sun. Between then and now, as we begin this Second Week of Lent, we rely on grace as we observe our Lenten disciplines with renewed vigor.

Walking in the footsteps of Abraham, how do I listen, trust and obey the voice of the Lord? What fears do I have as I journey down from the mountain of Transfiguration to the mountain of Calvary? As Jesus is always revealing his love and mercy to me, what is my inner response?

Mary, sustain me during my Lenten journey as I take up the cross that the Lord has given me.

Notes

First Reading: Daniel 9:4b-10

"Lord, great and awesome God, you who keep your merciful covenant toward those who love you and observe your commandments! We have sinned, been wicked and done evil; we have rebelled and departed from your commandments and your laws. We have not obeyed your servants the prophets, who spoke in your name to our kings, our princes, our fathers, and all the people of the land. Justice, O Lord, is on your side; we are shamefaced even to this day: we, the men of Judah, the residents of Jerusalem, and all Israel, near and far, in all the countries to which you have scattered them because of their treachery toward you. O LORD, we are shamefaced, like our kings, our princes, and our fathers, for having sinned against you. But yours, O Lord, our God, are compassion and forgiveness! Yet we rebelled against you and paid no heed to your command, O LORD, our God, to live by the law you gave us through your servants the prophets."

Responsorial Psalm: Psalm 79:8, 9, 11 and 13
Lord, do not deal with us according to our sins.

Remember not against us the iniquities of the past;
  may your compassion quickly come to us,
  for we are brought very low.
R. Lord, do not deal with us according to our sins.

Help us, O God our savior,
  because of the glory of your name;
Deliver us and pardon our sins
  for your name's sake.
R. Lord, do not deal with us according to our sins.

Let the prisoners' sighing come before you;
  with your great power free those doomed to death.
Then we, your people and the sheep of your pasture,
  will give thanks to you forever;
  through all generations we will declare your praise.
R. Lord, do not deal with us according to our sins.

Gospel Acclamation: see John 6:63c, 68c
Your words, Lord, are Spirit and life; you have the words of everlasting life.

✝ Gospel: Luke 6:36-38

Jesus said to his disciples: "Be merciful, just as your Father is merciful.

"Stop judging and you will not be judged. Stop condemning and you will not be condemned. Forgive and you will be forgiven. Give and gifts will be given to you; a good measure, packed together, shaken down, and overflowing, will be poured into your lap. For the measure with which you measure will in return be measured out to you."

Meditation:

Today's readings connect two essential elements of the Lenten journey: our absolute dependence on the mercy of God and our call to be merciful to one another. The prophet Daniel's prayer focuses on the first point, reminding us that the Lord is a God of compassion and forgiveness, while Jesus in the Gospel teaches the second point, that we are to be merciful as our Father is merciful.

Daniel describes our natural reaction to facing the truth of our own sin: "we are *shamefaced*." When we are shamefaced, we look down; we do not raise our eyes to Heaven. We find it hard to look other people in the eye. In particular, we look away from the one who confronts us or in any way makes us aware of our sin. Our body manifests the movements of our exposed soul. Our faces may turn red as we blush with shame. Shame comes with the painful recognition that "we have sinned, been wicked and done evil."

In contrast is the reaction of *defiance*. If we have a defiant face, our chin is up, we set our jaw; we stare down the one who has pointed out our wrong. Defiance feels less painful than shame; it makes us think we are standing up for ourselves. However, it is really worse. It leaves us firmly locked in the guilt we are trying to deny. Shame, too, can lock us in guilt, if we decide to sit in self-pity and self-condemnation. We make good use of shame when we allow it to alert us to our need for repentance, for repentance is the only way to freedom from the terrible condition of guilt.

In his prayer, Daniel is both honest and hopeful. We cannot pray if we are not honest, and we do not pray if we have no hope. Daniel acknowledges the whole dark condition of his people: "We have rebelled against you and paid no heed to your command, O LORD, our God." After recounting a whole list of defiant behaviors, for which the people can only be shamefaced, Daniel frankly admits that justice is on

69

the Lord's side. In justice, the people of Judah deserve nothing but punishment. But Daniel begs the Lord for *mercy*. He calls to mind the Lord's faithfulness to his "merciful covenant": "Yours, O Lord, our God, are compassion and forgiveness!"

We can pray like Daniel! We are shamefaced sinners, but the Lord has made a merciful covenant with us, beginning with our Baptism. He has been merciful to us from the beginning, from before we even knew that we should be ashamed. We have only to call upon him, to acknowledge and repent of our sin, and we can be sure that he will forgive us. No matter what we have done, the Lord's grace and mercy is more powerful. His mercy is constantly available to us in the Church through the Sacraments. In the Sacrament of Penance, we are fully renewed in the "merciful covenant" God has made with us.

As we acknowledge our sinfulness, we experience the mercy of God; and as we experience his mercy, we are moved to extend that mercy to others. When we are shamefaced, God treats us kindly; when we see the shame of others, he gives us the grace to be like him, so that we can pass on to them his own love and mercy. In today's Gospel Jesus teaches us to *be merciful* and not to *judge* or *condemn*. He teaches us to *forgive* and to *give*. He explicitly associates these acts of love for others with the love God has for us. As we enter into the flow of love, the floodgates of God's love open for us to receive even more. "The measure with which you measure will in return be measured out to you." This is a very beautiful way to understand the spiritual life.

This does *not* mean that God bases his love for us on what we do. He is not waiting to see how loving or merciful we will be before he decides to love or forgive us. He has already poured superabundant mercy upon us, "a good measure, packed together, shaken down, and overflowing." If we keep this in mind, we will find joy in giving to others and in forgiving them, because we are aware of how mercifully God treats us.

> *When have I been shamefaced because of my sins? How does this allow me to face the truth and the need of repentance? As I reflect on my relationship with others, how and why do I judge or condemn them?*

Mary, Mother of Marcy, teach me how to be merciful to others as Jesus is merciful to me.

70

First Reading: Isaiah 1:10, 16-20

Hear the word of the LORD,
    princes of Sodom!
Listen to the instruction of our God,
    people of Gomorrah!

    Wash yourselves clean!
Put away your misdeeds from before my eyes;
    cease doing evil; learn to do good.
Make justice your aim: redress the wronged,
    hear the orphan's plea, defend the widow.

Come now, let us set things right,
    says the LORD:
Though your sins be like scarlet,
    they may become white as snow;
Though they be crimson red,
    they may become white as wool.
If you are willing, and obey,
    you shall eat the good things of the land;
But if you refuse and resist,
    the sword shall consume you:
    for the mouth of the LORD has spoken!

Responsorial Psalm: Psalm 50:8-9, 16bc-17, 21 and 23
To the upright I will show the saving power of God.

"Not for your sacrifices do I rebuke you,
    for your burnt offerings are before me always.
I take from your house no bullock,
    no goats out of your fold."
R. To the upright I will show the saving power of God.
"Why do you recite my statutes,
    and profess my covenant with your mouth,
Though you hate discipline
    and cast my words behind you?"
R. To the upright I will show the saving power of God.
"When you do these things, shall I be deaf to it?
    Or do you think that I am like yourself?
    I will correct you by drawing them up before your eyes.

He that offers praise as a sacrifice glorifies me;
    and to him that goes the right way I will show the salvation of God."
R. To the upright I will show the saving power of God.

Gospel Acclamation: Ezekiel 18:31
Cast away from you all the crimes you have committed, says the Lord,
and make for yourselves a new heart and a new spirit.

Gospel: Matthew 23:1-12
Jesus spoke to the crowds and to his disciples, saying, "The
scribes and the Pharisees have taken their seat on the chair of Moses.
Therefore, do and observe all things whatsoever they tell you, but do
not follow their example. For they preach but they do not practice. They
tie up heavy burdens hard to carry and lay them on people's shoulders,
but they will not lift a finger to move them. All their works are
performed to be seen. They widen their phylacteries and lengthen their
tassels. They love places of honor at banquets, seats of honor in
synagogues, greetings in marketplaces, and the salutation 'Rabbi.' As
for you, do not be called 'Rabbi.' You have but one teacher, and you are
all brothers. Call no one on earth your father; you have but one Father
in heaven. Do not be called 'Master'; you have but one master, the
Christ. The greatest among you must be your servant. Whoever exalts
himself will be humbled; but whoever humbles himself will be exalted."

Meditation:
On Sunday, we joined the disciples on the holy mountain and
received a precious instruction from the voice of the Father: "This
is my beloved Son …; Listen to him!" Today's readings teach us more
about *listening*, and about the necessity of putting into practice what we
hear from the Lord.

Through the prophet Isaiah, the Lord exhorts us to "*hear* the word
of the LORD" and to "*listen* to the instruction of our God." As he continues
to speak, it becomes clear that this listening implies taking a new course
of action. If we are listening to the Lord, then we will "cease doing evil"
and "learn to do good." If we are listening to the Lord properly and
hearing his word, then we will also "*hear* the orphan's plea." In other
words, when we hear the orphan, or any people in need, we are to hear
the Lord telling us to do something to help them.

Today's Psalm teaches us more about the right way to listen. We
must go beyond reciting the Lord's statutes and professing his covenant
with our mouths. The Lord is not looking for superficial "sacrifices" and

"burnt offerings" but for a response of obedience from the heart. If he sees that we "hate discipline" and cast his words behind us, he gives us a word of correction. Do we recite the statutes of the Church and take pride in being practicing Catholics? Fine, but do our actions show that we hate the discipline involved in being faithful to his word?

"Discipline" is a good word to ponder during Lent. We began the season with a reminder to take on the three Lenten disciplines of prayer, fasting, and almsgiving. Perhaps we have added some prayers to our routine, meditated on the Stations of the Cross, or made some voluntary acts of self-denial. It is possible to do all these praiseworthy things and still "hate" them – that is, without allowing our hearts to be changed. We can even grow resentful that we ever committed ourselves to doing them!

In today's Gospel, Jesus tells us to make sure that our *deeds* are consistent with our *words*. As the saying goes, "actions speak louder than words." The Lord points to the scribes and Pharisees as examples of what God does not want from us. "They preach but they do not practice." Jesus reminds us not to do works simply in order to be seen, simply so that others might praise us. It is a good discipline to do good works that no one can see – but it is hard to persevere in such works. We tire of service that no one notices. We find it even worse if someone else gets the credit! This only shows us the imperfection of our love. Our love of God and neighbor is so often tainted with self-love. Jesus teaches us that the greatest among us is not the one who *looks* the greatest, but the one who *serves*. If we serve quietly and humbly, we may become invisible to others, but in reality we will be greater.

After the news of a public tragedy is broadcast, many people will voice a commitment to "pray for the victims." However, in the tumultuous world of social media, this sentiment is often met with anger by non-believers. In their eyes, those who talk about praying need rather to take action. Sometimes a counter-message is circulated: "Don't just pray – do something!" People share an image showing the familiar red circle with a backslash through it, superimposed over the word "PRAY." Some non-believers are even insulted when someone says, "I'll pray for you." What they hear is, "You are pathetic, and you need to change."

Reactions like this are based on a terrible misunderstanding of the power of prayer. For us who have faith, authentic prayer IS doing something. Still, the world is correct in its distaste for hypocrisy. If we are exalting ourselves by our pious words which are only causing others to resist grace, then we should be humbled. Rather than proclaim that we will pray for someone, we should just do it. We can quietly pray and sacrifice for those who are suffering *without talking about it*. God's love and mercy can be communicated through us if we truly act with selfless love. When we cease doing evil and learn to do good, when we make justice our aim, redress the wronged, hear the orphan's plea and defend the widow, when we give a ride, share a meal, lend a listening ear without judgment or comment – then we are listening to the word of the Lord and putting it into practice.

> *During Lent, how am I striving to better hear the word of the Lord and to listen to his instruction? How is my love of God and neighbor tainted with self-love? How do I respond when I am blamed or despised by another or when nobody praises me?*

Mary, may I perform acts of charity only for the greater glory of your son Jesus.
Sts. Perpetua and Felicity, pray for us.

Perpetua was a 22-year-old married noblewoman and a nursing mother. **Felicity** was her maid and an expectant mother. Shortly after they both converted to Christianity, during the persecutions of the Emperor Septimius Severus, they were arrested for their faith. While in prison, Perpetua wrote an account of her sufferings in a diary known as *The Passion of Perpetua and Felicity*. "What a day of horror! Terrible heat, owing to the crowds! Rough treatment by the soldiers! To crown all, I was tormented with anxiety for my baby … but I obtained leave for my baby to remain in prison with me." They were mauled by wild beasts and beheaded on March 7, 203, in Carthage, North Africa.

Notes

First Reading: Jeremiah 18:18-20

The people of Judah and the citizens of Jerusalem said, "Come, let us contrive a plot against Jeremiah. It will not mean the loss of instruction from the priests, nor of counsel from the wise, nor of messages from the prophets. And so, let us destroy him by his own tongue; let us carefully note his every word."

Heed me, O LORD,
    and listen to what my adversaries say.
Must good be repaid with evil
    that they should dig a pit to take my life?
Remember that I stood before you
    to speak in their behalf,
    to turn away your wrath from them.

Responsorial Psalm: Psalm 31:5-6, 14, 15-16
Save me, O Lord, in your kindness.

You will free me from the snare they set for me,
    for you are my refuge.
Into your hands I commend my spirit;
    you will redeem me, O LORD, O faithful God.
R. Save me, O Lord, in your kindness.
I hear the whispers of the crowd, that frighten me from every side,
    as they consult together against me, plotting to take my life.
R. Save me, O Lord, in your kindness.
But my trust is in you, O LORD;
    I say, "You are my God."
In your hands is my destiny; rescue me
    from the clutches of my enemies and my persecutors.
R. Save me, O Lord, in your kindness.

Gospel Acclamation: John 8:12
I am the light of the world, says the Lord; whoever follows me will have the light of life.

Gospel: Matthew 20:17-28

As Jesus was going up to Jerusalem, he took the Twelve disciples aside by themselves, and said to them on the way, "Behold, we are going up to Jerusalem, and the Son of Man will be handed over to the chief priests and the scribes, and they will condemn him to death, and hand him over to the Gentiles to be mocked and scourged and crucified, and he will be raised on the third day."

Then the mother of the sons of Zebedee approached Jesus with her sons and did him homage, wishing to ask him for something. He said to her, "What do you wish?" She answered him, "Command that these two sons of mine sit, one at your right and the other at your left, in your kingdom." Jesus said in reply, "You do not know what you are asking. Can you drink the chalice that I am going to drink?" They said to him, "We can." He replied, "My chalice you will indeed drink, but to sit at my right and at my left, this is not mine to give but is for those for whom it has been prepared by my Father." When the ten heard this, they became indignant at the two brothers. But Jesus summoned them and said, "You know that the rulers of the Gentiles lord it over them, and the great ones make their authority over them felt. But it shall not be so among you. Rather, whoever wishes to be great among you shall be your servant; whoever wishes to be first among you shall be your slave. Just so, the Son of Man did not come to be served but to serve and to give his life as a ransom for many."

Meditation:

When Jesus was transfigured in glory on the mountain, James and John, the sons of Zebedee, were there. Though they spoke about the vision to no one, the splendor they had witnessed was unforgettable. That vision was given in order to strengthen their faith in Jesus, so that they would be able to persevere in the upcoming dark days of his Passion. However, it seems that an unintended side effect of the vision was that they grew deaf to any mention of suffering, for they were so caught up in their dreams of glory.

In today's Gospel, Jesus once again prophesies that he will suffer and die before being raised up, but James and John seem not to hear it at all. In fact, the Lord's grave prophecy is received in a very odd way by all the Twelve. They voice no concern for their Master. They do not rally to his side or vow to protect him or even ask him what they can do for him. No, there is no response at all! Instead, their thoughts immediately turn to themselves. The ears of James and John pick up only the part about being "raised." They pay no attention to the bracing message that the Cross must come before the Resurrection.

This sort of selective deafness is not unusual. We all have a tendency simply not to hear what we do not want to hear, especially if we are fixated on some personal agenda. Such is the case of the enemies of the prophet Jeremiah, whose evil intentions are exposed in today's first reading. Jeremiah has spoken in the name of the Lord to the men of Judah and the citizens of Jerusalem. A true and faithful prophet, he has pointed out their errors and called them to repentance. They do not want to hear it! They plot to use his own words as a weapon against him. Full of malice and pride, they reassure themselves that they will still be able to get instruction and counsel and messages from prophets. They are ready to accept whatever "good stuff" they can get from God. But having their sin pointed out to them is too annoying. *This prophet is too depressing. He has to go!*

Jeremiah knows of their plans. He is deeply troubled that it seems that the Lord will allow good to be repaid with evil. He has interceded for these men, to turn the Lord's wrath away from them and their wicked deeds, and now they are plotting against him. Still, Jeremiah does not retaliate with a plot against them. Rather he puts his trust in God, knowing that God alone can save him.

We read of a similar situation in Psalm 31. The psalmist is threatened by enemies who are setting a snare for him. His response is to turn to the Lord and reaffirm his trust in the Lord's steadfast love: "Into your hands I commend my spirit; you will redeem me, O LORD, O faithful God." Jesus prayed this very Psalm as he hung dying on the Cross (cf. Lk 23:46).

In today's Gospel, Jesus informs his disciples that he, too, is surrounded by men plotting against him. He does not say that he will plead with his Father for rescue. He fully accepts that this is the Father's will for him. His purpose in telling his followers is that he wants to prepare them for what is to come. When they badly misunderstand him, Jesus gives a further instruction which enlightens us on the reason why he will undergo his suffering. He reveals that he has "not come to be served but to serve and to give his life as a ransom for many."

We who strive to follow in the footsteps of the Lord are also called *to serve* and *to give our life*. This way of life is incomprehensible to anyone whose goal is worldly greatness. To us who have received the gift of faith, however, it shines out as the way of true greatness. If we live by the truth and in love, if we drink our share of the cup of the Lord's sufferings, we will not be appreciated by the world any more than Jeremiah was, any more than Jesus himself was, but we will enter into the "greatness" the Lord has in mind for us – a share in his eternal glory.

> *How am I like Jeremiah who does not retaliate with evil when his life is in danger? Why is it impossible to serve and give my life for another when my goal is worldly greatness? Knowing that the cross is the only way to salvation, why do I avoid it and not accept it in love?*

Mary, free me from all jealousy and desire to be number one in this world.
St. John of God, pray for us.

John of God was born in Portugal in 1495 to a once-prominent family that had become impoverished but was rich in faith. As a young man, he worked as a shepherd. Later he moved to Spain and experienced a spiritual conversion while listening to a sermon by St. John of Avila. He decided to devote his life to caring for the sick and the poor. Settling in Granada, Spain, he used all his energies to care for the neediest people in the city. Slowly he drew to himself dedicated disciples who felt called to join him, and he founded the Brothers Hospitallers of St. John of God. This order has been officially entrusted with medical and dental care of the popes. St. John, who died in 1550, is patron of hospitals, nurses, and the sick.

Notes

First Reading: Jeremiah 17:5-10

Thus says the LORD:
Cursed is the man who trusts in human beings,
who seeks his strength in flesh,
whose heart turns away from the LORD.
He is like a barren bush in the desert
that enjoys no change of season,
But stands in a lava waste,
a salt and empty earth.
Blessed is the man who trusts in the LORD,
whose hope is the LORD.
He is like a tree planted beside the waters
that stretches out its roots to the stream:
It fears not the heat when it comes,
its leaves stay green;
In the year of drought it shows no distress,
but still bears fruit.
More tortuous than all else is the human heart,
beyond remedy; who can understand it?
I, the LORD, alone probe the mind
and test the heart,
To reward everyone according to his ways,
according to the merit of his deeds.

Responsorial Psalm: Psalm 1:1-2, 3, 4 and 6
Blessed are they who hope in the Lord.

Blessed the man who follows not
the counsel of the wicked
Nor walks in the way of sinners,
nor sits in the company of the insolent,
But delights in the law of the LORD
and meditates on his law day and night.
R. Blessed are they who hope in the Lord.
He is like a tree
planted near running water,
That yields its fruit in due season,
and whose leaves never fade.
Whatever he does, prospers.
R. Blessed are they who hope in the Lord.

Not so, the wicked, not so;
 they are like chaff which the wind drives away.
For the LORD watches over the way of the just,
 but the way of the wicked vanishes.
R. Blessed are they who hope in the Lord.

Gospel Acclamation: see Luke 8:15
Blessed are they who have kept the word with a generous heart and yield a harvest through perseverance.

Gospel: Luke 16:19-31

Jesus said to the Pharisees: "There was a rich man who dressed in purple garments and fine linen and dined sumptuously each day. And lying at his door was a poor man named Lazarus, covered with sores, who would gladly have eaten his fill of the scraps that fell from the rich man's table. Dogs even used to come and lick his sores. When the poor man died, he was carried away by angels to the bosom of Abraham. The rich man also died and was buried, and from the netherworld, where he was in torment, he raised his eyes and saw Abraham far off and Lazarus at his side. And he cried out, 'Father Abraham, have pity on me. Send Lazarus to dip the tip of his finger in water and cool my tongue, for I am suffering torment in these flames.' Abraham replied, 'My child, remember that you received what was good during your lifetime while Lazarus likewise received what was bad; but now he is comforted here, whereas you are tormented. Moreover, between us and you a great chasm is established to prevent anyone from crossing who might wish to go from our side to yours or from your side to ours.' He said, 'Then I beg you, father, send him to my father's house, for I have five brothers, so that he may warn them, lest they too come to this place of torment.' But Abraham replied, 'They have Moses and the prophets. Let them listen to them.' He said, 'Oh no, father Abraham, but if someone from the dead goes to them, they will repent.' Then Abraham said, 'If they will not listen to Moses and the prophets, neither will they be persuaded if someone should rise from the dead.'"

Meditation:

The first reading sets up a contrast between "the man who trusts in human beings" and "the man who trusts in the LORD." The first is "cursed" and the second is "blessed." The prophet is not saying that the Lord curses us when we turn away from him. He is simply making a statement about the way life is. If we trust in human beings and seek our strength in flesh, we make ourselves like a barren bush. On the other hand, if we trust in the Lord, good spiritual fruit is the natural consequence. This is how God made us. Jeremiah's words here are something like the instruction manual we get when we buy a new product. The manual tells us to use the product a certain way and to buy only quality parts and to go only to authorized technicians. If we do not follow the manufacturer's directions, the machine will break down – and it will be our own fault.

The *simplicity* of this instruction gets easily obscured by the *complexity* of our expectations and desires. We make our own life more difficult for ourselves. The Lord describes the human heart very accurately as "more tortuous than all else." "Tortuous" means "having many twists and turns; complicated, long, and confusing." (The word "tortuous" is often confused with "torturous," which is associated with "torture.") The human heart *is* confusing and twisted! Who can understand it? Even when we have clear instructions from the manufacturer, we assume we can come up with a better way or a shortcut. Often we cannot understand our own motives, yet we are convinced that we have a good reason for our decisions. We can rationalize even the worst behavior, claiming that we acted with only the best of intentions, and that if things did not work out, it was someone else's fault!

The Lord tells us frankly that only he can understand our hearts. He alone is able to "probe the mind and test the heart." By ourselves we are truly "beyond remedy," but the Lord provides us with his own divine remedy, offering us all we need to thrive like a tree planted beside a stream. If we are wise, we rely on the constant nourishment of God's word, prayer, the Sacraments, and the guidance of the Church – without which our inner life is both tortuous *and* torturous.

While Jeremiah describes the difference between the condition of the "cursed" and the "blessed," the Gospel illustrates the contrast with the vivid parable of the rich man and Lazarus. The rich man chooses to plant a barren desert of earthly riches for himself. He sinks his roots into his purple clothing and splendid feasts. In his eagerness to get on with his life, he pays no attention to the poor beggar right at his gate. After both men die, we learn that the rich man actually did see Lazarus and even knows his name – but even in the afterlife, he thinks of him as his personal servant. The reason the rich man is so *thirsty* is that he has no love. We are made for love, love of God and love of neighbor. Without love, our hearts become a barren desert.

When the rich man asks that a warning be given to his five brothers, Father Abraham explains that they already have Moses and the prophets. It is not a question of being warned but of *listening* to the warnings they already have. "If they will not *listen* to Moses and the prophets, neither will they be persuaded if someone should rise from the dead." If we wonder why the testimony of one who rises from the dead would have no more impact than that of Moses and the prophets, the answer is because the message would be essentially the same, no matter who the messenger is. But the rich man is not a listener. He did not listen to Moses or the prophets – nor to the cry of Lazarus, who was sent personally to the rich man as a prophet, to alert him to the call of love.

We have an enormous advantage over the rich man, for we actually do have the testimony of one who has risen from the dead, Jesus Christ. In last Sunday's Gospel, God the Father directed our attention to Jesus, saying: "Listen to him!" Listening is an attitude of the heart. It allows the remedy of light and truth to enter into the depths of our tortuous condition. We are called to listen to Jesus, who speaks to us through Moses and the prophets, and through the poorest of the poor.

Lent reminds us that we will not find true life in splendid banquets and luxurious clothes. These things only distract us from life and twist our hearts more than ever. Our hearts are thirsting for something more; they are thirsting for God! His word, his mercy, his grace, his divine life shared with us – this is the stream of living water into which our spiritual roots must continually grow.

> *Am I in the habit of rationalizing? How? In what ways has love of money distracted me from the call to love my neighbor? When are my actions contrary to my words?*

Mary, grant me a listening heart.
St. Frances of Rome, pray for us.

Frances of Rome, a great mystic of the fifteenth century, was born in 1384 of a noble family. Her youthful desire was to become a religious, but at her father's wish she married Lorenzo de Ponziani at the age of twelve. Although this marriage was arranged, it lasted forty years and she bore three children. Frances was a devoted, loving wife who was remarkable for her charity to the poor and her zeal for souls. She founded the Oblates of the Tor de'Specchi to minister to the needs of Rome's poor. These women led the life of a religious, but without the strict cloister or formal vows, and devoted themselves to prayer and service to the sick and the poor. Frances also founded the first home for abandoned children in Rome. She received numerous spiritual gifts, including visions of her guardian angel and private revelations concerning purgatory and hell. Frances was known for her humility, her obedience and patience. She died in Rome in 1440.

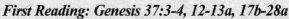

First Reading: Genesis 37:3-4, 12-13a, 17b-28a

Israel loved Joseph best of all his sons, for he was the child of his old age; and he had made him a long tunic. When his brothers saw that their father loved him best of all his sons, they hated him so much that they would not even greet him.

One day, when his brothers had gone to pasture their father's flocks at Shechem, Israel said to Joseph, "Your brothers, you know, are tending our flocks at Shechem. Get ready; I will send you to them."

So Joseph went after his brothers and caught up with them in Dothan. They noticed him from a distance, and before he came up to them, they plotted to kill him. They said to one another: "Here comes that master dreamer! Come on, let us kill him and throw him into one of the cisterns here; we could say that a wild beast devoured him. We shall then see what comes of his dreams."

When Reuben heard this, he tried to save him from their hands, saying, "We must not take his life. Instead of shedding blood," he continued, "just throw him into that cistern there in the desert; but do not kill him outright." His purpose was to rescue him from their hands and return him to his father. So when Joseph came up to them, they stripped him of the long tunic he had on; then they took him and threw him into the cistern, which was empty and dry.

They then sat down to their meal. Looking up, they saw a caravan of Ishmaelites coming from Gilead, their camels laden with gum, balm and resin to be taken down to Egypt. Judah said to his brothers: "What is to be gained by killing our brother and concealing his blood? Rather, let us sell him to these Ishmaelites, instead of doing away with him ourselves. After all, he is our brother, our own flesh." His brothers agreed. They sold Joseph to the Ishmaelites for twenty pieces of silver.

Responsorial Psalm: Psalm 105:16-17, 18-19, 20-21
Remember the marvels the Lord has done.

When the LORD called down a famine on the land
and ruined the crop that sustained them,
He sent a man before them,
Joseph, sold as a slave.
R. Remember the marvels the Lord has done.

They had weighed him down with fetters,
 and he was bound with chains,
Till his prediction came to pass
 and the word of the LORD proved him true.
R. Remember the marvels the Lord has done.
The king sent and released him,
 the ruler of the peoples set him free.
He made him lord of his house
 and ruler of all his possessions.
R. Remember the marvels the Lord has done.

Gospel Acclamation: John 3:16
God so loved the world that he gave his only-begotten Son; so that
everyone who believes in him might have eternal life.

✠ *Gospel: Matthew 21:33-43, 45-46*
 Jesus said to the chief priests and the elders of the people: "Hear
another parable. There was a landowner who planted a vineyard, put a
hedge around it, dug a wine press in it, and built a tower. Then he leased
it to tenants and went on a journey. When vintage time drew near, he
sent his servants to the tenants to obtain his produce. But the tenants
seized the servants and one they beat, another they killed, and a third
they stoned. Again he sent other servants, more numerous than the first
ones, but they treated them in the same way. Finally, he sent his son to
them, thinking, 'They will respect my son.' But when the tenants saw
the son, they said to one another, 'This is the heir. Come, let us kill him
and acquire his inheritance.' They seized him, threw him out of the
vineyard, and killed him. What will the owner of the vineyard do to
those tenants when he comes?" They answered him, "He will put those
wretched men to a wretched death and lease his vineyard to other
tenants who will give him the produce at the proper times." Jesus said
to them, "Did you never read in the Scriptures:
 The stone that the builders rejected
  has become the cornerstone;
 by the Lord has this been done,
  and it is wonderful in our eyes?
"Therefore, I say to you, the Kingdom of God will be taken away from
you and given to a people that will produce its fruit." When the chief
priests and the Pharisees heard his parables, they knew that he was
speaking about them. And although they were attempting to arrest him,
they feared the crowds, for they regarded him as a prophet.

Meditation:

On the Fridays of Lent, we recall the saving Passion of Jesus.

Today's readings, both of which refer to an obedient son who suffers at the hands of evil men, give us insight into the love that motivates Jesus to make a sacrificial offering of himself. This is the love in which we are being trained throughout our Lenten journey.

The obedient son in the first reading is Joseph, the beloved son of Israel. One day his father asks Joseph to make a journey for the sake of his brothers. Surely Joseph is aware of his brothers' hatred of him. They refuse even to greet him. Why, then, does he willingly travel alone to them? Because it is the will of his father.

We may wonder what Father Israel was thinking. How could he send his dear son into danger like that? On a purely human level, perhaps we can see here the wishful thinking and denial of one who loves. Israel probably did not want to admit the awful truth that his own sons hated each other so much. We do not want to see the things that cause us pain.

In this story, however, Israel also prefigures God the Father. Though he sees the tortuous condition of his sons, their animosity and their violent jealousy, he still loves them. He seeks a way to bring about a change of heart. *Maybe if I send Joseph to them, bringing them food and gifts, their hearts will soften, and they will love him, too.* Instead, the brothers turn from the heart of their father; they betray their own brother, selling him for twenty pieces of silver.

The obedient son in the Gospel is the beloved son of the vineyard owner. After the tenant farmers treat the man's servants with contempt and violence, the father sends his son. Again we may be puzzled by the father's willingness to place his own son in evident danger. In this case it seems the vineyard owner is doing some wishful thinking; he cannot imagine that anyone would not respect his own son. As an image of God the Father, the vineyard owner sees the son as a way for the tenants to be redeemed of their evil ways. Why does the son go? Because it is the will of his father.

We who know the whole story of Joseph, and even more, the story of Jesus, the obedient and sacrificial beloved Son of the Father, have the benefit of seeing the bigger picture. Today's Psalm recounts for us "the

85

marvels the Lord has done." One of the Lord's marvels is that in a time of famine he sent Joseph into Egypt: "He sent a man before them, Joseph, sold as a slave." In God's big plan, Joseph's presence in Egypt and all the sufferings he endured were for the good of the Chosen People. Joseph did not know this. He trusted his father and walked obediently into a confusing and dangerous situation.

As children of God our Father, we can be sent into situations where we know we are hated and are possibly even in danger. The missionaries who have spread the Gospel throughout history come to mind. Many have been rejected, tortured, and killed. In our own times, many faithful Christians, our brothers and sisters, are being mistreated and even killed; some have been crucified or beheaded. Why do missionaries keep going to dangerous places? Because the Father asks them to, and they trust that he has a bigger plan.

For most of us, our obedience to God does not put us in mortal danger. He "sends" us to our family, workplace, parish, or community. In obedient faith, we dedicate ourselves to service. In this life we may never see the big picture or the results of our faithfulness, but we trust that our loving Father knows what he is doing. Along the way, we are sometimes called to speak the truth in love, or challenge wrongdoing. We will be disliked or ignored or persecuted. Then why should we go? Why should we obey? Because it is the will of our good Father.

Was Joseph sold into slavery in vain? Was Jesus crucified in vain? No! So when the Lord allows us to pass through sufferings, we should not doubt him; we should not be afraid to follow his will. Faith tells us that the story is bigger than we can see right now. We put our trust in the goodness and love of our Father.

> *Pondering on my past, what are some sufferings that I endured which I later on realized were ultimately for my own good? Why do I find it difficult to speak the truth in love when I am challenging wrong doings? In my inner spirit, how do I handle envy and jealousy?*

Mary, show me how to be more obedient to the will of God each day.

First Reading: Micah 7:14-15, 18-20
Shepherd your people with your staff,
the flock of your inheritance,
That dwells apart in a woodland,
in the midst of Carmel.
Let them feed in Bashan and Gilead,
as in the days of old;
As in the days when you came from the land of Egypt,
show us wonderful signs.

Who is there like you, the God who removes guilt
and pardons sin for the remnant of his inheritance;
Who does not persist in anger forever,
but delights rather in clemency,
And will again have compassion on us,
treading underfoot our guilt?
You will cast into the depths of the sea all our sins;
You will show faithfulness to Jacob,
and grace to Abraham,
As you have sworn to our fathers
from days of old.

Responsorial Psalm: Psalm 103:1-2, 3-4, 9-10, 11-12
The Lord is kind and merciful.
Bless the LORD, O my soul;
and all my being, bless his holy name.
Bless the LORD, O my soul,
and forget not all his benefits.
R. The Lord is kind and merciful.
He pardons all your iniquities,
he heals all your ills.
He redeems your life from destruction,
he crowns you with kindness and compassion.
R. The Lord is kind and merciful.
He will not always chide,
nor does he keep his wrath forever.
Not according to our sins does he deal with us,
nor does he requite us according to our crimes.
R. The Lord is kind and merciful.

For as the heavens are high above the earth,
   so surpassing is his kindness toward those who fear him.
As far as the east is from the west,
   so far has he put our transgressions from us.
R. The Lord is kind and merciful.

Gospel Acclamation: Luke 15:18
I will get up and go to my father and shall say to him, Father, I have sinned against heaven and against you.

Gospel: Luke 15:1-3, 11-32
Tax collectors and sinners were all drawing near to listen to Jesus, but the Pharisees and scribes began to complain, saying, "This man welcomes sinners and eats with them." So to them Jesus addressed this parable. "A man had two sons, and the younger son said to his father, 'Father, give me the share of your estate that should come to me.' So the father divided the property between them. After a few days, the younger son collected all his belongings and set off to a distant country where he squandered his inheritance on a life of dissipation. When he had freely spent everything, a severe famine struck that country, and he found himself in dire need. So he hired himself out to one of the local citizens who sent him to his farm to tend the swine. And he longed to eat his fill of the pods on which the swine fed, but nobody gave him any. Coming to his senses he thought, 'How many of my father's hired workers have more than enough food to eat, but here am I, dying from hunger. I shall get up and go to my father and I shall say to him, "Father, I have sinned against heaven and against you. I no longer deserve to be called your son; treat me as you would treat one of your hired workers."' So he got up and went back to his father. While he was still a long way off, his father caught sight of him, and was filled with compassion. He ran to his son, embraced him and kissed him. His son said to him, 'Father, I have sinned against heaven and against you; I no longer deserve to be called your son.' But his father ordered his servants, 'Quickly, bring the finest robe and put it on him; put a ring on his finger and sandals on his feet. Take the fattened calf and slaughter it. Then let us celebrate with a feast, because this son of mine was dead, and has come to life again; he was lost, and has been found.' Then the celebration began. Now the older son had been out in the field and, on his way back, as he neared the house, he heard the sound of music and dancing. He called one of the servants and asked what this might mean. The servant said to him, 'Your brother has returned and your father has slaughtered the fattened calf because he has him back safe and sound.' He became angry, and when he refused to enter the house, his father came out and pleaded with him. He said to his father in reply,

'Look, all these years I served you and not once did I disobey your orders; yet you never gave me even a young goat to feast on with my friends. But when your son returns who swallowed up your property with prostitutes, for him you slaughter the fattened calf.' He said to him, 'My son, you are here with me always; everything I have is yours. But now we must celebrate and rejoice, because your brother was dead and has come to life again; he was lost and has been found.'"

Meditation:

Sometimes it happens that people look at the external disciplines associated with Lent and conclude that Christianity is a harsh and demanding religion, and that Christians believe in a harsh and demanding God. An attentive reading of the word of God dispels that false impression. Today's readings are overflowing with the *beauty of divine mercy*.

In the first reading the prophet Micah praises the attributes of God. He proclaims that the Lord "does not persist in anger forever, but delights rather in clemency." This short prophecy is full of expressions of mercy for us to ponder: God *removes guilt and pardons sin*; he will *have compassion on us* and *tread underfoot our guilt*; he will *cast all our sins into the depths of the sea*. This last statement, referring to the depths of the sea, calls to mind St. Faustina's description of God's mercy as an "ocean." She says that when Jesus died on the Cross, "the source of life gushed forth for souls and the ocean of mercy opened up for the whole world."

Today's Psalm, too, is bursting with words of mercy. We are reminded that the Lord *pardons all our iniquities*, he *heals all our ills*; he *does not deal with us according to our sins*. Instead, he puts our transgressions as far from us *as the east is from the west*. We can only be overwhelmed with joy and gratitude when we glimpse these extraordinary depths of God's kindness and mercy.

Surely these were the emotions of the prodigal son when he discovered, beyond all his hopes, that the father was actually *delighted* to have him back home. It seems too good to be true. No one could have expected that such a sinner would receive such a warm welcome! If the father allowed the boy back into the house at all, if he did not demand a public apology or require him to make restitution for squandering the family's estate, if he gave him the dignity of a trusted employee – we would consider that very merciful! But the father does nothing like that; his mercy goes beyond every boundary set by our measures of human justice. If this parable did not come from the heart of the Lord Jesus himself, the foremost Expert in the ways of the Father, we would be tempted to dismiss it as a pious exaggeration.

The part of us that finds the Father's mercy excessive is personified in the parable by the elder son. This son is not delighted; he is angry at the welcome given to the prodigal. This is not righteous anger but the anger of the self-righteous. He feels that a terrible injustice is being done to him. He resents being taken for granted, so unappreciated. His father has not even invited him to the party!

When we are caught in the trap of self-righteousness – that is, *pride* – we are blind to our own sin. Thus we cannot appreciate the great gift of mercy. We do not think we need mercy and we do not see any reason to be merciful to others. The more we see mercy, the more it looks like injustice. After all, we never get the reward that we deserve for doing our duty, while those who deserve punishment get treated better than we do. It is intolerably unfair.

The response of the father to his hard-hearted son is the response of the Lord to us when we are sitting in self-righteousness. The Father does not address the questions that so trouble us; he does not defend the wrongdoing of others nor affirm that we deserve better treatment. No, he says, "My son, you are here with me always; everything I have is yours." His love for us is that of a Father, not an employer. He does not love us more because we are good; he does not love us less because we are evil. Love moves him to give us *everything he has!* This is what the prodigal son learned in the end. His father is still willing to give, in spite of everything. This is what the elder son fails to see.

God does not owe us anything, but he gives us everything. When we focus on what kind of Father we have – not on what kind of brother we have, or what kind of son we ourselves are – then we will be moved to rejoice with the Father. Whether his mercy is extended to us or to our repentant brother, the only fitting response is to proclaim with the Father, "We must celebrate and rejoice!"

> *When have I been overwhelmed with joy and gratitude at the depths of God's mercy and kindness? How do I compare my actions to that of the forgiving Father, the prodigal son and his hard-hearted brother? How does mercy and forgiveness enable me to attain serenity of heart?*

Mary, Mother of Mercy, form my heart to be merciful and forgiving.

Third Week of Lent

"… whoever drinks the water I shall give will never thirst…"

John 4:14

Theme for the Week

Jesus offers living water to all who thirst for him. Our spiritual thirst can only be satisfied through a deeper faith encounter with him, the wellspring of all grace and mercy. The Season of Lent gives us a new opportunity to draw near to him and speak with him, to encounter him in prayer in a heart-to-heart dialogue. Let us persevere in faith so that we may encounter the Lord each day.

WATER: SYMBOL OF DIVINE GRACE
THAT GIVES ETERNAL LIFE
A Spiritual Reflection by Pope Francis

…The Gospel passage from today, the Third Sunday of Lent, tells us of Jesus' meeting with a Samaritan woman (cf. Jn 4:5-42). He is on a journey with his disciples and takes a break near a well in Samaria. The Samaritans were considered heretics by the Jews, and were very much despised as second-class citizens. Jesus is tired, thirsty. A woman arrives to draw water and he says to her: "Give me a drink" (v. 7). Breaking every barrier, he begins a dialogue in which he reveals to the woman *the mystery of living water,* that is, of the Holy Spirit, God's gift. Indeed, in response to the woman's surprised reaction, Jesus says: "If you knew the gift of God and who is saying to you, 'Give me a drink,' you would have asked him and he would have given you living water" (v. 10).

Water is the focus of this dialogue. On the one hand, water is an essential element that slakes the body's thirst and sustains life. On the other, water is a symbol of divine grace that gives eternal life. In the biblical tradition God is the source of living water: as it says in Psalms and in the Prophets: distancing oneself from God, the source of living water, and from his Law, leads to the worst drought. This is the experience of the People of Israel in the desert. During their long journey to freedom, as they were dying of thirst, they cried out against Moses and against God because there was no water. Thus, God willed Moses to make water flow from a rock, as a sign of the Providence of God, accompanying his people and giving them life (cf. Ex 17:1-7).

The Apostle Paul, too, interprets that rock as a symbol of Christ. He says: "And that rock was Christ" (1 Cor 10:4). It is the mysterious figure of his presence in the midst of the People of God on their journey. Christ, in fact, is the Temple from which, according to the prophets, flows the Holy Spirit, the living water which purifies and gives life. Whoever thirsts for salvation can draw freely from Jesus, and the Spirit will become a wellspring of full and eternal life in him/her. The promise of living water that Jesus made to the Samaritan woman becomes a reality in his Passion: from his pierced side flowed "blood and water" (Jn 19:34). Christ, the Lamb, immolated and risen, is the wellspring from which flows the Holy Spirit who remits sins and regenerates new life.

This gift is also the source of witness. Like the Samaritan woman, whoever personally encounters the living Jesus feels the need to talk about him to others, so that everyone might reach the point of proclaiming that Jesus "is truly the Savior of the world" (Jn 4:42), as the woman's fellow townspeople later said. Generated to new life through Baptism, we too are called to witness the life and hope that are within us. If our quest and our thirst are thoroughly quenched in Christ, we will manifest that salvation is not found in the "things" of this world, which ultimately produce drought, but in he who has loved us and will always love us: Jesus, our Savior, in the living water, that he offers us.

May Mary, Most Holy, help us nourish a desire for Christ, font of living water, the only one who can satisfy the thirst for life and love that we bear in our hearts.

Pope Francis, Angelus Message, March 15, 2020
© Copyright 2020 – Libreria Editrice Vaticana

First Reading: Exodus 17:3-7

In those days, in their thirst for water, the people grumbled against Moses, saying, "Why did you ever make us leave Egypt? Was it just to have us die here of thirst with our children and our livestock?" So Moses cried out to the LORD, "What shall I do with this people? A little more and they will stone me!" The LORD answered Moses, "Go over there in front of the people, along with some of the elders of Israel, holding in your hand, as you go, the staff with which you struck the river. I will be standing there in front of you on the rock in Horeb. Strike the rock, and the water will flow from it for the people to drink." This Moses did, in the presence of the elders of Israel. The place was called Massah and Meribah, because the Israelites quarreled there and tested the LORD, saying, "Is the LORD in our midst or not?"

Responsorial Psalm: Psalm 95:1-2, 6-7, 8-9
If today you hear his voice, harden not your hearts.

Come, let us sing joyfully to the LORD;
    let us acclaim the Rock of our salvation.
Let us come into his presence with thanksgiving;
    let us joyfully sing psalms to him.
R. If today you hear his voice, harden not your hearts.
Come, let us bow down in worship;
    let us kneel before the LORD who made us.
For he is our God,
    and we are the people he shepherds, the flock he guides.
R. If today you hear his voice, harden not your hearts.
Oh, that today you would hear his voice:
    "Harden not your hearts as at Meribah,
    as in the day of Massah in the desert.
Where your fathers tempted me;
    they tested me though they had seen my works."
R. If today you hear his voice, harden not your hearts.

Second Reading: Romans 5:1-2, 5-8

Brothers and sisters: Since we have been justified by faith, we have peace with God through our Lord Jesus Christ, through whom we have gained access by faith to this grace in which we stand, and we boast in hope of the glory of God.

And hope does not disappoint, because the love of God has been poured out into our hearts through the Holy Spirit who has been given to us. For Christ, while we were still helpless, died at the appointed time for the ungodly. Indeed, only with difficulty does one die for a just person, though perhaps for a good person one might even find courage to die. But God proves his love for us in that while we were still sinners Christ died for us.

Gospel Acclamation: see John 4:42, 15
Lord, you are truly the Savior of the world; give me living water, that I may never thirst again.

 Gospel: John 4:5-42
(Short Form: John 4:5-15, 19b-26, 39a, 40-42)
Jesus came to a town of Samaria called Sychar, near the plot of land that Jacob had given to his son Joseph. Jacob's well was there. Jesus, tired from his journey, sat down there at the well. It was about noon.

A woman of Samaria came to draw water. Jesus said to her, "Give me a drink." His disciples had gone into the town to buy food. The Samaritan woman said to him, "How can you, a Jew, ask me, a Samaritan woman, for a drink?" – For Jews use nothing in common with Samaritans. – Jesus answered and said to her, "If you knew the gift of God and who is saying to you, 'Give me a drink,' you would have asked him and he would have given you living water." The woman said to him, "Sir, you do not even have a bucket and the cistern is deep; where then can you get this living water? Are you greater than our father Jacob, who gave us this cistern and drank from it himself with his children and his flocks?" Jesus answered and said to her, "Everyone who drinks this water will be thirsty again; but whoever drinks the water I shall give will never thirst; the water I shall give will become in him a spring of water welling up to eternal life." The woman said to him, "Sir, give me this water, so that I may not be thirsty or have to keep coming here to draw water."

Jesus said to her, "Go call your husband and come back." The woman answered and said to him, "I do not have a husband." Jesus answered her, "You are right in saying, 'I do not have a husband.' For you have had five husbands, and the one you have now is not your husband. What you have said is true." The woman said to him, "Sir, I can see that you are a prophet. Our ancestors worshiped on this mountain; but you people say that the place to worship is in Jerusalem." Jesus said to her, "Believe me, woman, the hour is coming when you will worship the Father neither on this mountain nor in Jerusalem. You people worship what you do not understand; we worship what we understand, because salvation is from the Jews. But the hour is coming, and is now here, when true worshipers will worship the Father in Spirit and truth; and indeed the Father seeks such people to worship him. God is Spirit, and those who worship him must worship in Spirit and truth." The woman said to him, "I know that the Messiah is coming, the one called the Christ; when he comes, he will tell us everything." Jesus said to her, "I am he, the one speaking with you."

At that moment his disciples returned, and were amazed that he was talking with a woman, but still no one said, "What are you looking for?" or "Why are you talking with her?" The woman left her water jar and went into the town and said to the people, "Come see a man who told me everything I have done. Could he possibly be the Christ?" They went out of the town and came to him. Meanwhile, the disciples urged him, "Rabbi, eat." But he said to them, "I have food to eat of which you do not know." So the disciples said to one another, "Could someone have brought him something to eat?" Jesus said to them, "My food is to do the will of the one who sent me and to finish his work. Do you not say, 'In four months the harvest will be here'? I tell you, look up and see the fields ripe for the harvest. The reaper is already receiving payment and gathering crops for eternal life, so that the sower and reaper can rejoice together. For here the saying is verified that 'One sows and another reaps.' I sent you to reap what you have not worked for; others have done the work, and you are sharing the fruits of their work."

Many of the Samaritans of that town began to believe in him because of the word of the woman who testified, "He told me everything I have done." When the Samaritans came to him, they invited him to stay with them; and he stayed there two days. Many more began to believe in him because of his word, and they said to the woman, "We no longer believe because of your word; for we have heard for ourselves, and we know that this is truly the savior of the world."

Meditation:
In this Season of Lent, we have gone into the "desert" with Jesus, leaving "Egypt," which can symbolize our slavery to the ways of the world. Now that we have been journeying for two and a half weeks, we might begin to feel like the Israelites in the first reading. Our flesh grumbles against God, "Why did you ever make us leave Egypt?"

We can feel like we are dying, in a sense, as we thirst for the comforts and pleasures which our fallen nature craves. Especially if we are experiencing trials, we can begin to wonder, "Is the LORD in our midst or not?"

The reading reveals to us that the Lord is very much in the midst of his people. He tells Moses to go to the rock in Horeb, saying, "I will be standing there in front of you on the rock." He tells Moses to strike the rock, and when Moses does so, water flows out from the rock to satisfy the people's thirst.

Throughout the Scriptures, rock is used to signify something that is firm, sure, reliable. For example, Jesus tells his followers to build their houses on the "rock" of his words (cf. Mt 7:24-27). And he calls Peter the "rock" upon which he will securely build his Church (cf. Mt 16:18). We know that rock is hard; it is not easy to dig into. It is much easier to build on sand since it is easy to dig into sand and move it around. But as Jesus tells us, sand does not provide a firm foundation. It washes away when a storm comes.

During this season of Lent, God is calling us to dig into the "rock" of his word. This is where he is to be found; this is where he is "standing" in our midst. He is not found in the shifting sands of the world's ways, as pleasant as those are to our comfort-loving, self-seeking nature. If we want to find the true "water" which will quench our thirst for eternal life, we need to "strike the rock." That is, we need to do the hard work of turning away from the desires of our flesh and "dig into" God's word.

Today's Psalm gives us a practical first step: "If today you hear his voice, harden not your hearts." We will see this refrain repeated several times throughout this week, so we know that it is an important lesson which Mother Church means for us to learn. The word of God often challenges us and convicts us. It calls us out of our self-focus and leads us to sacrificial love for others. It sheds light on the disordered ways in which we often live and guides us toward repentance. Because we tend to resist this process, to reject God's word rather than allow it to challenge us, we need this repeated exhortation *not* to harden our hearts against his word but to welcome it with humility and gratitude.

A wonderful example of how to welcome the word is given to us by the Samaritan woman. She must have found Jesus' words very challenging. Even the fact that a Jewish rabbi was speaking to her at all would have surprised her. Then he tells her that she should be asking him for living water so that she would never thirst again. It would have been easy for her to dismiss him as a crazy person. But instead she listens to him with an open heart, asking questions so that she can better understand what he is saying, and then simply asking him to give her the water of which he speaks.

When Jesus tells her to go and call her husband, in all humility she admits that she has no husband – basically that she is living in a state of adultery. She does not try to hide her condition from Jesus, nor does she react with indignation. What a beautiful example she is of coming before the Lord in humility and truth, listening to his words and acting on them! Jesus' next words apply to her first of all: "The hour is coming, and is now here, when true worshipers will worship the Father in Spirit and truth; and indeed the Father seeks such people to worship him." This very woman is someone to whom the Father has sent Jesus to seek out and save, so that she could worship in Spirit and truth!

If we, also, will humble ourselves like this woman, listening to the Lord's word to us in all humility and openness of heart, then we too can be blessed. It is hard work to reject the grumbling and complaining of our fallen nature and to "dig into" the Lord's word in prayer, spiritual reading, and the Sacraments. But this is where our hope is, as St. Paul teaches us in the reading from Romans. Only through faith in Jesus Christ do we have access to the "grace in which we stand." When we rely on him, we have a sure hope that "does not disappoint, because the love of God has been poured out" – like living water – "into our hearts through the Holy Spirit who has been given to us."

> *Am I still longing for the comforts and pleasures that I gave up at the beginning of Lent? In what ways do I harden my heart against God's word instead of welcoming it with humility and gratitude? How can I imitate the humility and truth of the Samaritan woman?*

Mary, open my heart to listen to God's word in humility and faith.

First Reading: 2 Kings 5:1-15ab

Naaman, the army commander of the king of Aram, was highly esteemed and respected by his master, for through him the LORD had brought victory to Aram. But valiant as he was, the man was a leper. Now the Arameans had captured in a raid on the land of Israel a little girl, who became the servant of Naaman's wife. "If only my master would present himself to the prophet in Samaria," she said to her mistress, "he would cure him of his leprosy." Naaman went and told his lord just what the slave girl from the land of Israel had said. "Go," said the king of Aram. "I will send along a letter to the king of Israel." So Naaman set out, taking along ten silver talents, six thousand gold pieces, and ten festal garments. To the king of Israel he brought the letter, which read: "With this letter I am sending my servant Naaman to you, that you may cure him of his leprosy."

When he read the letter, the king of Israel tore his garments and exclaimed: "Am I a god with power over life and death, that this man should send someone to me to be cured of leprosy? Take note! You can see he is only looking for a quarrel with me!" When Elisha, the man of God, heard that the king of Israel had torn his garments, he sent word to the king: "Why have you torn your garments? Let him come to me and find out that there is a prophet in Israel."

Naaman came with his horses and chariots and stopped at the door of Elisha's house. The prophet sent him the message: "Go and wash seven times in the Jordan, and your flesh will heal, and you will be clean." But Naaman went away angry, saying, "I thought that he would surely come out and stand there to invoke the LORD his God, and would move his hand over the spot, and thus cure the leprosy. Are not the rivers of Damascus, the Abana and the Pharpar, better than all the waters of Israel? Could I not wash in them and be cleansed?" With this, he turned about in anger and left.

But his servants came up and reasoned with him. "My father," they said, "if the prophet had told you to do something extraordinary, would you not have done it? All the more now, since he said to you, 'Wash and be clean,' should you do as he said." So Naaman went down and plunged into the Jordan seven times at the word of the man of God. His flesh became again like the flesh of a little child, and he was clean.

He returned with his whole retinue to the man of God. On his arrival he stood before him and said, "Now I know that there is no God in all the earth, except in Israel."

Responsorial Psalm: Psalm 42:2, 3; 43:3, 4
Athirst is my soul for the living God.
When shall I go and behold the face of God?

As the hind longs for the running waters,
    so my soul longs for you, O God.

R. *Athirst is my soul for the living God.*
When shall I go and behold the face of God?

Athirst is my soul for God, the living God.
    When shall I go and behold the face of God?

R. *Athirst is my soul for the living God.*
When shall I go and behold the face of God?

Send forth your light and your fidelity;
    they shall lead me on
And bring me to your holy mountain,
    to your dwelling-place.

R. *Athirst is my soul for the living God.*
When shall I go and behold the face of God?

Then will I go in to the altar of God,
    the God of my gladness and joy;
Then will I give you thanks upon the harp,
    O God, my God!

R. *Athirst is my soul for the living God.*
When shall I go and behold the face of God?

Gospel Acclamation: see Psalm 130:5, 7
I hope in the LORD, I trust in his word; with him there is kindness and plenteous redemption.

Gospel: Luke 4:24-30

Jesus said to the people in the synagogue at Nazareth: "Amen, I say to you, no prophet is accepted in his own native place. Indeed, I tell you, there were many widows in Israel in the days of Elijah when the sky was closed for three and a half years and a severe famine spread over the entire land. It was to none of these that Elijah was sent, but only to a widow in Zarephath in the land of Sidon. Again, there were many lepers in Israel during the time of Elisha the prophet; yet not one of them was cleansed, but only Naaman the Syrian." When the people in the synagogue heard this, they were all filled with fury. They rose up, drove him out of the town, and led him to the brow of the hill on which their town had been built, to hurl him down headlong. But he passed through the midst of them and went away.

Meditation:

Yesterday we pondered the beautiful way in which the Samaritan woman responded to Jesus. She took in his word with a humble, open heart, and thus was able to receive a great blessing for herself – and to be the source of blessing for her whole village as well.

In today's Gospel, we see a very different reaction to Jesus' words on the part of the people of Nazareth. In Luke's Gospel, this event comes near the beginning of Jesus' ministry. He has been preaching throughout Galilee. Now he comes to his hometown, reads a prophecy about the Messiah from the Book of Isaiah, and then says to the people, "Today this scripture passage is fulfilled in your hearing." They marvel at this, and begin to ask one another, "Isn't this the son of Joseph?" (Lk 4:21-22).

The people harden their hearts against Jesus. We can imagine what they are thinking: *Who does this guy think he is? The Messiah? We know him; he's just the son of Joseph. How could he be anyone special?* From Jesus' next words, we learn that he knows what they are thinking – that if he wants to convince them that he is, in fact, the Messiah, he will have to do some amazing thing to prove it. "Surely you will quote me this proverb, 'Physician, cure yourself,' and say, 'Do here in your native place the things that we heard were done in Capernaum'" (Lk 4:23). Then he goes on to talk about Elijah and the widow, and the healing of Naaman the Syrian leper.

Jesus is warning the people not to make the mistake of thinking that God cannot work through ordinary things and familiar people. In our pride, we often find it difficult to hear God speaking to us through those who are near to us. How often we are willing to listen to and act on something that an "expert" says, while our spouse or close friends find themselves saying, "I've said that to you many times, but you would never accept it coming from me!" Jesus is warning the people of Nazareth to avoid this kind of proud hard-heartedness. But they did not heed his warning. Instead they tried to throw him off the top of a hill! It is striking that, outside of the events of the Passion, this is the most violent opposition Jesus meets anywhere in the Gospels – and it comes from his own townspeople!

In the first reading Naaman has a similar first reaction when Elisha instructs him to go wash in the River Jordan. He becomes indignant, thinking to himself, *How dare this prophet dismiss me with so little*

101

show! How dare he not even come out of his house to meet me and heal me personally! Doesn't he know who I am, how important I am? I'm not going to wash in his stupid river!

This is an excellent illustration of the hardness of heart against which we are being warned all this week. When we are proud and hard-hearted, we find it very hard to hear God speaking to us and working through the simple, ordinary events and people in our daily lives. We are not open to carefully considering the words of our family members, our friends, or our coworkers, and we do not think that God might be speaking to us through them, especially if their words are challenging. Yet, as Naaman's servants reasoned with him, of course it is precisely through the ordinary people and events that God most commonly speaks to us, if we are humble enough to hear him.

Today's Psalm gives us a wonderful teaching on how we can open ourselves most fruitfully to hear God's word to us. The psalmist says that his soul is "athirst ... for the living God." His soul longs for God like a deer longs for running water. He is yearning to see the face of God, and he begs God earnestly to send forth his light and his fidelity to lead him to God's dwelling place. He finds in God his gladness and joy, giving thanks to him for his goodness. If this is our attitude towards God's word – longing with all our heart to receive it as the living water which can quench our soul's thirst, and begging God to send us his light in whatever way he chooses to do so – then we can truly experience the kind of healing and restoration which Naaman experienced.

Let us put aside all pride and self-importance and take as our prayer for today the Gospel Acclamation: "I hope in the LORD, I trust in his word; with him there is kindness and plenteous redemption."

> What are some of the ways that God has worked in my life in ordinary things? How do I resemble Naaman's first reaction to the prophet Elijah? Why do I find it hard to receive advice or help from someone whom I think less of?

Mary, grant me the humility to accept and rejoice in God's providence.

First Reading: Daniel 3:25, 34-43
Azariah stood up in the fire and prayed aloud:

"For your name's sake, O Lord, do not deliver us up forever,
or make void your covenant.
Do not take away your mercy from us,
for the sake of Abraham, your beloved,
Isaac your servant, and Israel your holy one,
To whom you promised to multiply their offspring
like the stars of heaven,
or the sand on the shore of the sea.
For we are reduced, O Lord, beyond any other nation,
brought low everywhere in the world this day
because of our sins.
We have in our day no prince, prophet, or leader,
no burnt offering, sacrifice, oblation, or incense,
no place to offer first fruits, to find favor with you.
But with contrite heart and humble spirit
let us be received;
As though it were burnt offerings of rams and bullocks,
or thousands of fat lambs,
So let our sacrifice be in your presence today
as we follow you unreservedly;
for those who trust in you cannot be put to shame.
And now we follow you with our whole heart,
we fear you and we pray to you.
Do not let us be put to shame,
but deal with us in your kindness and great mercy.
Deliver us by your wonders,
and bring glory to your name, O Lord."

 Responsorial Psalm: Psalm 25:4-5ab, 6 and 7bc, 8-9
Remember your mercies, O Lord.
Your ways, O LORD, make known to me;
teach me your paths,
Guide me in your truth and teach me,
for you are God my savior.
R. Remember your mercies, O Lord.

Remember that your compassion, O LORD,
    and your kindness are from of old.
In your kindness remember me,
    because of your goodness, O LORD.
R. Remember your mercies, O Lord.
Good and upright is the LORD;
    thus he shows sinners the way.
He guides the humble to justice,
    he teaches the humble his way.
R. Remember your mercies, O Lord.

Gospel Acclamation: Joel 2:12-13
Even now, says the LORD, return to me with your whole heart; for I am gracious and merciful.

✠ Gospel: Matthew 18:21-35
Peter approached Jesus and asked him, "Lord, if my brother sins against me, how often must I forgive him? As many as seven times?" Jesus answered, "I say to you, not seven times but seventy-seven times. That is why the Kingdom of heaven may be likened to a king who decided to settle accounts with his servants. When he began the accounting, a debtor was brought before him who owed him a huge amount. Since he had no way of paying it back, his master ordered him to be sold, along with his wife, his children, and all his property, in payment of the debt. At that, the servant fell down, did him homage, and said, 'Be patient with me, and I will pay you back in full.' Moved with compassion the master of that servant let him go and forgave him the loan. When that servant had left, he found one of his fellow servants who owed him a much smaller amount. He seized him and started to choke him, demanding, 'Pay back what you owe.' Falling to his knees, his fellow servant begged him, 'Be patient with me, and I will pay you back.' But he refused. Instead, he had him put in prison until he paid back the debt. Now when his fellow servants saw what had happened, they were deeply disturbed, and went to their master and reported the whole affair. His master summoned him and said to him, 'You wicked servant! I forgave you your entire debt because you begged me to. Should you not have had pity on your fellow servant, as I had pity on you?' Then in anger his master handed him over to the torturers until he should pay back the whole debt. So will my heavenly Father do to you, unless each of you forgives your brother from your heart."

Meditation:

Our Gospel Acclamation for today is a passage from the prophet Joel: "Even now, says the LORD, return to me with your whole heart; for I am gracious and merciful." We might remember that these were the very first words of the first reading from Ash Wednesday, the first words we heard from the Lord as we began this Lenten season. Two things are noteworthy in this passage – the Lord exhorts us to return to him *now*, and with a *whole heart.*

One of the most successful tactics of the evil one is to persuade us to put off turning to the Lord. We think to ourselves: *I'm busy today, I'll put in some prayer time tomorrow. I'll do a little spiritual reading over the weekend when I have more time. I'll put off going to Confession until next week, I will surely turn to the Lord – but later.* But the Lord tells us that, no, *right now* is the time to return to him. We can stop right in the middle of reading this meditation and say, *Lord, I turn my heart to you right now. I open myself completely to whatever you want to say to me or however you want to work in me. I give myself to you, Lord, right here and now.* Let us pause with this thought for a moment. And let us return to the Lord throughout the day, whenever we remember to do so, and take a moment to thank him.

The other thing which we note in the passage from Joel is that we are to turn to the Lord with our *whole heart.* What does it mean to turn to the Lord with our whole heart? We see a wonderful example given to us in the first reading today. Azariah (also called Abednego) is a young Jewish man in exile in Babylon. God's people had not been faithful to his covenant, and so he has allowed the kingdom to be conquered and the people sent into captivity. Azariah and his companions have remained faithful to God's laws, even to the extent of refusing the King's orders for everyone to bow down to an idol he had made. Because of this, the king has ordered Azariah and his companions to be cast into a white-hot furnace.

Even though he personally has striven to be faithful to God, Azariah is in a desperate situation. We might expect him to grumble and complain like the Israelites in the desert. Or he might even reject God's word completely, as the people of Nazareth did. Instead, we see him turn to the Lord with his *whole heart.* He confesses that he and his people are in a tragic condition because of their sins. He does not pridefully put a judgment on God that his ways are not fair, nor does he insist that God act according to Azariah's will. He says to God, *We have been brought low due to our sins, and now we look to you for your kindness and mercy.*

The Psalm for today echoes the same sentiment of whole-hearted turning to God. The psalmist appeals to God to guide him in his paths out of his mercy and kindness. He also states that it is the humble (literally, the *anawim*) to whom God shows the way to the fullness of life.

Jesus assures us in the Gospel that we *can* confidently look to God for mercy. After all, in the parable the first servant owes the king a "huge amount" which would have been impossible for him to repay, and the king forgives him the entire debt. Therefore we should never fear to come before the Lord, especially in this Lenten season, and throw ourselves at his mercy, no matter how we might have sinned. His mercy is always greater than any sin of ours.

Despite the great mercy of the king, however, the first servant nevertheless ends up in a terrible condition. Why should this be so, if the king is merciful? We saw on Sunday that God's mercy is like the living water which Jesus offered to give to the Samaritan woman. It is like a flowing stream, bringing life into the parched desert of our broken condition. However, the stream of God's mercy cannot flow where there is a blockage. If there is pride, hard-heartedness, self-seeking, complaining, refusing to forgive – these things block the flow of God's grace. They close off our hearts from receiving it. No matter how endless God's mercy is, we will not benefit from it if we close ourselves off from it. We open ourselves to receive God's mercy by allowing it to flow through us to others. It is only in sharing God's gifts that we can ever truly receive them ourselves.

Let us, then, heed the word of the Lord by turning to him right now, with humble, contrite hearts, asking him to bathe us in his mercy, and resolving to show his mercy in turn to those whom we meet today.

What hinders me from returning to the Lord in prayer throughout the day? How does the humble prayer of Azariah echo in my heart? How can my pride, complaining, and hard-heartedness block God's mercy?

Mary, open my heart to God's endless mercy.

First Reading: Deuteronomy 4:1, 5-9

Moses spoke to the people and said: "Now, Israel, hear the statutes and decrees which I am teaching you to observe, that you may live, and may enter in and take possession of the land which the LORD, the God of your fathers, is giving you. Therefore, I teach you the statutes and decrees as the LORD, my God, has commanded me, that you may observe them in the land you are entering to occupy. Observe them carefully, for thus will you give evidence of your wisdom and intelligence to the nations, who will hear of all these statutes and say, 'This great nation is truly a wise and intelligent people.' For what great nation is there that has gods so close to it as the LORD, our God, is to us whenever we call upon him? Or what great nation has statutes and decrees that are as just as this whole law which I am setting before you today?

"However, take care and be earnestly on your guard not to forget the things which your own eyes have seen, nor let them slip from your memory as long as you live, but teach them to your children and to your children's children."

Responsorial Psalm: Psalm 147:12-13, 15-16, 19-20
Praise the Lord, Jerusalem.

Glorify the LORD, O Jerusalem;
    praise your God, O Zion.
For he has strengthened the bars of your gates;
    he has blessed your children within you.
R. Praise the Lord, Jerusalem.
He sends forth his command to the earth;
    swiftly runs his word!
He spreads snow like wool;
    frost he strews like ashes.
R. Praise the Lord, Jerusalem.
He has proclaimed his word to Jacob,
    his statutes and his ordinances to Israel.
He has not done thus for any other nation;
    his ordinances he has not made known to them.
R. Praise the Lord, Jerusalem.

Gospel Acclamation: see John 6:63c, 68c
Your words, Lord, are Spirit and life; you have the words of everlasting life.

Gospel: Matthew 5:17-19

Jesus said to his disciples: "Do not think that I have come to abolish the law or the prophets. I have come not to abolish but to fulfill. Amen, I say to you, until heaven and earth pass away, not the smallest letter or the smallest part of a letter will pass from the law, until all things have taken place. Therefore, whoever breaks one of the least of these commandments and teaches others to do so will be called least in the Kingdom of heaven. But whoever obeys and teaches these commandments will be called greatest in the Kingdom of heaven."

Meditation:

"Your words, Lord, are Spirit and life; you have the words of everlasting life." This Gospel Acclamation moves us to open our hearts to God's word, which is the subject of today's readings. We are challenged to consider what value we place on the Lord's word in our own life.

In the first reading, Moses urges the people to obey God's "statutes and decrees," and he explains why it is best for them to do so. They should carefully observe the laws which God is giving them, "that you may live, and may enter in and take possession of the land which the LORD, the God of your fathers, is giving you."

In the Gospel, Jesus likewise exhorts his followers to be diligent in following God's word, even the smallest part of it. He says that he has not come to abolish the law of God but to fulfill it. Whoever follows and teaches the law will be great in the Kingdom of Heaven, but whoever breaks God's law and teaches others to do so will be least in the Kingdom of Heaven.

When we read about God's "statutes," "laws," and "decrees," however, we may notice a certain negative reaction in our hearts and minds. In human society, laws and decrees are developed by human leaders, whether in government, in our workplace, or in our community. These are rules which someone in authority wants us to follow. Sometimes these are good and promote what is beneficial, but at other times they are merely asserting the preference of those who are in charge. Authorities can use their power to serve their own interests, which might not be good for us. In such situations it is natural for us to grow suspicious of "laws" and "decrees," and to examine them carefully to see if they are, in fact, good. If we determine that they are not, we might refuse to follow, or rebel against them.

We also have a tendency to be self-willed. No matter how good the rule which is given to us, we do not want to follow simply because we do not want to be told by another what to do.

We need to be careful not to approach God's word with this kind of suspicion and self-will. As Moses assures us, God's word is the way to find life, and to enter into our homeland, which is ultimately Heaven. God's word is not a matter of arbitrary rules which he imposes for his own benefit. God needs nothing from us! Rather, his word is like a map which shows us the way to arrive at our destination. If we are lost and someone gives us directions to where we are trying to go, we do not resent their directions and refuse to follow. We are grateful to them for setting us on the right way.

The Liturgy today invites us to stop and fix firmly in our minds and hearts that this is what God's word is for us – divine directions, showing us how to come home to him. We are so blessed that God has drawn close to us, as Moses says, to lead us in his way! No wonder the psalmist urges us, "Glorify the LORD, O Jerusalem; praise your God, O Zion." Why? Because the Lord "has proclaimed his word to Jacob, his statutes and his ordinances to Israel." No wonder Jesus tells us not to neglect the smallest part of God's word, and to take care to teach his word to others! We rejoice that God gives us his word so that we can come surely and swiftly into his presence, and not get lost along the way.

Let us thank the Lord today for his kindness in sharing his word with us, and let us repent of any way in which we have resisted his word. Let us follow the exhortation of James 1:21: "Humbly welcome the word that has been planted in you and is able to save your souls."

What holds me back from faithfully observing God's law? In what ways do I find it difficult to follow the Lord and observe his precepts? Being self-willed, what enables me to put God's plan before mine?

Mary, free me from all self-willfulness and pride.

First Reading: Jeremiah 7:23-28

Thus says the LORD:
This is what I commanded my people:
Listen to my voice;
then I will be your God and you shall be my people.
Walk in all the ways that I command you,
so that you may prosper.

But they obeyed not, nor did they pay heed.
They walked in the hardness of their evil hearts
and turned their backs, not their faces, to me.
From the day that your fathers left the land of Egypt even to this day,
I have sent you untiringly all my servants the prophets.
Yet they have not obeyed me nor paid heed;
they have stiffened their necks and done worse than their fathers.
When you speak all these words to them,
they will not listen to you either;
when you call to them, they will not answer you.
Say to them:
This is the nation that does not listen
to the voice of the LORD, its God,
or take correction.
Faithfulness has disappeared;
the word itself is banished from their speech.

Responsorial Psalm: Psalm 95:1-2, 6-7, 8-9
If today you hear his voice, harden not your hearts.

Come, let us sing joyfully to the LORD;
let us acclaim the Rock of our salvation.
Let us come into his presence with thanksgiving;
let us joyfully sing psalms to him.
R. If today you hear his voice, harden not your hearts.

Come, let us bow down in worship;
let us kneel before the LORD who made us.
For he is our God,
and we are the people he shepherds, the flock he guides.
R. If today you hear his voice, harden not your hearts.

'Oh, that today you would hear his voice:
"Harden not your hearts as at Meribah,
as in the day of Massah in the desert,
Where your fathers tempted me;
they tested me though they had seen my works."
R. If today you hear his voice, harden not your hearts.

Gospel Acclamation: Joel 2:12-13
Even now, says the LORD, return to me with your whole heart, for I am gracious and merciful.

Gospel: Luke 11:14-23
Jesus was driving out a demon that was mute, and when the demon had gone out, the mute man spoke and the crowds were amazed. Some of them said, "By the power of Beelzebul, the prince of demons, he drives out demons." Others, to test him, asked him for a sign from heaven. But he knew their thoughts and said to them, "Every kingdom divided against itself will be laid waste and house will fall against house. And if Satan is divided against himself, how will his kingdom stand? For you say that it is by Beelzebul that I drive out demons. If I, then, drive out demons by Beelzebul, by whom do your own people drive them out? Therefore they will be your judges. But if it is by the finger of God that I drive out demons, then the Kingdom of God has come upon you. When a strong man fully armed guards his palace, his possessions are safe. But when one stronger than he attacks and overcomes him, he takes away the armor on which he relied and distributes the spoils. Whoever is not with me is against me, and whoever does not gather with me scatters."

Meditation:
As we ponder the Lord's word given to us in the daily Mass readings, we notice that certain phrases are repeated. This is an indication that we need to pay careful attention to these points, because they are especially important. Today we have two of these repetitions. First of all, the Psalm is the same one which we read on Sunday, and it even refers to the events of the first reading on Sunday, when the Israelites grumbled against the Lord in the desert. Secondly, the Gospel Acclamation is repeated from Tuesday. Mother Church is pleading with us not to harden our hearts, but rather to come before the Lord with our whole hearts, looking to him for his gracious mercy.

Why do we need to be reminded of these things? We have only to ponder the first reading to find the answer. While Jeremiah is speaking about the people of Israel in his time, he could just as well be speaking about us. Wherever we happen to be living, it can truly be said of us: "This is the nation that does not listen to the voice of the LORD, its God, or take correction." The Lord can certainly say of our world today, "They walked in the hardness of their evil hearts and turned their backs, not their faces, to me."

The world gives abundant evidence of the terrible condition of "hardness of heart." Nowadays little thought is given to listening to God's voice or following his way. The spirit of our times is one of fierce independence and pride, where each person feels that he can decide for himself what his "reality" is, and each seeks his own advantage above all else.

Today's Gospel gives us an example of what hardness of heart can do to us. Jesus drives out a demon from a mute man, and the crowds are amazed. Certainly they should be amazed, for this is obviously something out of the ordinary, beyond human power. But then they begin to say that he has done this by the power of the evil one. Jesus points out the absurdity of this idea. Why would Satan drive out Satan? Only one stronger than he could drive him out, and that stronger one can only be God. What they are saying makes no sense. But they cling to their idea because otherwise they would have to acknowledge, as Jesus tells them, that "the Kingdom of God has come upon you."

In the hardness of their hearts, the people reject the Kingdom of God because they want to be the kings and queens of their own private kingdoms. This is the same kind of hard-heartedness that King Herod displayed when he murdered the baby boys of Bethlehem. When one's heart is hard enough, one will go to any length at all to refuse to acknowledge the Kingdom of God.

We also see in the Gospel that "Others, to test him, asked him for a sign from Heaven." Again, this is an absurd request. Jesus just performed a powerful sign from Heaven! He healed a mute man. And everyone in the crowd has heard of many other miracles which Jesus has done by this time. But if we do not want to accept that God is working in our life, we can simply continue to ask for "proof" again and again, and no sign will ever be enough to move us.

While this spirit of rebellion against God's word is clearly at work in the world today, we need to admit that it has taken root also in our own hearts, at least to some extent. So we can take the Lord's words today, not merely as a warning to our world, but as an exhortation to us personally. He says to us, *Harden not your heart. Return to me with your whole heart, even now.* As we move to respond to his merciful call to repentance, we can take the exhortation of the Psalm as a helpful instruction. Not only should we not rebel against the Lord's word to us, we should thank him with great joy for revealing to us the way to fullness of life! Let us kneel before him and bow down in praise and worship of him, acclaiming him as our Good Shepherd. This is the posture of a humble, open heart, a heart which is being guided into the Kingdom of God.

> *In what ways do I turn my back to the Lord? How and why do I stubbornly cling to my own opinion like the people in today's Gospel? In what areas of my life has the spirit of rebellion against God's word taken root?*

Mary, may I always open my heart to the word of your Son Jesus Christ.

Notes

113

First Reading: Hosea 14:2-10

Thus says the LORD:
Return, O Israel, to the LORD, your God;
  you have collapsed through your guilt.
Take with you words,
  and return to the LORD;
Say to him, "Forgive all iniquity,
  and receive what is good, that we may render
  as offerings the bullocks from our stalls.
Assyria will not save us,
  nor shall we have horses to mount;
We shall say no more, 'Our god,'
  to the work of our hands;
  for in you the orphan finds compassion."

I will heal their defection, says the LORD,
  I will love them freely;
  for my wrath is turned away from them.
I will be like the dew for Israel:
  he shall blossom like the lily;
He shall strike root like the Lebanon cedar,
  and put forth his shoots.
His splendor shall be like the olive tree
  and his fragrance like the Lebanon cedar.
Again they shall dwell in his shade
  and raise grain;
They shall blossom like the vine,
  and his fame shall be like the wine of Lebanon.

Ephraim! What more has he to do with idols?
  I have humbled him, but I will prosper him.
"I am like a verdant cypress tree"–
  Because of me you bear fruit!

Let him who is wise understand these things;
  let him who is prudent know them.
Straight are the paths of the LORD,
  in them the just walk,
  but sinners stumble in them.

Responsorial Psalm: Psalm 81:6c-8a, 8bc-9, 10-11ab, 14 and 17
I am the Lord your God: hear my voice.

An unfamiliar speech I hear:
"I relieved his shoulder of the burden;
his hands were freed from the basket.
In distress you called, and I rescued you."
R. *I am the Lord your God: hear my voice.*

"Unseen, I answered you in thunder;
I tested you at the waters of Meribah.
Hear, my people, and I will admonish you;
O Israel, will you not hear me?"
R. *I am the Lord your God: hear my voice.*

"There shall be no strange god among you
nor shall you worship any alien god.
I, the LORD, am your God
who led you forth from the land of Egypt."
R. *I am the Lord your God: hear my voice.*

"If only my people would hear me,
and Israel walk in my ways,
I would feed them with the best of wheat,
and with honey from the rock I would fill them."
R. *I am the Lord your God: hear my voice.*

Gospel Acclamation: Matthew 4:17
Repent, says the Lord; the Kingdom of heaven is at hand.

Gospel: Mark 12:28-34
One of the scribes came to Jesus and asked him, "Which is the first of all the commandments?" Jesus replied, "The first is this: *Hear, O Israel! The Lord our God is Lord alone! You shall love the Lord your God with all your heart, with all your soul, with all your mind, and with all your strength.* The second is this: *You shall love your neighbor as yourself.* There is no other commandment greater than these." The scribe said to him, "Well said, teacher. You are right in saying, *He is One and there is no other than he.* And *to love him with all your heart, with all your understanding, with all your strength, and to love your neighbor as yourself* is worth more than all burnt offerings and sacrifices." And when Jesus saw that he answered with understanding, he said to him, "You are not far from the Kingdom of God." And no one dared to ask him any more questions.

Meditation:

This week the Lord has been speaking to us through the Liturgy, urging us not to harden our hearts against his word, but to receive it with open, humble hearts – as the Samaritan woman did in all simplicity on Sunday. If we are striving to do that, then we are ready to hear the most important instruction which he gives us in the Gospel today. Jesus proclaims the first commandment of God, from Deuteronomy 6:4-5: *"Hear, O Israel! The Lord our God is Lord alone! You shall love the Lord your God with all your heart, with all your soul, with all your mind, and with all your strength."*

The Lord tells us that we must respond to him with our *whole* hearts; we must give our hearts to him alone. If we want to enter into the Kingdom of God, then we cannot divide our love and give some to God and some to others. As the Psalm for today says, "There shall be no strange god among you, nor shall you worship any alien god." And the repentant people in the first reading promise, "We shall say no more, 'Our god,' to the work of our hands."

God's word today invites us to examine our hearts and minds and see how we might be setting up other "gods" to which we devote some of our hearts and to which we look for some of our security. Are we focused on acquiring wealth and possessions, thinking that this will provide us with safety and comfort? Are we seeking to gain power and prestige, in an effort to have control over our lives? Do we spend our time pursuing pleasure through food and drink, entertainment, social media, sex, drugs, etc.? We are challenged today to take a hard look and see where we might be setting up rivals to God in our hearts and minds.

When we identify how we have failed to give God our wholehearted love and worship, then we can hear him say to us in the Gospel Acclamation, "Repent." Or as he urges us in the first reading, "Return, O Israel, to the LORD, your God …. Take with you words, and return to the LORD." If we will do this, then he promises us, "I will heal their defection, … I will love them freely." And even more beautifully he assures us in the Psalm: "If only my people would hear me, and Israel walk in my ways, I would feed them with the best of wheat, and with honey from the rock I would fill them."

The Lord has been instructing us all week in the truth that his word is not an unjust imposition or burden on us. Rather, as he told the Samaritan woman, it is a spring of living water which can satisfy our thirst for eternal life. His Kingdom is truly at hand, and we can begin to live in it even now, in this life, if we will truly *hear* his word, which means taking it in, pondering it deeply as the most important thing in our lives, and striving to put it into practice.

One practical way in which we can do this is to heed the second half of Jesus' instruction in the Gospel – to love our neighbor as ourselves. This means to take our focus off ourselves and our own concerns and desires, and work to be a blessing in the lives of those around us. If we are doing this, then we are taking on the very mind and heart of God, who is always pouring himself out in love for us.

Let us turn to the Lord today with repentance for any way in which we have failed to give him the first place in our lives, and resolve to love him with our whole hearts. With confidence in his mercy, let us give ourselves in love to our neighbor in whatever way God leads us.

> *What are some of the other gods that I have set up in my heart as I look for security? How do I experience God's word as a spring of living water which satisfies my thirst for eternal life? What efforts will I make to focus my attention on the needs and concerns of others rather than myself?*

Mary, as your heart and eyes were always focused on others, guide me in your ways.
St. Patrick, pray for us.

Born around 385 in Great Britain, **Patrick** was captured and sold as a slave in Ireland. After working some years there as a shepherd, learning the language and culture, he escaped back to his homeland, where he was ordained a priest and eventually a bishop. Full of missionary zeal, he returned to Ireland, where he tirelessly preached the Gospel, converted many to the faith and established the Church. He died at County Down around 461. He is the patron saint of Ireland and Nigeria.

First Reading: Hosea 6:1-6

"Come, let us return to the LORD,
   it is he who has rent, but he will heal us;
he has struck us, but he will bind our wounds.
He will revive us after two days;
   on the third day he will raise us up,
   to live in his presence.
Let us know, let us strive to know the LORD;
   as certain as the dawn is his coming,
   and his judgment shines forth like the light of day!
He will come to us like the rain,
   like spring rain that waters the earth."

What can I do with you, Ephraim?
What can I do with you, Judah?
Your piety is like a morning cloud,
   like the dew that early passes away.
For this reason I smote them through the prophets,
   I slew them by the words of my mouth;
For it is love that I desire, not sacrifice,
   and knowledge of God rather than burnt offerings.

Responsorial Psalm: Psalm 51:3-4, 18-19, 20-21ab
   It is mercy I desire, and not sacrifice.

Have mercy on me, O God, in your goodness;
   in the greatness of your compassion wipe out my offense.
Thoroughly wash me from my guilt
   and of my sin cleanse me.
R. It is mercy I desire, and not sacrifice.
For you are not pleased with sacrifices;
   should I offer a burnt offering, you would not accept it.
My sacrifice, O God, is a contrite spirit;
   a heart contrite and humbled, O God, you will not spurn.
R. It is mercy I desire, and not sacrifice.
Be bountiful, O LORD, to Zion in your kindness
   by rebuilding the walls of Jerusalem;
Then shall you be pleased with due sacrifices,
   burnt offerings and holocausts.
R. It is mercy I desire, and not sacrifice.

✝ *Gospel: Luke 18:9-14*

Jesus addressed this parable to those who were convinced of their own righteousness and despised everyone else. "Two people went up to the temple area to pray; one was a Pharisee and the other was a tax collector. The Pharisee took up his position and spoke this prayer to himself, 'O God, I thank you that I am not like the rest of humanity – greedy, dishonest, adulterous – or even like this tax collector. I fast twice a week, and I pay tithes on my whole income.' But the tax collector stood off at a distance and would not even raise his eyes to heaven but beat his breast and prayed, 'O God, be merciful to me a sinner.' I tell you, the latter went home justified, not the former; for everyone who exalts himself will be humbled, and the one who humbles himself will be exalted."

Meditation:

Today's reading from Hosea begins with what sounds like a good attitude for our Lenten journey: "Come, let us return to the LORD." Indeed, we have seen all week that the Lord *has* been calling us to turn back to him with our whole hearts. It seems that the people have gotten the message, that they are truly turning their hearts and minds to the Lord, as they say: "Let us know, let us strive to know the LORD; as certain as the dawn is his coming, and his judgment shines forth like the light of day!"

Sadly, we learn from the context of the passage that the people's nice words at the beginning of the reading are insincere. Even their expectation that God will revive them and raise them up in two or three days is presumptuous. If they truly knew and acknowledged their sin before the Lord, they would simply be pleading humbly for his mercy, not putting demands on him to restore them quickly according to their time frame.

We can understand why God seems to be frustrated with them as he asks them in the second part of the reading, "What can I do with you?" He tells them that their piety is "like a morning cloud, like the dew that early passes away." Morning clouds and dew in Palestine evaporate very quickly when the sun comes up. Their idea of "returning to the Lord," then, turns out to be little more than an attempt to control God. They have found themselves in some trouble, and they think that if they simply perform a few external rituals and sacrifices, God will be obliged to save them. They have no real intention of converting and seeking his will; they only want to find the right "formula" to make God do their will.

What *can* God do with such hard-hearted people? Here he says, "I smote them through the prophets, I slew them by the words of my mouth." He chastised them for their sins. We know that God always looks upon his people with mercy. Sometimes, though, the way to reach people who will not hear any other way is to allow them to experience the consequences of their misguided behavior. This too is mercy. God allows people to go through some hardship in this life so that they will turn from their sin and not come to a much more tragic condition in eternity.

Jesus in the Gospel also warns us against external shows of piety which do not come from a true heart. The Pharisee in the parable does not come into the temple to worship God. He comes in to make a show of his holiness, and to congratulate himself on his superiority over "the rest of humanity." Jesus says that people who act in this way will be humbled. Again, it is truly merciful on the part of God to humble the proud. *God himself is the humblest one of all.* He freely emptied himself of his divine glory in the Incarnation, choosing to be born in a stable to a poor family in an insignificant town, wandering the countryside with no possessions, and finally allowing himself to be tortured and killed, all for love of us. How could a proud, self-glorifying heart ever be joined eternally to such a humble Lord? Impossible! But God longs to be united with us completely in Heaven, so he does all that he can to humble our proud hearts, to make them ready to be joined to his humble heart.

We can see, then, the fullness of the wonderful promise which Jesus makes as he speaks about the tax collector in the Gospel. He says of him, "the latter went home justified, ... the one who humbles himself will be exalted." It is the tax collector who is more prepared than the

Pharisee to be eternally united to God! If he continues on the way of humility, he will reach a height of exaltation which is beyond our imagining!

The readings are telling us to be careful not to make only an outward show of turning to the Lord, especially during this season of Lent. The Psalm shows us clearly the kind of heartfelt repentance which the Lord is looking for from us. It is "a heart contrite and humbled" which God can exalt to the highest place with himself.

The psalmist begs God: "Thoroughly wash me from my guilt and of my sin cleanse me." We can recall the story of Naaman the Syrian army commander who was healed of his leprosy in Monday's reading. At first his pride was an obstacle to him being healed, but when he humbled himself to follow God's ways rather than insist on his own ways, then he was restored to health. Let us learn from him to welcome God's work in humbling us and softening our hard hearts, in whatever way he sees best to do that, so that we, too, might one day be washed clean by his mercy, and counted among the truly exalted ones!

> *What are some of the demands I make on the Lord? In what ways do I try to manipulate God to do my will? How do I compare my actions with the Pharisee and the tax collector in the Temple?*

Mary, during this Lent, continue to form my heart in humility and contriteness.
St. Cyril of Jerusalem, pray for us.

Little is known about the early life of **Cyril of Jerusalem**. Historians say that he was probably born of Christian parents around 314 and was brought up in Jerusalem. He was ordained by St. Maximus, who was bishop of Jerusalem at that time, and after his death in 348, Cyril became the next bishop. He strongly upheld the divinity of Christ and zealously defended the Church, especially against the Arian heresy. For this he was exiled three times. His *Catecheses*, in which he explained to the people the true teachings of the faith and of scriptures, and also the traditions of the Church, reveal his pastoral zeal. He has given us the earliest detailed account of the rites of Baptism, Confirmation, and Holy Eucharist, and has left us clear insights into the Eucharist as a sacrifice. He died in 386.

Fourth Week of Lent

I am the light of the world, says the Lord;
whoever follows me will have the light of life.

Gospel Acclamation (John 8:12)

Theme for the Week

Through his Passion, Death and Resurrection, Jesus reveals himself as the Light of the World. He has come to save us from sin, which is the very root of spiritual darkness. The season of Lent is a grace-filled time for us to commit to live in the light of Christ. Let us not remain blind in sin, but welcome the light of Christ and live as children of light.

JESUS IS THE LIGHT THAT BRIGHTENS OUR DARKNESS
A Spiritual Reflection by Pope Francis

At the center of the Liturgy of this Fourth Sunday of Lent there is the theme of *light*. The Gospel (cf. Jn 9:1-41) recounts the episode of the man blind from birth, to whom Jesus gives sight. This miraculous sign confirms Jesus' affirmation that "I am the light of the world" (v. 5), the light that brightens our darkness. Jesus is thus. He operates illumination on two levels: a physical level and a spiritual level: the blind person first receives the *sight* of the eyes and then is led to *faith* in the "Son of Man" (v. 35), that is, in Jesus. It is all a journey. Today it would be good if you were all to take a copy of the Gospel according to John, chapter nine, and read this passage: it is so good and it will do us good to read it once or twice more. The wonders that Jesus performs are not spectacular gestures, but have the purpose of leading to faith through a journey of inner transformation.

The doctors of the law – who were there in a group – persist in not admitting the miracle, and ask the healed man insidious questions. But he disconcerts them with the power of reality: "One thing I do know. I was blind and now I see" (v. 25). Amidst the distrust and hostility of those who surround him and interrogate him, incredulous, he takes a route that leads him to gradually discover the identity of the One who opened his eyes and to confess his faith in Him. At first he considers Him a prophet (cf. v. 17); then he recognizes Him as one Who comes from God (cf. v. 33); finally he welcomes Him as the Messiah and prostrates himself before Him (cf. vv. 36-38). He understood that by giving him sight Jesus displayed "the works of God" (cf. v. 3).

May we too have this experience! With the light of faith he who was blind discovers his new identity. He is now a "new creature," able to see his life and the world around him in a new light because he has entered into communion with Christ; he has entered into another dimension. He is no longer a beggar marginalized by the community; he is no longer a slave to blindness and prejudice. His path of enlightenment is a metaphor for the path of liberation from sin to which we are called. Sin is like a dark veil that covers our face and prevents us from clearly seeing ourselves and the world; the Lord's forgiveness takes away this blanket of shadow and darkness and gives us new light.

The Lenten period that we are living is an opportune and valuable time to approach the Lord, asking for His mercy, in the different forms that Mother Church proposes to us.

The healed blind man, who now sees both with the eyes of the body and with those of the soul, is the image of every baptized person, who, immersed in Grace, has been pulled out of the darkness and placed in the light of faith. But it is not enough to *receive* the light, one must *become light*. Each one of us is called to receive the divine light in order to manifest it with our whole life. The first Christians, the theologians of the first centuries, used to say that the community of Christians, that is the Church, is the "mystery of the moon," because it gave light, but it was not its own light, it was the light it received from Christ. We too can be "mystery of the moon": giving light received from the sun, which is Christ, the Lord. Saint Paul reminds us of this today: "Live as children of light; for the fruit of the light consists in all goodness, righteousness and truth" (*Eph* 5:8-9). The seed of new life placed in us in Baptism is like the spark of a fire, which first of all purifies us, burning the evil in our hearts, and allows us to shine and illuminate – with the light of Jesus.

May Mary Most Holy help us to imitate the blind man of the Gospel, so that we can be flooded with the light of Christ and set out with Him on the way of salvation.

Pope Francis, Angelus Message, March 22, 2020
© Copyright 2020 - Libreria Editrice Vaticana

First Reading: 1 Samuel 16:1b, 6-7, 10-13a

The LORD said to Samuel: "Fill your horn with oil, and be on your way. I am sending you to Jesse of Bethlehem, for I have chosen my king from among his sons."

As Jesse and his sons came to the sacrifice, Samuel looked at Eliab and thought, "Surely the LORD's anointed is here before him." But the LORD said to Samuel: "Do not judge from his appearance or from his lofty stature, because I have rejected him. Not as man sees does God see, because man sees the appearance but the LORD looks into the heart." In the same way Jesse presented seven sons before Samuel, but Samuel said to Jesse, "The LORD has not chosen any one of these." Then Samuel asked Jesse, "Are these all the sons you have?" Jesse replied, "There is still the youngest, who is tending the sheep." Samuel said to Jesse, "Send for him; we will not begin the sacrificial banquet until he arrives here." Jesse sent and had the young man brought to them. He was ruddy, a youth handsome to behold and making a splendid appearance. The LORD said, "There – anoint him, for this is the one!" Then Samuel, with the horn of oil in hand, anointed David in the presence of his brothers; and from that day on, the spirit of the LORD rushed upon David.

Responsorial Psalm: Psalm 23:1-3a, 3b-4, 5, 6
The Lord is my shepherd; there is nothing I shall want.

The LORD is my shepherd; I shall not want.
In verdant pastures he gives me repose;
beside restful waters he leads me;
he refreshes my soul.
R. The Lord is my shepherd; there is nothing I shall want.

He guides me in right paths
for his name's sake.
Even though I walk in the dark valley
I fear no evil; for you are at my side
with your rod and your staff
that give me courage.
R. The Lord is my shepherd; there is nothing I shall want.

You spread the table before me
in the sight of my foes;
you anoint my head with oil;
my cup overflows.
R. The Lord is my shepherd; there is nothing I shall want.

Only goodness and kindness follow me
    all the days of my life;
and I shall dwell in the house of the LORD
    for years to come.
R. The Lord is my shepherd; there is nothing I shall want.

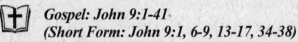

Second Reading: Ephesians 5:8-14

Brothers and sisters: You were once darkness, but now you are light in the Lord. Live as children of light, for light produces every kind of goodness and righteousness and truth. Try to learn what is pleasing to the Lord. Take no part in the fruitless works of darkness; rather expose them, for it is shameful even to mention the things done by them in secret; but everything exposed by the light becomes visible, for everything that becomes visible is light. Therefore, it says:
"Awake, O sleeper,
    and arise from the dead,
    and Christ will give you light."

Gospel Acclamation: John 8:12

I am the light of the world, says the Lord; whoever follows me will have the light of life.

Gospel: John 9:1-41
(Short Form: John 9:1, 6-9, 13-17, 34-38)

As Jesus passed by he saw a man blind from birth. His disciples asked him, "Rabbi, who sinned, this man or his parents, that he was born blind?" Jesus answered, "Neither he nor his parents sinned; it is so that the works of God might be made visible through him. We have to do the works of the one who sent me while it is day. Night is coming when no one can work. While I am in the world, I am the light of the world." When he had said this, he spat on the ground and made clay with the saliva, and smeared the clay on his eyes, and said to him, "Go wash in the Pool of Siloam" – which means Sent –. So he went and washed, and came back able to see.

His neighbors and those who had seen him earlier as a beggar said, "Isn't this the one who used to sit and beg?" Some said, "It is," but others said, "No, he just looks like him." He said, "I am." So they said to him, "How were your eyes opened?" He replied, "The man called Jesus made clay and anointed my eyes and told me, 'Go to Siloam and wash.' So I went there and washed and was able to see." And they said to him, "Where is he?" He said, "I don't know."

They brought the one who was once blind to the Pharisees. Now Jesus had made clay and opened his eyes on a sabbath. So then the Pharisees also asked him how he was able to see. He said to them, "He put clay on my eyes, and I washed, and now I can see." So some of the Pharisees said, "This man is not from God, because he does not keep the sabbath." But others said, "How can a sinful man do such signs?" And there was a division among them. So they said to the blind man again, "What do you have to say about him, since he opened your eyes?" He said, "He is a prophet."

Now the Jews did not believe that he had been blind and gained his sight until they summoned the parents of the one who had gained his sight. They asked them, "Is this your son, who you say was born blind? How does he now see?" His parents answered and said, "We know that this is our son and that he was born blind. We do not know how he sees now, nor do we know who opened his eyes. Ask him, he is of age; he can speak for himself." His parents said this because they were afraid of the Jews, for the Jews had already agreed that if anyone acknowledged him as the Christ, he would be expelled from the synagogue. For this reason his parents said, "He is of age; question him."

So a second time they called the man who had been blind and said to him, "Give God the praise! We know that this man is a sinner." He replied, "If he is a sinner, I do not know. One thing I do know is that I was blind and now I see." So they said to him, "What did he do to you? How did he open your eyes?" He answered them, "I told you already and you did not listen. Why do you want to hear it again? Do you want to become his disciples, too?" They ridiculed him and said, "You are that man's disciple; we are disciples of Moses! We know that God spoke to Moses, but we do not know where this one is from." The man answered and said to them, "This is what is so amazing, that you do not know where he is from, yet he opened my eyes. We know that God does not listen to sinners, but if one is devout and does his will, he listens to him. It is unheard of that anyone ever opened the eyes of a person born blind. If this man were not from God, he would not be able to do anything." They answered and said to him, "You were born totally in sin, and are you trying to teach us?" Then they threw him out.

When Jesus heard that they had thrown him out, he found him and said, "Do you believe in the Son of Man?" He answered and said, "Who is he, sir, that I may believe in him?" Jesus said to him, "You have seen him, and the one speaking with you is he." He said, "I do believe, Lord," and he worshiped him. Then Jesus said, "I came into this world for judgment, so that those who do not see might see, and those who do see might become blind."

Some of the Pharisees who were with him heard this and said to him, "Surely we are not also blind, are we?" Jesus said to them, "If you were blind, you would have no sin; but now you are saying, 'We see,' so your sin remains."

Meditation:

As we progress through the Lenten season towards Holy Week, we are given a Gospel that reveals the spiritual progress of a man blind from birth. The account begins with Jesus and the disciples seeing this man and discussing his situation of blindness. Blindness, like any infirmity or sickness, was considered a curse and was therefore seen as a result of sin. This idea is reflected in the insult that the Pharisees throw at the man after his cure: "You were born totally in sin…." Thus, the disciples ask Jesus if the man's disability is due to his own sin or the sin of his parents. Jesus' reply is decisive and instructive: one's disability is not the result of sin but is rather a canvas upon which "the works of God might be made visible." Against the darkness of the situation of this blind man, Jesus will reveal himself to be the light of the world. Similarly, we can say that the darkness of our sin condition, which we are addressing in Lent through prayer, sacrifice, and charity, is the backdrop upon which the bright light of Easter will shine.

To experience the light of Easter, we must go through the journey from blindness to sight, like the man born blind. The Lord himself guides us through the journey. As today's Psalm reminds us, the Lord is our shepherd; therefore we lack nothing that we need. When we are in danger of stumbling because of our blindness, he guides us in right paths. As we walk through dark valleys, our Shepherd is at our side. Our blindness, then, or whatever weakness or infirmity we may have, is not merely a handicap, but a condition that moves us to dependence on the Lord. It sets the stage for the Lord to display his greatness.

Jesus uses *clay* and then *washing* as the means of healing the blind man. Mention of clay recalls the story of *creation*, where "God formed the man out of the dust of the ground and blew into his nostrils the breath of life, and the man became a living being" (Gen 2:7). This image reminds us that whatever blindness we are experiencing, it is not what defines us. The truth of our personhood is that we are created in the image and likeness of God, and this truth is at the source of our vision. The action of washing is a reminder of *Baptism*, the precious gift by which we were submerged and brought to life again through Jesus Christ. We rose from the font healed and filled with grace, empowered to live a new life, free from sin. Like the blind man, through clay and washing – through our creation in God's likeness and our new creation in Baptism – we are able to see!

After being prodded to say more about Jesus, the man cured from blindness declares, "He is a prophet!" The Jews had a long and respected tradition of prophecy. The prophets of old spoke in the name of God. Sometimes they were referred to as "seers" because they saw things from God's perspective; they also enabled those who listened to them to "see" the will of God. One of the first great prophets in the Old Testament was Samuel, whom we see in action in today's first reading.

The Lord tells Samuel to anoint a new king from among the sons of Jesse of Bethlehem. But the instructions are incomplete: Jesse has eight sons; which one has the Lord chosen? Samuel cannot tell on his own. In order to be faithful to his mission, he must abandon any tendency to judge by appearances. God has a different standard: "Not as man sees does God see, because man sees the appearance but the LORD looks into the heart." The chosen son is the one whom everyone considered the least qualified, the youngest, David. Samuel knows it because the Lord reveals it to him. The prophet can "see" and reveal because he listens. When the man in the Gospel declares that Jesus is a prophet, he also takes on the role of a prophet. He who can now see is revealing Jesus to them. This is also our call: as the Lord gives us new sight, we are to share it with others.

The man's journey is not yet complete. Jesus is more than a prophet. Alas, worldly people find it hard to comprehend and accept spiritual things. The man healed from blindness is relentlessly challenged, maligned, discredited, and shamed. But all the insults and threats bear fruit: he recognizes and accepts Jesus more and more deeply. Only when he is thrown out of the temple can he complete his spiritual journey. Jesus finds him in what looks like a cursed situation and invites him to take another step of faith. "Do you believe in the Son of Man?... the one speaking with you is he." The man receives his spiritual sight, expresses his faith, and worships Jesus as Lord. Worship of the Lord is the ultimate destination of our spiritual journey.

What made it possible for the man healed from blindness to progress to the point of deep belief? Mysteriously, it was the experience of being rejected and thrown out. We can understand this to be his conformity to Jesus Christ, who will himself be rejected, attacked, discredited, and shamed. Like a cursed man, he will die on the Cross. The way of the Cross, the path of following Jesus, is the underlying truth of our Lenten journey. Lent leads us to the Paschal Triduum. In this journey, we discover – if the eyes of our hearts are open – that suffering can lead us to deeper vision, to knowing Jesus, and to true worship. St. Paul proclaims to us: "You were once darkness, but now you are light in the Lord. Live as children of light!"

> *Do I experience my blindness - any weakness or infirmity - as a means to become dependent on the Lord? How does this lead me to a deeper knowledge of Jesus? Why do I tend to judge on appearances and not by the actions of another?*

Mary, may the light of your faith continue to guide me through my journey in Lent.

Notes

130

Liturgical Note:
The Marriage of Joseph and Mary

In the Jewish tradition, the joyful celebration of marriage lasted for one full week. This tradition is reflected in the one-week period which connects the *Solemnity of St. Joseph, Spouse of the Blessed Virgin Mary* (March 19) with the *Solemnity of the Annunciation* (March 25). These two solemnities can be regarded together as liturgical "companion feasts" representing the union of these two holy spouses, Joseph and Mary.

Joseph and Mary were truly married, for by their free consent they made a life-long gift of themselves to one another in a covenant of love. We celebrate the feast of Joseph first, identified as Mary's true husband, because the Annunciation takes place only after their betrothal establishes the legal bond between them. When Gabriel is sent to her, Mary is already Joseph's bride, his wife (cf. Mt 1:20, 24), though their marriage has not been consummated. The Savior is to be born into a family, as the child of a married couple. The Holy Family, like every family, is founded on marriage. This shows how highly God regards his beautiful plan for marriage and family life.

In contemporary society, God's plan is badly obscured by error and confusion. In the face of modern trends which claim that almost any sexual relationship may be called "marriage," and which regard "sexual fulfillment" as the one essential value in a relationship, Joseph and Mary together stand as truly counter-cultural witnesses. They lift our minds to the possibility of a profound and tender love not expressed by conjugal relations. They inspire us to persevere in fidelity to our vocation of selfless committed love, and to make our every relationship a "home" which welcomes and nurtures the life of Jesus Christ.

March 20, Monday
Solemnity of Saint Joseph, Spouse of the Blessed Virgin Mary

First Reading: 2 Samuel 7:4-5a, 12-14a, 16

The LORD spoke to Nathan and said: "Go, tell my servant David, 'When your time comes and you rest with your ancestors, I will raise up your heir after you, sprung from your loins, and I will make his kingdom firm. It is he who shall build a house for my name. And I will make his royal throne firm forever. I will be a father to him, and he shall be a son to me. Your house and your kingdom shall endure forever before me; your throne shall stand firm forever.'"

Responsorial Psalm: Psalm 89:2-3, 4-5, 27, 29
The son of David will live for ever.

The promises of the LORD I will sing forever,
    through all generations my mouth shall proclaim your faithfulness,
For you have said, "My kindness is established forever";
    in heaven you have confirmed your faithfulness.
R. *The son of David will live for ever.*
"I have made a covenant with my chosen one,
    I have sworn to David my servant:
Forever will I confirm your posterity
    and establish your throne for all generations."
R. *The son of David will live for ever.*
"He shall say of me, 'You are my father,
    my God, the Rock, my savior.'
Forever I will maintain my kindness toward him,
    and my covenant with him stands firm."
R. *The son of David will live for ever.*

Second Reading: Romans 4:13, 16-18, 22

Brothers and sisters: It was not through the law that the promise was made to Abraham and his descendants that he would inherit the world, but through the righteousness that comes from faith. For this reason, it depends on faith, so that it may be a gift, and the promise may be guaranteed to all his descendants, not to those who only adhere to the law but to those who follow the faith of Abraham, who is the father of all of us, as it is written, *I have made you father of many nations.* He is our father in the sight of God, in whom he believed, who gives life to the dead and calls into being what does not exist. He believed, hoping against hope, that he would become *the father of many nations,* according to what was said, *Thus shall your descendants be.* That is why *it was credited to him as righteousness.*

Gospel Acclamation: Psalm 84:5

Blessed are those who dwell in your house, O Lord; they never cease to praise you.

✝ Gospel: Matthew 1:16, 18-21, 24

Jacob was the father of Joseph, the husband of Mary. Of her was born Jesus who is called the Christ.

Now this is how the birth of Jesus Christ came about. When his mother Mary was betrothed to Joseph, but before they lived together, she was found with child through the Holy Spirit. Joseph her husband, since he was a righteous man, yet unwilling to expose her to shame, decided to divorce her quietly. Such was his intention when, behold, the angel of the Lord appeared to him in a dream and said, "Joseph, son of David, do not be afraid to take Mary your wife into your home. For it is through the Holy Spirit that this child has been conceived in her. She will bear a son and you are to name him Jesus, because he will save his people from their sins." When Joseph awoke, he did as the angel of the Lord had commanded him and took his wife into his home.

or *Luke 2:41-51a*.

Each year Jesus' parents went to Jerusalem for the feast of Passover, and when he was twelve years old, they went up according to festival custom. After they had completed its days, as they were returning, the boy Jesus remained behind in Jerusalem, but his parents did not know it. Thinking that he was in the caravan, they journeyed for a day and looked for him among their relatives and acquaintances, but not finding him, they returned to Jerusalem to look for him. After three days they found him in the temple, sitting in the midst of the teachers, listening to them and asking them questions, and all who heard him were astounded at his understanding and his answers. When his parents saw him, they were astonished, and his mother said to him, "Son, why have you done this to us? Your father and I have been looking for you with great anxiety." And he said to them, "Why were you looking for me? Did you not know that I must be in my Father's house?" But they did not understand what he said to them. He went down with them and came to Nazareth, and was obedient to them.

✶ Meditation:

Today we celebrate a man who is both a true son of Abraham and a true son of David, St. Joseph, the Spouse of the Blessed Virgin Mary. Joseph's quiet humility and obedient faith do not attract much attention, so he is often overlooked. As we ponder his life, however, we discover his extraordinary greatness. He is a giant of faith, the greatest Saint in history, after his beloved wife.

We know very few details about Joseph's life. He was certainly a descendant of King David, and was probably born in Bethlehem. King David is mentioned in today's first reading, where the Lord promises him that his offspring will reign forever. David's son Solomon succeeded him on the throne and was the first to "build a house" for the Lord's name, but Solomon did not reign forever. The prophecy points to a mysterious future "son of David," Jesus Christ, who will reign as an Eternal King. But the prophecy is fulfilled by means of the free participation of Joseph, since it is only through him that Jesus can rightly be called "Son of David." Joseph himself was addressed by the angel as "son of David," but he was not a king; he was a simple carpenter.

The first virtue of Joseph that appears in the Scriptures comes from his description as "a righteous man." He is firmly determined to do what is right. Since he knows he is not the father of Mary's unborn child, he chooses the most honorable solution he can find; he decides to break off their betrothal. From Joseph's response to this moment of crisis, we can learn an important lesson. To be righteous, we must be decisive. It is better to decide on the best possible course of action and to go forward with trust in the Lord than to linger in indecision. Many people, especially the youth, have the attitude that it is better not to commit to anything, so as to leave all one's options open. Thus, they neither progress humanly nor discover their true vocation from God. Joseph is not like that. He does not let fear prevent him from doing what is right. He is a man of prudent decision and prompt action.

The Lord intervenes by way of an angel who appears to Joseph in a dream. When Joseph learns that God wants him to take Mary home as his wife, he immediately changes the whole course of his life, in obedience to the will of God. This is a supreme example of faith. Faith is not weakness. It is not an irrational approach to life. It is a whole-hearted "yes" to the will of God. Joseph shows us how to act in faith: as soon as he *knows* God's will, he *does* it.

The Liturgy compares the faith of Joseph to the faith of Abraham, our father in faith. St. Paul writes about Abraham in the second reading, teaching us that *faith* was the key to his inheriting all that was promised.

It is faith that opens the way to salvation. Righteousness comes from faith. Just as Abraham believed that God "calls into being what does not exist," Joseph believed that God called into being Mary's Child, the one who "will save his people from their sins."

This kind of faith, strong and enduring, has the quality of producing abundant spiritual offspring. Abraham is the spiritual father of all who believe as he did. We are not physical descendants of Abraham, but we follow in the line of his faith. In the same way we can look to Joseph as our spiritual father. We become his descendants by believing as he did. We do indeed believe what Joseph believes: that Mary conceived by the power of the Holy Spirit, and that Jesus her Son is the only begotten Son of God, born of the Father before all ages.

Today's feast moves us not only to believe what Joseph believes, but also to love those whom he loves – Jesus and Mary. Joseph teaches us that there is no contradiction between loving Jesus and loving Mary. As a devoted and faithful husband and father, he put his life at the service of them both, without concern for his personal benefit. His whole life shows us that the very best we can do for our families and loved ones is to dedicate ourselves to the will of God. The more deeply we live by faith, the more fully we can give ourselves in love.

> *Why do I have the tendency to linger in indecision instead of going forward, trusting in the Lord like Joseph? What lessons can I learn from the faith of Abraham and St. Joseph? How do I imitate St. Joseph's humility, faithfulness and righteousness?*

Mary, Spouse of St. Joseph, grant me an increase of faith and commitment.

St. Joseph, pray for us.

Prayer to St. Joseph, Protector of the Anawim

Beloved St. Joseph, Protector of the Anawim, watch over us day and night, preserve us from occasions of sin and obtain for us purity of soul and body. Grant us a spirit of sacrifice, humility, and courage, a burning love for Jesus in the Eucharist, and a tender love for Mary our Mother.

St. Joseph, be with us living, be with us dying, and intercede for us to Jesus our merciful Savior. Amen.

First Reading: Ezekiel 47:1-9, 12

The angel brought me, Ezekiel, back to the entrance of the temple of the LORD, and I saw water flowing out from beneath the threshold of the temple toward the east, for the façade of the temple was toward the east; the water flowed down from the right side of the temple, south of the altar. He led me outside by the north gate, and around to the outer gate facing the east, where I saw water trickling from the right side. Then when he had walked off to the east with a measuring cord in his hand, he measured off a thousand cubits and had me wade through the water, which was ankle-deep. He measured off another thousand and once more had me wade through the water, which was now knee-deep. Again he measured off a thousand and had me wade; the water was up to my waist. Once more he measured off a thousand, but there was now a river through which I could not wade; for the water had risen so high it had become a river that could not be crossed except by swimming. He asked me, "Have you seen this, son of man?" Then he brought me to the bank of the river, where he had me sit. Along the bank of the river I saw very many trees on both sides. He said to me, "This water flows into the eastern district down upon the Arabah, and empties into the sea, the salt waters, which it makes fresh. Wherever the river flows, every sort of living creature that can multiply shall live, and there shall be abundant fish, for wherever this water comes the sea shall be made fresh. Along both banks of the river, fruit trees of every kind shall grow; their leaves shall not fade, nor their fruit fail. Every month they shall bear fresh fruit, for they shall be watered by the flow from the sanctuary. Their fruit shall serve for food, and their leaves for medicine."

Responsorial Psalm: Psalm 46:2-3, 5-6, 8-9

The Lord of hosts is with us; our stronghold is the God of Jacob.

God is our refuge and our strength,
    an ever-present help in distress.
Therefore we fear not, though the earth be shaken
    and mountains plunge into the depths of the sea.
R. The Lord of hosts is with us; our stronghold is the God of Jacob.
There is a stream whose runlets gladden the city of God,
    the holy dwelling of the Most High.
God is in its midst; it shall not be disturbed;
    God will help it at the break of dawn.
R. The Lord of hosts is with us; our stronghold is the God of Jacob.

The LORD of hosts is with us;
    our stronghold is the God of Jacob.
Come! behold the deeds of the LORD,
    the astounding things he has wrought on earth.
R. The Lord of hosts is with us; our stronghold is the God of Jacob.

Gospel Acclamation: Psalm 51:12a, 14a

A clean heart create for me, O God; give me back the joy of your salvation.

Gospel: John 5:1-16

There was a feast of the Jews, and Jesus went up to Jerusalem. Now there is in Jerusalem at the Sheep Gate a pool called in Hebrew Bethesda, with five porticoes. In these lay a large number of ill, blind, lame, and crippled. One man was there who had been ill for thirty-eight years. When Jesus saw him lying there and knew that he had been ill for a long time, he said to him, "Do you want to be well?" The sick man answered him, "Sir, I have no one to put me into the pool when the water is stirred up; while I am on my way, someone else gets down there before me." Jesus said to him, "Rise, take up your mat, and walk." Immediately the man became well, took up his mat, and walked.

Now that day was a sabbath. So the Jews said to the man who was cured, "It is the sabbath, and it is not lawful for you to carry your mat." He answered them, "The man who made me well told me, 'Take up your mat and walk.'" They asked him, "Who is the man who told you, 'Take it up and walk'?" The man who was healed did not know who it was, for Jesus had slipped away, since there was a crowd there. After this Jesus found him in the temple area and said to him, "Look, you are well; do not sin any more, so that nothing worse may happen to you." The man went and told the Jews that Jesus was the one who had made him well. Therefore, the Jews began to persecute Jesus because he did this on a sabbath.

Meditation:

As we draw closer to Holy Week, Jesus asks us a direct question: "Do you want to be well?" We know that we are not well; we *need* healing. Our Lenten journey has perhaps made this even more painfully clear to us. We are beset by all sorts of wounds, physical, psychological, and spiritual. But do we *want* to be well? Do we want it enough to change our ways? Where do we go for healing?

Today's Gospel tells us about a place in Jerusalem called Bethesda where many sick people used to gather. There was a belief that when the waters of the pool were stirred up, the first one to enter would be healed. Archeologists have discovered near the site of this pool a shrine dedicated to Aesculapius, the Greek god of health, which indicates that even near the temple in Jerusalem there were pagan beliefs and practices. There was one man there who, after thirty-eight years of sickness, had almost no hope left of being healed or even helped by anyone, Aesculapius or anyone else.

We can imagine ourselves among the blind, the lame, and the disabled gathered by the pool, waiting and hoping for a healing. But what are we doing here? This place, amazing though it sounds, is a pagan shrine, full of superstitious practices. This is no place for a Christian! This is exactly the situation we place ourselves in when we seek help in ways or places that are incompatible with our faith – such as the wearing of charms, the consulting of mediums or palm-readers or horoscopes, delving into the occult, practicing sorcery, or believing in a variety of superstitions. All superstition is in some sense a "perverse excess of religion" (*CCC* 2110).

The *Catechism* warns us against any practice that suggests we can find health or help outside the will of God. "All practices of *magic* or *sorcery*, by which one attempts to tame occult powers, so as to place them at one's service and have a supernatural power over others – even if this were for the sake of restoring their health – are gravely contrary to the virtue of religion. These practices are even more to be condemned when accompanied by the intention of harming someone, or when they have recourse to the intervention of demons. Wearing charms is also reprehensible. *Spiritism* often implies divination or magical practices; the Church for her part warns the faithful against it. Recourse to so-called traditional cures does not justify either the invocation of evil powers or the exploitation of another's credulity" (*CCC* 2117).

When we are discouraged or in pain, if our faith is weak, we can be vulnerable to the lure of devious sources that claim they can "cure" us. Let us not be manipulated or deceived! Let us not be drawn away from the true faith! In the First Commandment the Lord instructs us, "You shall have no other gods before me." If we persist in superstitions even after we know better, we sin by not trusting in the Lord.

Jesus comes to us in our need, just as he approached the sick man at Bethesda. Like a Good Shepherd he searches for us when we go astray, or when we are looking for answers in the wrong places. He comes to save us. Jesus himself is the fulfillment of the beautiful prophecy of Ezekiel which we ponder today. From Jesus' heart flows an abundant river of life and overflowing mercy.

"Do you want to be well?" Jesus is most eager to heal us, as we learned also from Sunday's Gospel. In the account of the man born blind, there is no indication that he asked Jesus for a healing, but Jesus took the initiative and gave him sight. Today's case of the crippled man is similar; Jesus does not wait for him to ask for a healing. He does not postpone the healing to the next day to avoid persecution from the authorities who oppose healing on the Sabbath. He is not put off by the sick man's self-pity or complaints or superstitious beliefs. Jesus wants us, too, to know that he is here for us. He does not abandon us in our discouragement and resentment. We truly have someone to help us, the Lord himself, who wants to heal us!

Jesus' command, "Rise, take up your mat, and walk," is very compelling. The sick man immediately obeys. Yet despite the miraculous cure, he is afraid to stand up for Jesus when he is reminded by the Jews that carrying a mat is not allowed on the Sabbath. We can see in this man our own tendency to weaken when we are challenged. We have received many gifts of healing grace from the Lord, but before long, we are quite capable of blaming him instead of proclaiming him, or even of denying him when trials come, as if we never really met him. In this way, the crippled man stands in contrast to Sunday's example of the man born blind. Both men are cured physically, but only the blind man shows us what to do *after* we are cured: praise and thank the Lord!

Even if we are slow to respond to the Lord's goodness, even when we are stumbling around in fear and confusion, the Lord seeks us out *again*. Though he knows we may reject and betray him, he takes every risk for our sake. He wants us to know who he is. He cautions us: "Look, you are well; do not sin any more, so that nothing worse may happen to you." This Lenten message to us is not a condemnation or a threat. It is part of the river of divine grace flowing over us. The Lord wants us never to forget his love, never to go back to seeking answers in the wrong places. But do we want to be healed? And remain healed? Let us not waste the blessings that he has bestowed upon us. Let us entrust ourselves to him, allowing his power to work through us and set us free from the bondage of sin.

> *Do I believe in superstitions? Why? Do I not see it as being incompatible with my Christian faith? What are the other gods in my life that I am drawn to when I am in pain or discouraged? How can I allow the Lord to work through me and free me from the bondage of sin?*

Mary, may the power of Jesus' death and resurrection heal me and raise me up to a new life.

First Reading: Isaiah 49:8-15
Thus says the LORD:
In a time of favor I answer you,
   on the day of salvation I help you;
   and I have kept you and given you as a covenant to the people,
To restore the land
   and allot the desolate heritages,
Saying to the prisoners: Come out!
To those in darkness: Show yourselves!
Along the ways they shall find pasture,
   on every bare height shall their pastures be.
They shall not hunger or thirst,
   nor shall the scorching wind or the sun strike them;
For he who pities them leads them
   and guides them beside springs of water.
I will cut a road through all my mountains,
   and make my highways level.
See, some shall come from afar,
   others from the north and the west,
   and some from the land of Syene.
Sing out, O heavens, and rejoice, O earth,
   break forth into song, you mountains.
For the LORD comforts his people
   and shows mercy to his afflicted.

But Zion said, "The LORD has forsaken me;
   my Lord has forgotten me."
Can a mother forget her infant,
   be without tenderness for the child of her womb?
Even should she forget,
   I will never forget you.

Responsorial Psalm: Psalm 145:8-9, 13cd-14, 17-18
The Lord is gracious and merciful.
The LORD is gracious and merciful,
   slow to anger and of great kindness.
The LORD is good to all
   and compassionate toward all his works.
R. The Lord is gracious and merciful.

The LORD is faithful in all his words
    and holy in all his works.
The LORD lifts up all who are falling
    and raises up all who are bowed down.
R. The Lord is gracious and merciful.
The LORD is just in all his ways
    and holy in all his works.
The LORD is near to all who call upon him,
    to all who call upon him in truth.
R. The Lord is gracious and merciful.

Gospel Acclamation: John 11:25a, 26
I am the resurrection and the life, says the Lord; whoever believes in me will never die.

Gospel: John 5:17-30
    Jesus answered the Jews: "My Father is at work until now, so I am at work." For this reason they tried all the more to kill him, because he not only broke the sabbath but he also called God his own father, making himself equal to God.

    Jesus answered and said to them, "Amen, amen, I say to you, the Son cannot do anything on his own, but only what he sees the Father doing; for what he does, the Son will do also. For the Father loves the Son and shows him everything that he himself does, and he will show him greater works than these, so that you may be amazed. For just as the Father raises the dead and gives life, so also does the Son give life to whomever he wishes. Nor does the Father judge anyone, but he has given all judgment to the Son, so that all may honor the Son just as they honor the Father. Whoever does not honor the Son does not honor the Father who sent him. Amen, amen, I say to you, whoever hears my word and believes in the one who sent me has eternal life and will not come to condemnation, but has passed from death to life. Amen, amen, I say to you, the hour is coming and is now here when the dead will hear the voice of the Son of God, and those who hear will live. For just as the Father has life in himself, so also he gave to the Son the possession of life in himself. And he gave him power to exercise judgment, because he is the Son of Man. Do not be amazed at this, because the hour is coming in which all who are in the tombs will hear his voice and will come out, those who have done good deeds to the resurrection of life, but those who have done wicked deeds to the resurrection of condemnation.

"I cannot do anything on my own; I judge as I hear, and my judgment is just, because I do not seek my own will but the will of the one who sent me."

Meditation:
This week began with the Gospel account of Jesus performing a miraculous healing on the Sabbath – the man blind from birth. Yesterday we pondered another Sabbath healing, that of the man at Bethesda who was sick for thirty-eight years. Both miracles were met with opposition, but Jesus is undaunted. Today he declares firmly that he will continue to work, just as the Father still works until now.

Sin is opposition to this divine work. While the will of God fills us with light, sin envelops us in darkness. The more we look for and engage in illicit ways to ease our pains and miseries, the more we stumble, like a blind man groping for solutions in the dark. Sin afflicts our souls, rendering us not only helpless but also lifeless. It is like a Pandora's box; instead of finding a cure, we add more bruises and wounds to our list of complaints.

The Lord sees clearly the darkened condition into which we have fallen. He knows that by ourselves we cannot find a way out. We need someone to come and illumine our darkness. Thus, he comes and opens our eyes that we may see and cautions us not to sin again.

Today's Gospel is a continuation from yesterday. The Jews have learned that Jesus is the one who healed the sick man and told him to carry his mat. Instead of acknowledging the astounding deed of mercy Jesus has done, they begin to persecute him. Their knowledge and strict observance of the Law of Moses makes them think that they can stand in judgment over Jesus. Their envy of him only complicates the matter. What a dangerous combination! Pride and envy can make even the brightest person foolish! This is the sort of spiritual blindness that Jesus exposed on Sunday, when he told the Pharisees, "If you were blind, you would have no sin; but now you are saying, 'We see,' so your sin remains."

Spiritual blindness is not merely a thing of the past! It is happening in our society today and in our own hearts. There are people who argue that it is foolishness to defend the rights of the unborn or the disabled or the aged. They say it is better to dedicate our time and money to help those who will benefit society, not people who can never be profitable or return the favor. We do not agree with the aggressive perpetrators of these views, but often we do nothing to oppose them either. Our inaction implicates us as passive accomplices. We may not be blind to sins of commission, but do we see our own sins of omission?

Because of Jesus Christ, there is great hope for every sinner. His words bring us comfort and new life. He says that "the hour is coming and is now here when the dead will hear the voice of the Son of God, and those who hear will live." Though our souls have been deadened by sin, when we listen to and obey the word of God, we are restored to life. The power of the word resuscitates us and enables us to live a new and transformed life. Jesus promises most solemnly: "whoever hears my word and believes in the one who sent me has eternal life."

Today's first reading also gives us a wonderful dose of life-giving spiritual medicine. Through the prophet Isaiah, the Lord promises that even if we are in a prison or in darkness, he calls us forth into the light. "For the LORD comforts his people and shows mercy to his afflicted." It might happen that we feel forsaken, that our sufferings make us suspect that the Lord has forgotten all about us, since he is not taking care of us. The Lord strongly rejects this impression and corrects us. He assures us that his love for us is more tender and more reliable than the love of a mother for her infant child. "Even should she forget, I will never forget you!" This is truly a word of life, a word to hear, to ponder, and to treasure in faith.

> *How has listening to and obeying the word of God led me away from sin? What makes me spiritually blind? In our modern world, how have I been blind to sins of commission and omission?*

Mary, comfort me with your tender, motherly love.

Notes

First Reading: Exodus 32:7-14

The LORD said to Moses, "Go down at once to your people whom you brought out of the land of Egypt, for they have become depraved. They have soon turned aside from the way I pointed out to them, making for themselves a molten calf and worshiping it, sacrificing to it and crying out, 'This is your God, O Israel, who brought you out of the land of Egypt!'" The LORD said to Moses, "I see how stiff-necked this people is. Let me alone, then, that my wrath may blaze up against them to consume them. Then I will make of you a great nation."

But Moses implored the LORD, his God, saying, "Why, O LORD, should your wrath blaze up against your own people, whom you brought out of the land of Egypt with such great power and with so strong a hand? Why should the Egyptians say, 'With evil intent he brought them out, that he might kill them in the mountains and exterminate them from the face of the earth'? Let your blazing wrath die down; relent in punishing your people. Remember your servants Abraham, Isaac and Israel, and how you swore to them by your own self, saying, 'I will make your descendants as numerous as the stars in the sky; and all this land that I promised, I will give your descendants as their perpetual heritage.'" So the LORD relented in the punishment he had threatened to inflict on his people.

Responsorial Psalm: Psalm 106:19-20, 21-22, 23
Remember us, O Lord, as you favor your people.

Our fathers made a calf in Horeb
    and adored a molten image;
They exchanged their glory
    for the image of a grass-eating bullock.
R. Remember us, O Lord, as you favor your people.

They forgot the God who had saved them,
    who had done great deeds in Egypt,
Wondrous deeds in the land of Ham,
    terrible things at the Red Sea.
R. Remember us, O Lord, as you favor your people.

Then he spoke of exterminating them,
    but Moses, his chosen one,
Withstood him in the breach
    to turn back his destructive wrath.
R. Remember us, O Lord, as you favor your people.

Gospel Acclamation: John 3:16

God so loved the world that he gave his only-begotten Son, so that everyone who believes in him might have eternal life.

✝ *Gospel: John 5:31-47*

Jesus said to the Jews: "If I testify on my own behalf, my testimony is not true. But there is another who testifies on my behalf, and I know that the testimony he gives on my behalf is true. You sent emissaries to John, and he testified to the truth. I do not accept human testimony, but I say this so that you may be saved. He was a burning and shining lamp, and for a while you were content to rejoice in his light. But I have testimony greater than John's. The works that the Father gave me to accomplish, these works that I perform testify on my behalf that the Father has sent me. Moreover, the Father who sent me has testified on my behalf. But you have never heard his voice nor seen his form, and you do not have his word remaining in you, because you do not believe in the one whom he has sent. You search the Scriptures, because you think you have eternal life through them; even they testify on my behalf. But you do not want to come to me to have life.

"I do not accept human praise; moreover, I know that you do not have the love of God in you. I came in the name of my Father, but you do not accept me; yet if another comes in his own name, you will accept him. How can you believe, when you accept praise from one another and do not seek the praise that comes from the only God? Do not think that I will accuse you before the Father: the one who will accuse you is Moses, in whom you have placed your hope. For if you had believed Moses, you would have believed me, because he wrote about me. But if you do not believe his writings, how will you believe my words?"

Meditation:

The painful reality of our human condition is that we are fragile. We can be easily broken down and enslaved by sin. Our efforts at holiness are not consistent. Even when we strive to do what is right and good, as we do with greater effort in the Season of Lent, we are easily distracted and we often fail – not because we do not try but because we try to do it on our own. The good news is that the Lord never expected us to make ourselves perfect. It is his work. We find hope and comfort in the mercy of the Lord who searches for us and saves us. He not only restores us to his friendship but also teaches us how to remain in him.

The Israelites in Moses' time had personal experience of the great love of God and witnessed his power. When they cried out to him, he heard them and responded by bringing them out of Egypt, the place of slavery. Yet today's first reading recounts a crisis that quickly arose during their journey through the desert. While Moses was on the holy mountain, the people collapsed into idolatry. The Lord tells Moses, "Go down at once to your people whom you have brought out of the land of Egypt, for they have become depraved. They have soon turned aside from the way I pointed out to them, making for themselves a molten calf and worshipping it, sacrificing to it and crying out, 'This is your God, O Israel, who brought you out of Egypt!'"

This rapid fall from obedient faith to idolatry reveals the typical pattern of sin. When we sin, we become depraved. We "turn aside from the way" the Lord has pointed out to us. We do not sacrifice to a molten calf, but we find something or someone other than God to worship. Recall that not long before this incident with the calf, the people made a solemn promise of commitment to their covenant with God: "Everything that the Lord has said, we shall do" (Ex 24:3). We have made similar promises to the Lord in times of fervor, or when we were in great need. When we cried out to him from the place of slavery – that is, sin – the Lord heard our prayers and rescued us.

Now we are out of Egypt, thanks be to God, yet we still carry Egypt in our hearts. It is hard to discard our old ways and take on the new life of faith to which God calls us. In our fallen condition, we have a natural resistance to change. This is more a matter of human weakness than sin. The much more serious danger is *hardness of heart* – a resistance to God that arises not from weakness but from our own choices. This is the condition Jesus confronts in today's Gospel: "I know that you do not have the love of God in you…. How can you believe, when you accept praise from one another and do not seek the praise that comes from the only God? …. If you had believed Moses, you would have believed me."

In asking these questions, Jesus intensifies the focus on our interior life. In the first part of the Gospel, it is as if he is on trial, and he offers abundant testimony on his behalf. But it becomes clear that the people do not accept *any* testimony – neither that of John the Baptist, nor of Jesus' miracles ("works"), nor of the Father, nor of the Scriptures. This shows that there is something wrong with these people – and there is something wrong with us. The case against us is much stronger than the case against him. Jesus does not have to accuse us before the Father. The questions he asks are enough of an accusation: *Do we have the love of God in our hearts?*

Jesus has plenty of supportive testimony on his side, even though he really does not need it. But who will testify for us, guilty as we are? Who will intercede for us, as Moses interceded for the Israelites after they became so depraved that they worshipped a molten calf? Who will be our new Moses? The answer is *Jesus himself*. He is the one, our only Mediator, pleading for us at the right hand of the Father, even though we deserve punishment.

Because of Jesus' mediation, we do not need to fear what is described in the language of the Old Testament as the "blazing wrath" of God. We *do* need to fear that we might resist the fire of his love – that we might remain cold, indifferent to our only source of hope. With renewed faith, today we turn again to Jesus. He himself is the Way the Father has pointed out to us, "the Way, the Truth, and the Life" (Jn 14:6).

> *How have I been cold and indifferent to God? Why? In what ways does sin cause me to fall into depravity? How can I turn to God again and renew my faith in Him?*

Mary, intercede for me to your Son.
St. Turibius of Mogrovejo, pray for us.

Turibius of Mogrovejo was born of a noble family in Spain around the year 1538. His learning and virtuous reputation led to his appointment as chief judge of the Tribunal at Grenada. He was ordained a priest during this time, in 1578, and sent to Peru. There he was named Archbishop of Lima, Peru, in 1579. He began his mission work by traveling on foot, baptizing, and teaching the natives. He baptized and confirmed nearly half a million persons, among them St. Rose of Lima and St. Martin de Porres. He was a champion of the rights of the natives against the Spanish colonizers. In 1591 he founded the first seminary in the Americas. Worn out from all his labors, he died in 1606.

First Reading: Wisdom 2:1a, 12-22

The wicked said among themselves,
    thinking not aright:
"Let us beset the just one, because he is obnoxious to us;
    he sets himself against our doings,
Reproaches us for transgressions of the law
    and charges us with violations of our training.
He professes to have knowledge of God
    and styles himself a child of the LORD.
To us he is the censure of our thoughts;
    merely to see him is a hardship for us,
Because his life is not like that of others,
    and different are his ways.
He judges us debased;
    he holds aloof from our paths as from things impure.
He calls blest the destiny of the just
    and boasts that God is his Father.
Let us see whether his words be true;
    let us find out what will happen to him.
For if the just one be the son of God, he will defend him
    and deliver him from the hand of his foes.
With revilement and torture let us put him to the test
    that we may have proof of his gentleness
    and try his patience.
Let us condemn him to a shameful death;
    for according to his own words, God will take care of him."
These were their thoughts, but they erred;
    for their wickedness blinded them,
and they knew not the hidden counsels of God;
    neither did they count on a recompense of holiness
    nor discern the innocent souls' reward.

Responsorial Psalm: Psalm 34:17-18, 19-20, 21 and 23
The Lord is close to the brokenhearted.

The LORD confronts the evildoers,
    to destroy remembrance of them from the earth.
When the just cry out, the LORD hears them,
    and from all their distress he rescues them.
R. The Lord is close to the brokenhearted.

The LORD is close to the brokenhearted;
   and those who are crushed in spirit he saves.
Many are the troubles of the just man,
   but out of them all the LORD delivers him.
R. The Lord is close to the brokenhearted.
He watches over all his bones;
   not one of them shall be broken.
The LORD redeems the lives of his servants;
   no one incurs guilt who takes refuge in him.
R. The Lord is close to the brokenhearted.

Gospel Acclamation: Matthew 4:4b
One does not live on bread alone, but on every word that comes forth
from the mouth of God.

Gospel: John 7:1-2, 10, 25-30

Jesus moved about within Galilee; he did not wish to travel in
Judea, because the Jews were trying to kill him. But the Jewish feast of
Tabernacles was near.

But when his brothers had gone up to the feast, he himself also
went up, not openly but as it were in secret.

Some of the inhabitants of Jerusalem said, "Is he not the one they
are trying to kill? And look, he is speaking openly and they say nothing
to him. Could the authorities have realized that he is the Christ? But we
know where he is from. When the Christ comes, no one will know
where he is from." So Jesus cried out in the temple area as he was
teaching and said, "You know me and also know where I am from. Yet
I did not come on my own, but the one who sent me, whom you do not
know, is true. I know him, because I am from him, and he sent me." So
they tried to arrest him, but no one laid a hand upon him, because his
hour had not yet come.

Meditation:

In the Gospel of John, there is frequent mention of "testimony"
on behalf of Jesus. On Sunday we heard the testimony of the
man born blind, whom Jesus had cured. That man's testimony was
rejected because his birth defect identified him as a "sinner." In
yesterday's Gospel, Jesus gave an impressive list of authentic witnesses
who testify on his behalf – but they too were all rejected. In today's
Gospel, after some people claim to know where he is from and claim

that their knowledge of his origin proves that he cannot be the Messiah, Jesus offers some testimony of his own. He declares his true origin: he has not come on his own initiative; he was sent by the Father, "the One who sent me." Still, the people persist in their doubts because, as Jesus says, they do not know the Father.

We can miss the truth about others when we live in the narrowness of our own opinions. How do we respond to "testimony" on someone's behalf? For example, how do we respond when we discover something new about a friend or loved one? What do we do when we learn that someone whom we looked down on has improved in a remarkable way? Our reception of these people can tell us much about our own spiritual condition. Do we welcome the new insights we receive, even from surprising sources, or do we remain spiritually blind? Our own blindness is often imperceptible to us.

The way that sin blinds us is well described in today's first reading, which gives us an opportunity to listen in on the inmost thoughts of the wicked. They are in error in their thinking because "their wickedness blinded them." They are blind to how God rewards the just. In our own life, we do not usually think of ourselves as deliberately opposing goodness, as these wicked men do. As a rule we do not admit that we are opposed to justice and just people. Usually our inner voices simply find ways to justify ourselves for treating others badly, thinking they deserve it.

The Wisdom reading's description of how wicked men think gives us insight into how the wicked leaders of Jesus' time got to the point of crucifying him, the true Just One. In the Gospel, his opponents' hostility toward him is building up; some already find Jesus so intolerable that they are "trying to kill him." Jesus knows this. His obedience, however, is not to popular opinion, but to the Father, so he makes the decision to go to Jerusalem. He goes in secret, not because he is afraid but because the time is not yet right, "his hour had not yet come." He is doing what he was sent to do, steadily journeying toward the hour of the complete fulfillment of his mission. The key to understanding what Jesus is doing is his relationship with the Father. Jesus' mission is to reconcile us to the Father and to make the Father known.

There is a certain paradox being played out here, because we would think that revealing the Father would mean performing works of great power and authority, proving to the wicked that the Father is in charge of everything and, in a sense, forcing them to believe and obey. That is how we would do it. But this is not Jesus' way. God's ways are very different from ours. Jesus comes to reveal the Father, but not with force or domination. He comes in a way of obedience and humble service. He comes in suffering, even to the point of dying. This reveals the Father's love. This pattern, which is so contradictory to our nature, is repeated in everyone who follows the way of Jesus. This is what the Season of Lent is bringing us to: not to achieve greatness in the world, but to achieve great holiness by our obedience to the One who sends us, the Father.

> *How do I interiorly respond to the success of someone whom I have looked down upon? As I continue my Lenten journey, how am I striving to achieve great holiness? How am I following the ways of God?*

Mary, encourage me to joyfully bear any cross because of my witness to Jesus.

Notes

First Reading: Isaiah 7:10-14; 8:10

The LORD spoke to Ahaz, saying: Ask for a sign from the LORD, your God; let it be deep as the nether world, or high as the sky! But Ahaz answered, "I will not ask! I will not tempt the LORD!" Then Isaiah said: Listen, O house of David! Is it not enough for you to weary people, must you also weary my God? Therefore the Lord himself will give you this sign: the virgin shall be with child, and bear a son, and shall name him Emmanuel, which means "God is with us!"

Responsorial Psalm: Psalm 40:7-8a, 8b-9, 10, 11
Here I am, Lord; I come to do your will.

Sacrifice or oblation you wished not,
but ears open to obedience you gave me.
Holocausts or sin-offerings you sought not;
then said I, "Behold, I come."
R. Here I am, Lord; I come to do your will.
"In the written scroll it is prescribed for me,
To do your will, O my God, is my delight,
and your law is within my heart!"
R. Here I am, Lord; I come to do your will.
I announced your justice in the vast assembly;
I did not restrain my lips, as you, O LORD, know.
R. Here I am, Lord; I come to do your will.
Your justice I kept not hid within my heart;
your faithfulness and your salvation I have spoken of;
I have made no secret of your kindness and your truth
in the vast assembly.
R. Here I am, Lord; I come to do your will.

Second Reading: Hebrews 10:4-10

Brothers and sisters: It is impossible that the blood of bulls and goats takes away sins. For this reason, when Christ came into the world, he said:
"Sacrifice and offering you did not desire,
but a body you prepared for me;
in holocausts and sin offerings you took no delight.
Then I said, 'As is written of me in the scroll,
behold, I come to do your will, O God.'"

First he says, "Sacrifices and offerings, holocausts and sin offerings, you neither desired nor delighted in." These are offered according to the law. Then he says, "Behold, I come to do your will." He takes away the first to establish the second. By this "will," we have been consecrated through the offering of the Body of Jesus Christ once for all.

Gospel Acclamation: John 1:14ab
The Word became flesh and made his dwelling among us; and we saw his glory.

Gospel: Luke 1:26-38
The angel Gabriel was sent from God to a town of Galilee called Nazareth, to a virgin betrothed to a man named Joseph, of the house of David, and the virgin's name was Mary. And coming to her, he said, "Hail, full of grace! The Lord is with you." But she was greatly troubled at what was said and pondered what sort of greeting this might be. Then the angel said to her, "Do not be afraid, Mary, for you have found favor with God. Behold, you will conceive in your womb and bear a son, and you shall name him Jesus. He will be great and will be called Son of the Most High, and the Lord God will give him the throne of David his father, and he will rule over the house of Jacob forever, and of his Kingdom there will be no end." But Mary said to the angel, "How can this be, since I have no relations with a man?" And the angel said to her in reply, "The Holy Spirit will come upon you, and the power of the Most High will overshadow you. Therefore the child to be born will be called holy, the Son of God. And behold, Elizabeth, your relative, has also conceived a son in her old age, and this is the sixth month for her who was called barren; for nothing will be impossible for God." Mary said, "Behold, I am the handmaid of the Lord. May it be done to me according to your word." Then the angel departed from her.

Meditation:
Submission. In our world today, where pride, power, individualism, and autonomy dominate the cultural landscape, the word submission sounds so negative. It connotes weakness and failure. Only losers submit, and only because they are forced to. Today's feast, the Annunciation, dispels such worldly errors and shines a bright light on the true greatness of submission. Mary's "yes" to God is the most momentous *submission* ever to take place. It is an event the Church celebrates with great joy and solemnity nine months before the visible

fruit of Mary's "yes" appears for the first time at Christmas. Without Mary's submission to the will of God, Jesus would not have been born into the world. Salvation history would not have unfolded. We would still be languishing in the darkness. But Mary did submit herself totally to the supernatural message she received, and the whole world is bathed in divine light.

Mary gives us the gift of seeing, as if with her eyes, with her faith, what it means to humble oneself before the will of God. Her acceptance of what the angel tells her, despite her fear and confusion, shows us the beauty of saying "yes" to God, no matter how impossible the circumstances may appear. Gabriel's assurance to Mary is enough to dispel any lingering hesitation: "For nothing will be impossible for God."

Submission to God is not defeat; it is not beneath our dignity. It is using our freedom properly, in the best possible way, to give glory to God. According to the *Catechism*, "To adore God is to acknowledge, in respect and absolute submission, the 'nothingness of the creature' who would not exist but for God. To adore God is to praise and exalt him and to humble oneself, as Mary did in the Magnificat, confessing with gratitude that he has done great things and holy is his name" (*CCC* 2097). Submission is our decision to release our control, stepping aside so that God can take over. It is giving up the pilot's seat so that God can fly the plane. It is John the Baptist saying, "He must increase; I must decrease" (Jn 3:30). It is our saying to God: *Empty me of me and fill me with yourself.*

There is a divine foundation to every act of submission to the will of God: the absolute submission of the Son to the Father. Jesus brought this perfect eternal "yes" into the world, saying, "I come to do your will, O God." He made a perfect offering of himself on the Cross, and now, as the Letter to the Hebrews explains, "we have been consecrated through the offering of the Body of Jesus Christ once for all." Mary too was sanctified by Jesus' sacrifice, though she is a unique case because she was sanctified in advance, preparing her for her future role as Mother of God. This is why Gabriel could address her as "full of grace."

When Mary said, "May it be done to me according to your word," she conceived Jesus by the power of the Holy Spirit. She was forever changed – physically, mentally, emotionally, spiritually – once she

154

allowed the Word to be made flesh in her. By God's grace, this pattern is repeated in us whenever we make a wholehearted "yes" to God. We too are changed forever. We are filled with the Holy Spirit, and Jesus Christ lives and grows within us. In time, his presence in the "womb" of our hearts becomes evident through our words and deeds, as we "give birth" to him in acts of selfless love and service for others.

There is another option, however. The tragic case of King Ahaz reminds us that it is also possible to refuse to submit to God. God tells Ahaz to ask for a sign, any kind of sign, but the king rejects God's offer – which is a foolish thing to do! Ahaz disguises his pride behind a façade of humility. The truth is he does not *want* a sign. It would involve him in too direct an interaction with God, and his decision not to submit would be exposed. The wise prophet Isaiah tells Ahaz that even if he will not accept God's offer, God is going to give a sign anyway: the virginal conception and birth of a Child who will be "Emmanuel," "God is with us."

Just as we can say "yes" like Mary, we can say "no" like Ahaz. We can refuse the gifts God offers to us. Why would anyone say "no" to God? Our nature tends to react with fear when God draws near. *What does he expect of me? Can I do it? What else will he ask? What will I have to give up if I say yes? What if he asks me to do something I do not want to do?* These fears, if we listen to them, hold us back from saying "yes." They are the seeds of a "no."

Today's feast urges us not to be afraid! Because of Mary's "yes," God is with us! And if God is with us, who can be against us? The road to glory is in submission to his will. Together with our spiritual Mother, we repeat from our hearts, *"May it be done according to your word."*

> *How does the total submission of Mary to the will of God inflame my heart to follow in her footsteps? Why is it so difficult for me to step aside and let God take over my life? How have I experienced "giving birth to Jesus" in acts of selfless love and service for others?*

Mary, may the example of your fiat sustain me when I find it difficult to do God's will.

Fifth Week of Lent

*"I am the resurrection and the life;
whoever believes in me, even if he dies, will live,
and everyone who lives and believes in me
will never die."*

John 11:25-26

Theme for the Week

Through his Death on the Cross and his glorious Resurrection, Jesus has destroyed our death and offered us life. No tomb is beyond his power to open. Jesus gives new and eternal life to our mortal bodies by his Spirit living in us. Let us surrender our lives to him with complete faith and walk in his Risen Life.

GOD'S DOMINION OVER LIFE AND DEATH
THROUGH JESUS CHRIST
A Spiritual Reflection by Pope Francis

The Gospel passage for this fifth Sunday of Lent is the resurrection of Lazarus (cf. Jn 11:1-45). Lazarus was Martha and Mary's brother; they were good friends of Jesus. When Jesus arrives in Bethany, Lazarus has already been dead for four days. Martha runs towards the Master and says to Him: "If you had been here, my brother would not have died!" (v. 21). Jesus replies to her: "Your brother will rise again" (v. 23) and adds: "I am the resurrection and the life; he who believes in me, though he die, yet shall he live" (v. 25). Jesus makes himself seen as the Lord of life, he who is capable of giving life even to the dead. Then Mary and other people arrive, in tears, and so Jesus — the Gospel says — "was deeply moved in spirit and troubled.... Jesus wept" (vv. 33, 35). With this turmoil in his heart, he goes to the tomb, thanks the Father who always listens to him, has the tomb opened and cries aloud: "Lazarus, come out!" (v. 43). And Lazarus emerges with "his hands and feet bound with bandages and his face wrapped with a cloth" (v. 44).

Here we can experience firsthand that God is life and gives life, yet takes on the tragedy of death. Jesus could have avoided the death of his friend Lazarus, but he wanted to share in our suffering for the death of people dear to us, and above all, he wished to demonstrate God's dominion over death. In this Gospel passage we see that the faith of man and the omnipotence of God, of God's love, seek each other and finally meet. It is like a two-lane street: the faith of man and the omnipotence of God's love seek each other and finally meet. We see this in the cry of Martha and Mary, and of all of us with them: "If you had been here!" And God's answer is not a speech, no, God's answer to the problem of death is Jesus: "I am the resurrection and the life" ... have faith. Amid grief, continue to have faith, even when it seems that death has won. Take away the stone from your heart! Let the Word of God restore life where there is death.

Today, too, Jesus repeats to us: "Take away the stone." God did not create us for the tomb, but rather he created us for life, [which is] beautiful, good, joyful. But "through the devil's envy death entered the world" (Wis 2:24) says the Book of Wisdom, and Jesus Christ came to free us from its bonds.

We are thus called to take away the stones of all that suggests death: for example, the hypocrisy with which faith is lived, is death; the destructive criticism of others, is death; insults, slander, are death; the marginalization of the poor, is death. The Lord asks us to remove these stones from our hearts, and life will then flourish again around us. Christ lives, and those who welcome him and follow him come into contact with life. Without Christ, or outside of Christ, not only is life not present, but one falls back into death.

The resurrection of Lazarus is also a sign of the regeneration that occurs in the believer through Baptism, with full integration within the Paschal Mystery of Christ. Through the action and power of the Holy Spirit, the Christian is a person who journeys in life as a new creature: a creature for life, who goes towards life.

May the Virgin Mary help us to be compassionate like her Son Jesus, who made our suffering his own. May each of us be close to those who are in difficulty, becoming for them a reflection of God's love and tenderness, which frees us from death and makes life victorious.

Pope Francis, Angelus Message, March 29, 2020

First Reading: Ezekiel 37:12-14

Thus says the Lord GOD: O my people, I will open your graves and have you rise from them, and bring you back to the land of Israel. Then you shall know that I am the LORD, when I open your graves and have you rise from them, O my people! I will put my spirit in you that you may live, and I will settle you upon your land; thus you shall know that I am the LORD. I have promised, and I will do it, says the LORD.

Responsorial Psalm: Psalm 130:1-2, 3-4, 5-6, 7-8
With the Lord there is mercy and fullness of redemption.

Out of the depths I cry to you, O LORD;
　　LORD, hear my voice!
Let your ears be attentive
　　to my voice in supplication.
R. With the Lord there is mercy and fullness of redemption.
If you, O LORD, mark iniquities,
　　LORD, who can stand?
But with you is forgiveness,
　　that you may be revered.
R. With the Lord there is mercy and fullness of redemption.
I trust in the LORD;
　　my soul trusts in his word.
More than sentinels wait for the dawn,
　　let Israel wait for the LORD.
R. With the Lord there is mercy and fullness of redemption.
For with the LORD is kindness
　　and with him is plenteous redemption;
and he will redeem Israel
　　from all their iniquities.
R. With the Lord there is mercy and fullness of redemption.

Second Reading: Romans 8:8-11

Brothers and sisters: Those who are in the flesh cannot please God. But you are not in the flesh; on the contrary, you are in the spirit, if only the Spirit of God dwells in you. Whoever does not have the Spirit of Christ does not belong to him. But if Christ is in you, although the body is dead because of sin, the spirit is alive because of righteousness. If the Spirit of the One who raised Jesus from the dead dwells in you, the One who raised Christ from the dead will give life to your mortal bodies also, through his Spirit dwelling in you.

Gospel Acclamation: John 11:25a, 26

I am the resurrection and the life, says the Lord; whoever believes in me, even if he dies, will never die.

 Gospel: John 11:1-45
(Short Form: John 11:3-7, 17, 20-27, 33b-45)

Now a man was ill, Lazarus from Bethany, the village of Mary and her sister Martha. Mary was the one who had anointed the Lord with perfumed oil and dried his feet with her hair; it was her brother Lazarus who was ill. So the sisters sent word to Jesus saying, "Master, the one you love is ill." When Jesus heard this he said, "This illness is not to end in death, but is for the glory of God, that the Son of God may be glorified through it." Now Jesus loved Martha and her sister and Lazarus. So when he heard that he was ill, he remained for two days in the place where he was. Then after this he said to his disciples, "Let us go back to Judea." The disciples said to him, "Rabbi, the Jews were just trying to stone you, and you want to go back there?" Jesus answered, "Are there not twelve hours in a day? If one walks during the day, he does not stumble, because he sees the light of this world. But if one walks at night, he stumbles, because the light is not in him." He said this, and then told them, "Our friend Lazarus is asleep, but I am going to awaken him." So the disciples said to him, "Master, If he is asleep, he will be saved." But Jesus was talking about his death, while they thought that he meant ordinary sleep. So then Jesus said to them clearly, "Lazarus has died. And I am glad for you that I was not there, that you may believe. Let us go to him." So Thomas, called Didymus, said to his fellow disciples, "Let us also go to die with him."

When Jesus arrived, he found that Lazarus had already been in the tomb for four days. Now Bethany was near Jerusalem, only about two miles away. And many of the Jews had come to Martha and Mary to comfort them about their brother. When Martha heard that Jesus was coming, she went to meet him; but Mary sat at home. Martha said to Jesus, "Lord, if you had been here, my brother would not have died. But even now I know that whatever you ask of God, God will give you." Jesus said to her, "Your brother will rise." Martha said to him, "I know he will rise, in the resurrection on the last day." Jesus told her, "I am the resurrection and the life; whoever believes in me, even if he dies, will live, and everyone who lives and believes in me will never die. Do you believe this?" She said to him, "Yes, Lord. I have come to believe that you are the Christ, the Son of God, the one who is coming into the world."

When she had said this, she went and called her sister Mary secretly, saying, "The teacher is here and is asking for you." As soon as she heard this, she rose quickly and went to him. For Jesus had not yet come into the village, but was still where Martha had met him. So when the Jews who were with her in the house comforting her saw Mary get up quickly and go out, they followed her, presuming that she was going to the tomb to weep there. When Mary came to where Jesus was and saw him, she fell at his feet and said to him, "Lord, if you had been here, my brother would not have died." When Jesus saw her weeping and the Jews who had come with her weeping, he became perturbed and deeply troubled, and said, "Where have you laid him?" They said to him, "Sir, come and see." And Jesus wept. So the Jews said, "See how he loved him." But some of them said, "Could not the one who opened the eyes of the blind man have done something so that this man would not have died?"

So Jesus, perturbed again, came to the tomb. It was a cave, and a stone lay across it. Jesus said, "Take away the stone." Martha, the dead man's sister, said to him, "Lord, by now there will be a stench; he has been dead for four days." Jesus said to her, "Did I not tell you that if you believe you will see the glory of God?" So they took away the stone. And Jesus raised his eyes and said, "Father, I thank you for hearing me. I know that you always hear me; but because of the crowd here I have said this, that they may believe that you sent me." And when he had said this, he cried out in a loud voice, "Lazarus, come out!" The dead man came out, tied hand and foot with burial bands, and his face was wrapped in a cloth. So Jesus said to them, "Untie him and let him go."

Now many of the Jews who had come to Mary and seen what he had done began to believe in him.

Meditation:

Last Sunday, Jesus revealed himself as the Light of the World who overcame the darkness of the man blind from birth. Today, Jesus reveals himself as the Resurrection and the Life who overcomes the death of his friend Lazarus. The Lord has been continuously revealing to us who he is, in and through our life situations, no matter how dark and desperate they may be. As our Lenten journey leads us to the greatest revelation of Christ in our liturgical calendar – that is, in the Paschal Triduum – we hope that our prayer, sacrifice, and charity are making us more and more receptive to God's revelation.

Today's Gospel sets before us the siblings Martha, Mary, and Lazarus as models of receptivity to the Lord. Their house in Bethany, because of its proximity to Jerusalem, was a favorite stopover of the Lord Jesus, who was also their personal friend. When Lazarus fell ill, the sisters did not hesitate to inform the Lord. Upon receiving the news, Jesus makes his mysterious declaration: "This illness is not to end in death, but is for the glory of God, that the Son of God may be glorified through it." It looks to everyone like Lazarus's illness *did* end in death. Only Jesus knows how God will be glorified through the events to come.

When he arrives in Bethany, days after receiving the message, Martha goes out to meet him. We can see in Martha's actions one aspect of receptivity to the Lord: actively seeking him. Martha had been depicted in a previous Gospel story as someone who busies herself in providing hospitality (cf. Lk 10:38-42). In that story she was anxious, but in today's Gospel, Martha is an example of faith. In the dialogue that ensues between her and Jesus, we see Martha's faith deepening as she is guided by the Lord. Martha's first words express her faith in what Jesus can do: "Lord, if you had been here, my brother would not have died. But even now, I know that whatever you ask of God, God will give you." She knows him as a miracle worker and a powerful intercessor.

The Lord offers her a hopeful response: "Your brother will rise." When Martha welcomes this message, but then sets its fulfillment in the distant future, "in the resurrection on the last day," Jesus invites her to take a further step of faith. He reveals that he himself is "the resurrection and the life." Faith in him is life, such that one who believes "will never die." Now Martha makes a profession of deep faith: "Yes, Lord. I have come to believe that you are the Christ, the Son of God, the One who is coming into the world." Though her brother is still lying dead in the tomb, she sees beyond death to life in Christ. This vision of faith becomes possible because she actively seeks the Lord.

Martha's sister Mary learns that Jesus has come, and she promptly meets him and pleads with him. Her first words are the same as her sister's, but her gestures are different. Mary "fell at his feet." Prostrate before him, she also wept, and her companions wept with her. We can see in Mary's actions another aspect of receptivity to the Lord: humility. We began our Lenten season with an act of humility: we received ashes on our forehead and were told that we are dust, and to dust we shall return. Lent reminds us of our nothingness before God, which makes us humble. Acknowledgement of our sin also humbles us and moves us to contrition. The whole self-emptying journey of Lent is meant to make space in our hearts for the abundant outpouring of God's merciful love. We ponder and follow Mary's attitude and actions. Humility and contrition deeply move our Lord; he becomes "perturbed and deeply troubled."

In his Letter to the Romans, St. Paul describes the path of self-emptying in terms of being "in the spirit," as opposed to the pursuit of self-glorification which is being "in the flesh." Our Lenten practices of fasting and abstinence train us to resist the demands of our flesh with all its cravings, to free us of disordered attachments. But we do not stop there. Our practice of almsgiving or charity completes our self-emptying for the benefit of others. This two-step process opens us up for the Spirit of God to dwell in us and work in our lives. As Jesus Christ will show us next week, his total self-emptying on the Cross for our benefit does not end in death but in a glorious Resurrection. St. Paul confidently encourages us to live this truth: "the One who raised Christ from the dead will give life to your mortal bodies also, through his Spirit dwelling in you." We cannot raise ourselves from death, but "out of the depths" we can cry to the Lord. A humble and contrite heart, a heart that attends to the needs of others, the Lord can fill with the grace of his Resurrection.

What of Lazarus? What does he teach us about welcoming the revelation of God? All we know of him is that he was sick, then dead, then buried. He seems beyond any hope or help. But nothing is impossible for God! No matter how hopeless our condition or how dead our nature may be – like the vast valley of dry bones that Ezekiel saw in his vision (cf. Ez 37) – we can receive new life. Ezekiel's prophecy was that the Lord would open his people's graves and have them rise from them. This prophecy is fulfilled in part with the dramatic raising of Lazarus. Lazarus testifies to the Lord's saving power simply by being alive! But the prophecy comes to its more glorious completion with the Resurrection of the Lord. Our hope, today and tomorrow, now and forever, whether we are alive or dead, is in Jesus' victorious power over death. This is where the Season of Lent is headed. We are following our Lord who is our Resurrection and our Life, with whom "there is mercy and fullness of redemption."

> *How do I actively seek the Lord like Martha? In the dark and desperate situations in my life, how does the Lord reveal himself to me personally? As I continue my journey in Lent, how am I being reminded of my nothingness before God?*

Mary, be with me in my sufferings and trials that will lead me to Jesus' glorious Resurrection.

First Reading: Daniel 13:1-9, 15-17, 19-30, 33-62
(Short Form: Daniel 13:41c-62)

In Babylon there lived a man named Joakim, who married a very beautiful and God-fearing woman, Susanna, the daughter of Hilkiah; her pious parents had trained their daughter according to the law of Moses. Joakim was very rich; he had a garden near his house, and the Jews had recourse to him often because he was the most respected of them all.

That year, two elders of the people were appointed judges, of whom the Lord said, "Wickedness has come out of Babylon: from the elders who were to govern the people as judges." These men, to whom all brought their cases, frequented the house of Joakim. When the people left at noon, Susanna used to enter her husband's garden for a walk. When the old men saw her enter every day for her walk, they began to lust for her. They suppressed their consciences; they would not allow their eyes to look to heaven, and did not keep in mind just judgments.

One day, while they were waiting for the right moment, she entered the garden as usual, with two maids only. She decided to bathe, for the weather was warm. Nobody else was there except the two elders, who had hidden themselves and were watching her. "Bring me oil and soap," she said to the maids, "and shut the garden doors while I bathe."

As soon as the maids had left, the two old men got up and hurried to her. "Look," they said, "the garden doors are shut, and no one can see us; give in to our desire, and lie with us. If you refuse, we will testify against you that you dismissed your maids because a young man was here with you."

"I am completely trapped," Susanna groaned. "If I yield, it will be my death; if I refuse, I cannot escape your power. Yet it is better for me to fall into your power without guilt than to sin before the Lord." Then Susanna shrieked, and the old men also shouted at her, as one of them ran to open the garden doors. When the people in the house heard the cries from the garden, they rushed in by the side gate to see what had happened to her. At the accusations by the old men, the servants felt very much ashamed, for never had any such thing been said about Susanna.

When the people came to her husband Joakim the next day, the two wicked elders also came, fully determined to put Susanna to death. Before all the people they ordered: "Send for Susanna, the daughter of Hilkiah, the wife of Joakim." When she was sent for, she came with her parents, children and all her relatives. All her relatives and the onlookers were weeping.

In the midst of the people the two elders rose up and laid their hands on her head. Through tears she looked up to heaven, for she trusted in the Lord wholeheartedly. The elders made this accusation: "As we were walking in the garden alone, this woman entered with two girls and shut the doors of the garden, dismissing the girls. A young man, who was hidden there, came and lay with her. When we, in a corner of the garden, saw this crime, we ran toward them. We saw them lying together, but the man we could not hold, because he was stronger than we; he opened the doors and ran off. Then we seized her and asked who the young man was, but she refused to tell us. We testify to this." The assembly believed them, since they were elders and judges of the people, and they condemned her to death.

But Susanna cried aloud: "O eternal God, you know what is hidden and are aware of all things before they come to be: you know that they have testified falsely against me. Here I am about to die, though I have done none of the things with which these wicked men have charged me."

The Lord heard her prayer. As she was being led to execution, God stirred up the holy spirit of a young boy named Daniel, and he cried aloud: "I will have no part in the death of this woman." All the people turned and asked him, "What is this you are saying?" He stood in their midst and continued, "Are you such fools, O children of Israel! To condemn a woman of Israel without examination and without clear evidence? Return to court, for they have testified falsely against her."

Then all the people returned in haste. To Daniel the elders said, "Come, sit with us and inform us, since God has given you the prestige of old age." But he replied, "Separate these two far from each other that I may examine them."

After they were separated one from the other, he called one of them and said: "How you have grown evil with age! Now have your past sins come to term: passing unjust sentences, condemning the innocent, and freeing the guilty, although the Lord says, 'The innocent and the just you shall not put to death.' Now, then, if you were a witness, tell me under what tree you saw them together." "Under a mastic tree," he answered. Daniel replied, "Your fine lie has cost you your head, for the angel of God shall receive the sentence from him and split you in two." Putting him to one side, he ordered the other one to be brought. Daniel said to him, "Offspring of Canaan, not of Judah, beauty has seduced you, lust has subverted your conscience. This is how you acted with the daughters of Israel, and in their fear they yielded to you; but a daughter of Judah did not tolerate your wickedness. Now, then, tell me under what tree you surprised them together." "Under an oak," he said. Daniel replied, "Your fine lie has cost you also your head, for the angel of God waits with a sword to cut you in two so as to make an end of you both."

The whole assembly cried aloud, blessing God who saves those who hope in him. They rose up against the two elders, for by their own words Daniel had convicted them of perjury. According to the law of Moses, they inflicted on them the penalty they had plotted to impose on their neighbor: they put them to death. Thus was innocent blood spared that day.

 Responsorial Psalm: Psalm 23:1-3a, 3b-4, 5, 6
Even though I walk in the dark valley I fear no evil;
for you are at my side.

The LORD is my shepherd; I shall not want.
    In verdant pastures he gives me repose;
Beside restful waters he leads me;
    he refreshes my soul.

R. Even though I walk in the dark valley I fear no evil;
    for you are at my side.

He guides me in right paths
    for his name's sake.
Even though I walk in the dark valley
    I fear no evil; for you are at my side
With your rod and your staff
    that give me courage.

R. Even though I walk in the dark valley I fear no evil;
    for you are at my side.

You spread the table before me
    in the sight of my foes;
You anoint my head with oil;
    my cup overflows.

R. Even though I walk in the dark valley I fear no evil;
    for you are at my side.

Only goodness and kindness follow me
    all the days of my life;
And I shall dwell in the house of the LORD
    for years to come.

R. Even though I walk in the dark valley I fear no evil;
    for you are at my side.

Gospel Acclamation: Ezekiel 33:11

I take no pleasure in the death of the wicked man, says the Lord, but rather in his conversion, that he may live.

Gospel: John 8:1-11

Jesus went to the Mount of Olives. But early in the morning he arrived again in the temple area, and all the people started coming to him, and he sat down and taught them. Then the scribes and the Pharisees brought a woman who had been caught in adultery and made her stand in the middle. They said to him, "Teacher, this woman was caught in the very act of committing adultery. Now in the law, Moses commanded us to stone such women. So what do you say?" They said this to test him, so that they could have some charge to bring against him. Jesus bent down and began to write on the ground with his finger. But when they continued asking him, he straightened up and said to them, "Let the one among you who is without sin be the first to throw a stone at her." Again he bent down and wrote on the ground. And in response, they went away one by one, beginning with the elders. So he was left alone with the woman before him. Then Jesus straightened up and said to her, "Woman, where are they? Has no one condemned you?" She replied, "No one, sir." Then Jesus said, "Neither do I condemn you. Go, and from now on do not sin any more."

Meditation:

The journey of Lent is an interior journey, a pilgrimage into the depths of our hearts. As we progress, we face our deepest hopes and fears, and our conscience is laid bare before the gaze of the Lord. Today's readings are delightful to the heart that is eager for light, for they are full of rich instruction for the formation of our conscience.

The interior life of the two wicked judges in the Book of Daniel is described very well: "They suppressed their consciences; they would not allow their eyes to look to heaven, and did not keep in mind just judgments." Young Daniel has the wisdom and the courage to identify not only what their moral condition is but also its cause: the serious sin of lust. "Beauty has seduced you; lust has subverted your conscience." These men, like many who get caught in the trap of sin, think they can remain hidden from God. Like a child playing "peek-a-boo," they think to themselves, *If I close my eyes to him, then he can't see me.* These are grown men, however, not children, and this is no child's game. They are risking the mortal life of innocent Susanna, and they are endangering their own immortal souls. In their sinful decisions, all the hallmarks of mortal sin are present: grave matter, full knowledge, and deliberate consent (cf. *CCC* 1857).

The two judges are so wicked and corrupt that we can easily distance ourselves from them, saying to ourselves with proud satisfaction, *Thank God, I am not like them!* Are we indeed unlike them? We are not like them in the obvious sense, but as we probe our hearts more deeply, we uncover our own hidden sins, our secret areas of pride, resentment, envy, jealousy, and judgment. Self-righteousness can be a worse sin than lust. The holy Season of Lent, especially these final two weeks, is a time to ask the Holy Spirit to show us our sinfulness and lead us to repentance. Have I gone to Confession lately?

In the first reading, the innocent Susanna is saved and the sinners are put to death. Since we are identifying ourselves as sinners, this could become a discouraging meditation – until we recall that there is another way to deal with sinners: mercy! This is the wonderful lesson of today's Gospel, the account of the woman caught in adultery. Jesus turns what looks like a disaster into a moment of conversion and freedom. When we are caught and our sin is exposed, we may think the humiliation is too much to bear, but, painful as it may be, God's mercy is at work even in such moments.

The woman's accusers try to use the case of the woman as a trap for Jesus. They have no concern for her, or even for justice according to the law. Perhaps the man who was involved in her adulterous act is even there among her accusers. Jesus avoids their trap by turning the question of judgment around and shining the light of their own conscience back onto themselves. "Let the one among you who is without sin be the first to throw a stone at her." Without any further need for discussion, each man takes an honest look at himself and finds himself convicted. They walk away, one by one.

Jesus then has a personal and private conversation with the woman. (She must have been the one to tell this story afterward; Jesus would never have said a word about it to anyone.) He reveals the divine response to sin. There are two parts. First, he forgives the woman: "I do not condemn you." Then he counsels her to follow a new way, the path of conversion: "From now on, do not sin any more." The spiritual effect on the woman is as profound as the raising of Lazarus, which we pondered yesterday. She was condemned, as good as dead, but Jesus raises her to new life. He restores her dignity as a child of God and sets her free.

In this Gospel story, the Lord Jesus pierces the conscience of all sinners. With his word of truth, with his patient silence, with his compassion, he shows us that he knows our sins and their just consequences, yet he does not condemn us. He has come not to condemn us but to save us (cf. Jn 3:17). He tells us, *"Do not sin any more!"*

> *How do today's readings aid me in the formation of my conscience? As I probe my heart, what are some of the secret areas of my life that I am afraid to face and admit? In what ways do I "cast stones at others" by judging and condemning them?*

Mary, Mother of Mercy, teach me to be merciful and loving to all.

Notes

First Reading: Numbers 21:4-9

From Mount Hor the children of Israel set out on the Red Sea road, to bypass the land of Edom. But with their patience worn out by the journey, the people complained against God and Moses, "Why have you brought us up from Egypt to die in this desert, where there is no food or water? We are disgusted with this wretched food!"

In punishment the LORD sent among the people saraph serpents, which bit the people so that many of them died. Then the people came to Moses and said, "We have sinned in complaining against the LORD and you. Pray the LORD to take the serpents away from us." So Moses prayed for the people, and the LORD said to Moses, "Make a saraph and mount it on a pole, and whoever looks at it after being bitten will live." Moses accordingly made a bronze serpent and mounted it on a pole, and whenever anyone who had been bitten by a serpent looked at the bronze serpent, he lived.

Responsorial Psalm: Psalm 102:2-3, 16-18, 19-21
O Lord, hear my prayer, and let my cry come to you.

O LORD, hear my prayer,
    and let my cry come to you.
Hide not your face from me
    in the day of my distress.
Incline your ear to me;
    in the day when I call, answer me speedily.
R. O Lord, hear my prayer, and let my cry come to you.
The nations shall revere your name, O LORD,
    and all the kings of the earth your glory,
When the LORD has rebuilt Zion
    and appeared in his glory;
When he has regarded the prayer of the destitute,
    and not despised their prayer.
R. O Lord, hear my prayer, and let my cry come to you.
Let this be written for the generation to come,
    and let his future creatures praise the LORD:
"The LORD looked down from his holy height,
    from heaven he beheld the earth,
To hear the groaning of the prisoners,
    to release those doomed to die."
R. O Lord, hear my prayer, and let my cry come to you.

Gospel Acclamation:

The seed is the word of God, Christ is the sower; all who come to him will live for ever.

Gospel: John 8:21-30

Jesus said to the Pharisees: "I am going away and you will look for me, but you will die in your sin. Where I am going you cannot come." So the Jews said, "He is not going to kill himself, is he, because he said, 'Where I am going you cannot come'?" He said to them, "You belong to what is below, I belong to what is above. You belong to this world, but I do not belong to this world. That is why I told you that you will die in your sins. For if you do not believe that I AM, you will die in your sins." So they said to him, "Who are you?" Jesus said to them, "What I told you from the beginning. I have much to say about you in condemnation. But the one who sent me is true, and what I heard from him I tell the world." They did not realize that he was speaking to them of the Father. So Jesus said to them, "When you lift up the Son of Man, then you will realize that I AM, and that I do nothing on my own, but I say only what the Father taught me. The one who sent me is with me. He has not left me alone, because I always do what is pleasing to him." Because he spoke this way, many came to believe in him.

Meditation:

In the forty days of Lent, the Church invites us to reflect on the forty years that the Israelites spent in the desert. Their experience sheds light on our own spiritual journey through the "forty years" of our life on earth. In today's reading, the Israelites complain against God and Moses. They were willing to make the journey out of Egypt, but only until it became too difficult, only until it no longer fulfilled their expectations. They never considered the possibility that as they obeyed the Lord and followed him, he might allow them to experience hardships along their journey.

We too are quite willing to follow the Lord – until we experience discomfort or disappointment. Then we complain. Our hearts feel overburdened and we begin to criticize God's ways. We act as if we know what is good for us better than God does. Rather than trusting in the will of the Lord, we expect the circumstances in life to match our hopes. The truth is, however, that we do not know the mind of God; we only know what we perceive through our own limited perspective. Thus, we assume that he should not allow suffering to touch us. Yet we do suffer. Pain is part of life, part of our journey of faith.

God is not disconnected or distant from us in our times of trial. The Psalm response expresses the plea that arises to him from our hearts: "O Lord, hear my prayer, and let my cry come to you!" He does hear our cries for help. He never despises our prayers. God does not hide his face from us in the day of our distress. Rather, he reaches out to save us, sometimes in most surprising ways. God uses even the evil consequences of our own sins as a means to save us. He sent the seraph serpents to the Israelites as a punishment, and then, when they humbled themselves before him, he transformed the punishment into a means of salvation. When the Israelites gazed upon the bronze serpent, mounted on a pole, they recovered. It became an instrument of hope and healing.

The lifting up of the bronze serpent foretells the lifting up of Jesus Christ on the Cross. He is the divinely provided solution to the problem of sin. Sin, as we know, is an offense against the goodness of God. However, the harm that we do when we sin is really against ourselves, not God. It is much like being bitten by a poisonous snake. If we do not extract the poison, our condition goes from bad to worse. Sin will eventually kill us – and "mortal" sin *does* kill us spiritually – unless we receive an antidote. This is why Jesus in today's Gospel warns the Pharisees, "If you do not believe that I AM, you will die in your sins." He is saying, in effect, *I do not want you to die in your sins! Open your hearts to receive the remedy which the Father in his mercy is providing for you!*

We easily lose patience with our daily journey. After all, we will always be prone to sin. Thus, we will always need to rely upon the Lord Jesus Christ. He took on the punishment, the suffering and death due to our sins. He hangs on the Cross and brings good out of evil. When we gaze with faith upon the Cross of Christ, we are healed. The very evidence of our sin, the very reason why we deserve condemnation, now offers us salvation. As we humbly recognize our own weakness, we can stop dwelling on our crosses and gaze upon the Cross of our Savior and Lord.

In what ways do I complain to the Lord like the Israelites in the desert? Why do I easily lose patience as I go on my own spiritual journey of "forty years" of earthly life? How do I experience the life of the Risen Christ who suffered and died on the Cross for me?

Mary, fix my eyes to gaze on Jesus crucified for my sins.

First Reading: Daniel 3:14-20, 91-92, 95

King Nebuchadnezzar said: "Is it true, Shadrach, Meshach, and Abednego, that you will not serve my god, or worship the golden statue that I set up? Be ready now to fall down and worship the statue I had made, whenever you hear the sound of the trumpet, flute, lyre, harp, psaltery, bagpipe, and all the other musical instruments; otherwise, you shall be instantly cast into the white-hot furnace; and who is the God who can deliver you out of my hands?" Shadrach, Meshach, and Abednego answered King Nebuchadnezzar, "There is no need for us to defend ourselves before you in this matter. If our God, whom we serve, can save us from the white-hot furnace and from your hands, O king, may he save us! But even if he will not, know, O king, that we will not serve your god or worship the golden statue that you set up."

King Nebuchadnezzar's face became livid with utter rage against Shadrach, Meshach, and Abednego. He ordered the furnace to be heated seven times more than usual and had some of the strongest men in his army bind Shadrach, Meshach, and Abednego and cast them into the white-hot furnace.

Nebuchadnezzar rose in haste and asked his nobles, "Did we not cast three men bound into the fire?" "Assuredly, O king," they answered. "But," he replied, "I see four men unfettered and unhurt, walking in the fire, and the fourth looks like a son of God." Nebuchadnezzar exclaimed, "Blessed be the God of Shadrach, Meshach, and Abednego, who sent his angel to deliver the servants who trusted in him; they disobeyed the royal command and yielded their bodies rather than serve or worship any god except their own God."

Responsorial Psalm: Daniel 3:52, 53, 54, 55, 56
  Glory and praise for ever!
"Blessed are you, O Lord, the God of our fathers,
    praiseworthy and exalted above all forever;
· And blessed is your holy and glorious name,
    praiseworthy and exalted above all for all ages."
R. Glory and praise for ever!
"Blessed are you in the temple of your holy glory,
    praiseworthy and exalted above all forever."
R. Glory and praise for ever!

"Blessed are you on the throne of your Kingdom,
   praiseworthy and exalted above all forever."
R. Glory and praise for ever!
"Blessed are you who look into the depths
   from your throne upon the cherubim;
   praiseworthy and exalted above all forever."
R. Glory and praise for ever!
"Blessed are you in the firmament of heaven,
   praiseworthy and glorious forever."
R. Glory and praise for ever!

Gospel Acclamation: see Luke 8:15
Blessed are they who have kept the word with a generous heart and yield a harvest through perseverance.

✝ *Gospel: John 8:31-42*

Jesus said to those Jews who believed in him, "If you remain in my word, you will truly be my disciples, and you will know the truth, and the truth will set you free." They answered him, "We are descendants of Abraham and have never been enslaved to anyone. How can you say, 'You will become free'?" Jesus answered them, "Amen, amen, I say to you, everyone who commits sin is a slave of sin. A slave does not remain in a household forever, but a son always remains. So if the Son frees you, then you will truly be free. I know that you are descendants of Abraham. But you are trying to kill me, because my word has no room among you. I tell you what I have seen in the Father's presence; then do what you have heard from the Father."

They answered and said to him, "Our father is Abraham." Jesus said to them, "If you were Abraham's children, you would be doing the works of Abraham. But now you are trying to kill me, a man who has told you the truth that I heard from God; Abraham did not do this. You are doing the works of your father!" So they said to him, "We were not born of fornication. We have one Father, God." Jesus said to them, "If God were your Father, you would love me, for I came from God and am here; I did not come on my own, but he sent me."

Meditation:

Today's readings continue to remind us that in the journey of life our faith will be challenged. On Sunday we saw the faith of Martha and Mary being challenged when their brother Lazarus died. On Monday we saw Susanna's faith challenged as she clung to the Lord in the face of injustice and the threat of execution. Some people are being challenged even in our own day to the point of death – martyrdom. Most of us find our faith challenged in more subtle ways.

In the first reading, King Nebuchadnezzar questions Shadrach, Meshach, and Abednego in a way similar to how the serpent questioned Adam and Eve in the garden. "Is it true…?" "Did God really say…?" Most of the challenges to our faith begin in this fashion, in the guise of innocent questions which sow the seed of doubt. *Is it true that Catholics believe marriage is between one woman and one man? Is it true that Catholics must attend Mass on Sunday? Do you think God really cares whether you do this or not?* The questions are limitless. Some ask out of ignorance; others ask out of disbelief and disdain. Either way, our faith is put to the test. We must be ready to hold fast, and strive to answer with truth in love.

In the case of Shadrach, Meshach, and Abednego, their commitment to the truth of who the real God is sets them free from the unjust demands of the king. They are determined to remain faithful to God, regardless of the consequences. Even if God will not save them from the white-hot furnace, they will still not serve any false god or golden idol.

If we are open to truth, the effect of such a witness of faith is that it inspires us to believe. When someone is willing to risk death for what he believes, we are inclined to listen to him. King Nebuchadnezzar, however, is not moved to faith. Sensing a defiance of his royal authority, he becomes very angry, "livid with utter rage." The king is not receptive to the truth until the Lord miraculously saves the three young men from all harm in the furnace. Then Nebuchadnezzar is humbled and moved to respect the God of Israel. He realizes that they were right to disobey his royal command; he is impressed by their willingness to "yield their bodies rather than serve or worship any god except their own God."

In the Gospel, Jesus challenges the faith of "those Jews who believed in him." Initially, they respond to Jesus with pride. They take offense at the implication that they are slaves. When Jesus speaks of being set free, he is not referring to slavery in the usual sense. Since the Jews object, he patiently explains to them what he means: "Everyone who commits sin is a slave of sin." Sin does indeed enslave us. It is similar to an addiction; the more one indulges, the more one craves until all freedom is sacrificed for the indulgence of the sin.

This is one reason why our faith must be challenged in order for us to grow — because otherwise, we settle into the slavery of sin, without even thinking about it. Jesus, the Son of God, sent by the Father, has come to set us free from sin. "A son always remains" as a member of the family; this is Jesus' rightful place as the Son of the Father, and he alone has the power to free those who are slaves of sin. Through his Cross we are no longer slaves but sons and daughters of the Father. "If you remain in my word, you will truly be my disciples, and you will know the truth, and the truth will set you free…. If the Son frees you, you will truly be free."

As the conversation continues, Jesus' listeners find his statements more and more challenging. They begin to cling to their claim that Abraham is their father, and when Jesus questions that, they cry out in exasperation, "We have one Father, God." There is truth in what they say, but it is the truth of what we may call intellectual faith. Faith has not yet found a home in their hearts. In every challenge to our faith, Jesus is inviting us to deepen our conviction that God is our Father, and that we are his beloved children. We do not need to fear that the "furnace" of his divine love will destroy us, for the Father's will is that we be truly free, "unfettered and unhurt," walking in intimate communion with him, through his Son, in the power of the Holy Spirit, who is the "fire" of divine love.

> *As I continue my Lenten journey, how is my faith being challenged in subtle ways? How can I imitate the faith of the three young men when I am called to witness to the truth? What habits or addictions can sway me away from the worship of the true God?*

Mary, may the "furnace" of divine love ever burn in my heart.

Notes

First Reading: Genesis 17:3-9

When Abram prostrated himself, God spoke to him: "My covenant with you is this: you are to become the father of a host of nations. No longer shall you be called Abram; your name shall be Abraham, for I am making you the father of a host of nations. I will render you exceedingly fertile; I will make nations of you; kings shall stem from you. I will maintain my covenant with you and your descendants after you throughout the ages as an everlasting pact, to be your God and the God of your descendants after you. I will give to you and to your descendants after you the land in which you are now staying, the whole land of Canaan, as a permanent possession; and I will be their God."

God also said to Abraham: "On your part, you and your descendants after you must keep my covenant throughout the ages."

Responsorial Psalm: Psalm 105:4-5, 6-7, 8-9
The Lord remembers his covenant for ever.

Look to the LORD in his strength;
    seek to serve him constantly.
Recall the wondrous deeds that he has wrought,
    his portents, and the judgments he has uttered.
R. The Lord remembers his covenant for ever.

You descendants of Abraham, his servants,
    sons of Jacob, his chosen ones!
He, the LORD, is our God;
    throughout the earth his judgments prevail.
R. The Lord remembers his covenant for ever.

He remembers forever his covenant
    which he made binding for a thousand generations –
Which he entered into with Abraham
    and by his oath to Isaac.
R. The Lord remembers his covenant for ever.

Gospel Acclamation: Psalm 95:8
If today you hear his voice, harden not your hearts.

Gospel: John 8:51-59

Jesus said to the Jews: "Amen, amen, I say to you, whoever keeps my word will never see death." So the Jews said to him, "Now we are sure that you are possessed. Abraham died, as did the prophets, yet you say, 'Whoever keeps my word will never taste death.' Are you greater than our father Abraham, who died? Or the prophets, who died? Who do you make yourself out to be?" Jesus answered, "If I glorify myself, my glory is worth nothing; but it is my Father who glorifies me, of whom you say, 'He is our God.' You do not know him, but I know him. And if I should say that I do not know him, I would be like you a liar. But I do know him and I keep his word. Abraham your father rejoiced to see my day; he saw it and was glad." So the Jews said to him, "You are not yet fifty years old and you have seen Abraham?" Jesus said to them, "Amen, amen, I say to you, before Abraham came to be, I AM." So they picked up stones to throw at him; but Jesus hid and went out of the temple area.

Meditation:

"What's in a name?" So asks Juliet in Shakespeare's famous play, musing that Romeo would still be the same man even if he had a different name. In the Bible, however, one's name, and especially the change of a name, is very significant. Today the Liturgy begins and ends with the significance of a name. It begins with the change of Abram's name to Abraham; it ends with Jesus claiming for himself the divine Name, I AM. These are moments of revelation, declarations both of personal identity and of divine mission.

In the case of our father in faith, "Abram" is translated as "exalted father," while "Abraham" means something even more exalted, "father of a multitude" – showing that Abraham's mission is truly to be the spiritual father of all who believe in the one true God. Though Abraham is a great patriarch, father of kings and of a host of nations, none of this originated from him. It was all the work of God who chose him, called him, and made a sacred covenant with him. Abraham did not fully understand what God's plan was, nor did he know how it could ever come about, since at the time he was already almost one hundred years old, and he had only one son, Ishmael, son of his wife's slave girl. The greatness of Abraham is his absolute faith. He knew that God had made a promise, and he lived in certainty – not by sight but by faith – that God would be true to that promise. Abraham passed on this faith to his descendants and taught them to remain faithful to the covenant.

Despite his great faith and preeminence, Abraham eventually died, just like everyone else. Death is one certainty that does not require faith to accept; it is obvious that everyone dies. The people in conversation with Jesus in today's Gospel have not yet seen that he has power even over death, since this encounter takes place before he raised Lazarus from the tomb. When he declares, "Whoever keeps my word will never see death," his listeners are shocked. This Jesus must be possessed! He talks as if he is greater than Abraham!

They are not prepared for the even greater shock that hits them when Jesus solemnly declares, "Before Abraham came to be, I AM." *I AM* is the Name God used for himself when he revealed himself to Moses in the burning bush. Only God can use the holy Name for himself. At this point the people judge Jesus to be not possessed but an arrogant blasphemer. His implicit claim to precede Abraham, and to be greater than him, and much worse, to be equal to God himself, merits the punishment of being stoned to death. Obviously, the lesson of mercy that Jesus gave in Monday's Gospel, the forgiveness of the adulteress, made no lasting impact on them. Even if they are convinced that Jesus is guilty, which of them is free from sin, so that he can cast the first stone at him?

In a few days we will follow Jesus as he enters Jerusalem and is acclaimed as a king. Not long afterward, he will be mocked as an imposter and killed as a blasphemer. But his true identity is revealed today. He is the divine and eternal I AM. He is God-with-us. Though innocent, he will be treated as guilty. He will die not for his sins but for ours, so that we will never see death.

The key which gains access to his victory over death is faith in him. This is why the Liturgy today focuses on Abraham, because we need to respond to Jesus with the same absolute faith with which Abraham responded to the Lord. Our father Abraham rejoiced to see Jesus' day. He saw it by faith, not by sight. We share in his joy when we share his faith. Our faith will be challenged when what we see seems to contradict what we believe – when we see Jesus, the I AM, suffering, and when we ourselves experience suffering. Strong faith, however, like the faith of Abraham, endures in the absence of light. This is the faith to which we are called.

> *How does my faith compare with that of Abraham? In what ways have I been unfaithful to my covenant with God? Why is it difficult to live in faith when I cannot understand the ways of the Lord in my life?*

Mary, increase my faith as I prepare to participate fully in the Paschal Mystery of your Son Jesus.

First Reading: Jeremiah 20:10-13

I hear the whisperings of many:
    "Terror on every side!
Denounce! let us denounce him!"
All those who were my friends
    are on the watch for any misstep of mine.
"Perhaps he will be trapped; then we can prevail,
    and take our vengeance on him."
But the LORD is with me, like a mighty champion:
    my persecutors will stumble, they will not triumph.
In their failure they will be put to utter shame,
    to lasting, unforgettable confusion.
O LORD of hosts, you who test the just,
    who probe mind and heart,
Let me witness the vengeance you take on them,
    for to you I have entrusted my cause.
Sing to the LORD,
    praise the LORD,
For he has rescued the life of the poor
    from the power of the wicked!

Responsorial Psalm: Psalm 18:2-3a, 3bc-4, 5-6, 7
In my distress I called upon the Lord, and he heard my voice.
I love you, O LORD, my strength,
    O LORD, my rock, my fortress, my deliverer.
R. In my distress I called upon the Lord, and he heard my voice.
My God, my rock of refuge,
    my shield, the horn of my salvation, my stronghold!
Praised be the LORD, I exclaim,
    and I am safe from my enemies.
R. In my distress I called upon the Lord, and he heard my voice.
The breakers of death surged round about me,
    the destroying floods overwhelmed me;
The cords of the nether world enmeshed me,
    the snares of death overtook me.
R. In my distress I called upon the Lord, and he heard my voice.
In my distress I called upon the LORD
    and cried out to my God;
From his temple he heard my voice,
    and my cry to him reached his ears.
R. In my distress I called upon the Lord, and he heard my voice.

Your words, Lord, are Spirit and life; you have the words of everlasting life.

✝ *Gospel: John 10:31-42*

The Jews picked up rocks to stone Jesus. Jesus answered them, "I have shown you many good works from my Father. For which of these are you trying to stone me?" The Jews answered him, "We are not stoning you for a good work but for blasphemy. You, a man, are making yourself God." Jesus answered them, "Is it not written in your law, 'I said, "You are gods"'? If it calls them gods to whom the word of God came, and Scripture cannot be set aside, can you say that the one whom the Father has consecrated and sent into the world blasphemes because I said, 'I am the Son of God'? If I do not perform my Father's works, do not believe me; but if I perform them, even if you do not believe me, believe the works, so that you may realize and understand that the Father is in me and I am in the Father." Then they tried again to arrest him; but he escaped from their power.

He went back across the Jordan to the place where John first baptized, and there he remained. Many came to him and said, "John performed no sign, but everything John said about this man was true." And many there began to believe in him.

Meditation:

With Good Friday only one week away, we continue to ponder the growing violent resistance against Jesus and his mission. The experience of the prophet Jeremiah is a kind of prophetic foreshadowing of Jesus' Passion. In today's reading, Jeremiah is in a dire situation. His friends – or those who used to be his friends – have turned against him. Now they are thinking to themselves, "Perhaps he will be trapped; then we can prevail, and take our vengeance on him."

The only way Jeremiah can face such suffering and persecution is by the strength he gains through his faith in God. He entrusts himself to the Lord and sings his praises for rescuing "the life of the poor from the power of the wicked." We notice that Jeremiah has not yet been rescued from persecution, but he already sees in faith that the Lord will deliver him. Because he knows that the Lord is with him, "like a mighty champion," he can sing out as if the Lord has already accomplished the great deed of saving him.

In Jeremiah's confidence in God and in his frank description of his sufferings we find a prophecy pointing toward Jesus' own experience. Jesus too will be denounced, betrayed, and abandoned even by his friends. Though innocent, he will be treated as guilty, so that we who are guilty can be restored to innocence through his suffering. He is confident that he too will be rescued from all harm because of the love of his Father. Though it looks humanly impossible, Jesus knows that the apparent defeat will be reversed. He deliberately takes the place of the whole human family, not only in suffering for us, but also in rising again in glory for us.

In the Gospel, the Jews are again ready to stone Jesus. His response is another merciful attempt to open their eyes to the good that he has done for them: "I have shown you many good works from my Father. For which of these are you trying to stone me?" The Jews say they are not stoning him for his good deeds but for blasphemy. Whatever good works he did no longer matter; whatever truths he uttered no longer matter either. None of the obvious proofs of his goodness can make sense to them for they have closed their hearts and their minds. Jesus knows that he will soon be delivered into the hands of evil men, but he remains totally in charge. He is not losing his life against his will; he is laying it down in sacrifice. He makes a freewill offering of himself according to his Father's plan. Therefore Jesus does not back down from revealing the truth about his relationship with the Father: "The Father is in me and I am in the Father."

Though Jesus' words may confuse or amaze us, we have no justification for rejecting him. There is another way to respond: *faith*. When Jesus crosses back over to the other side of the Jordan, he finds that many people are willing to put faith in him. They are the fruit of the ministry of John the Baptist. By his preaching, John called the people to repentance and prepared them to open their minds and hearts to Jesus.

Here we can see some of the obstacles that the word of God warns us about. If we do not repent of our sins, we are not ready to welcome the truth. And if we carry biases or judgmental attitudes in our hearts, we will resist the Lord and his messengers. It is not right for us to let a strong dislike of a person move us to close our heart to him. A closed heart cannot listen to the truth. A listening heart can hear the truth, even a challenging truth, from anyone. The good deeds of others and their true words are gifts to us from God, who calls us to welcome him in faith.

> *How has the strength and faith of the Prophet Jeremiah inspired me? As I continue to follow Jesus to Calvary, how am I interiorly preparing for this journey? When have I been denounced, betrayed or abandoned because of my faith in Jesus?*

Mary, give me the strength and courage to be steadfast as I journey with Jesus to Calvary.

Notes

First Reading: Ezekiel 37:21-28

Thus says the Lord GOD: I will take the children of Israel from among the nations to which they have come, and gather them from all sides to bring them back to their land. I will make them one nation upon the land, in the mountains of Israel, and there shall be one prince for them all. Never again shall they be two nations, and never again shall they be divided into two kingdoms.

No longer shall they defile themselves with their idols, their abominations, and all their transgressions. I will deliver them from all their sins of apostasy, and cleanse them so that they may be my people and I may be their God. My servant David shall be prince over them, and there shall be one shepherd for them all; they shall live by my statutes and carefully observe my decrees. They shall live on the land that I gave to my servant Jacob, the land where their fathers lived; they shall live on it forever, they, and their children, and their children's children, with my servant David their prince forever. I will make with them a covenant of peace; it shall be an everlasting covenant with them, and I will multiply them, and put my sanctuary among them forever. My dwelling shall be with them; I will be their God, and they shall be my people. Thus the nations shall know that it is I, the LORD, who make Israel holy, when my sanctuary shall be set up among them forever.

Responsorial Psalm: Jeremiah 31:10, 11-12abcd, 13
The Lord will guard us, as a shepherd guards his flock.

Hear the word of the LORD, O nations,
    proclaim it on distant isles, and say:
He who scattered Israel, now gathers them together,
    he guards them as a shepherd his flock.
R. The Lord will guard us, as a shepherd guards his flock.
The LORD shall ransom Jacob,
    he shall redeem him from the hand of his conqueror.
Shouting, they shall mount the heights of Zion,
    they shall come streaming to the LORD's blessings:
The grain, the wine, and the oil,
    the sheep and the oxen.
R. The Lord will guard us, as a shepherd guards his flock.
Then the virgins shall make merry and dance,
    and young men and old as well.
I will turn their mourning into joy,
    I will console and gladden them after their sorrows.
R. The Lord will guard us, as a shepherd guards his flock.

Gospel Acclamation: Ezekiel 18:31
Cast away from you all the crimes you have committed, says the Lord,
and make for yourselves a new heart and a new spirit.

✝ Gospel: John 11:45-56

Many of the Jews who had come to Mary and seen what Jesus
had done began to believe in him. But some of them went to the
Pharisees and told them what Jesus had done. So the chief priests and
the Pharisees convened the Sanhedrin and said, "What are we going to
do? This man is performing many signs. If we leave him alone, all will
believe in him, and the Romans will come and take away both our land
and our nation." But one of them, Caiaphas, who was high priest that
year, said to them, "You know nothing, nor do you consider that it is
better for you that one man should die instead of the people, so that the
whole nation may not perish." He did not say this on his own, but since
he was high priest for that year, he prophesied that Jesus was going to
die for the nation, and not only for the nation, but also to gather into one
the dispersed children of God. So from that day on they planned to kill
him.

So Jesus no longer walked about in public among the Jews, but he
left for the region near the desert, to a town called Ephraim, and there
he remained with his disciples.

Now the Passover of the Jews was near, and many went up from
the country to Jerusalem before Passover to purify themselves. They
looked for Jesus and said to one another as they were in the temple area,
"What do you think? That he will not come to the feast?"

Meditation:

Throughout this week we have been pondering the plight of
people caught in hopeless situations. Lazarus died before Jesus
arrived; Susanna was falsely accused by wicked judges; the woman
caught in adultery was threatened with stoning; Shadrach, Meshach and
Abednego were thrown into a fiery furnace; and the prophet Jeremiah
suffered fierce opposition and threats to his life by the very people to
whom God sent him. Each one entrusted his or her cause to God, crying
out for mercy and help. The Old Testament sign of the help that God
sends is the mysterious figure of the bronze serpent hung on a pole. We
will see the fulfillment of this symbol of hope and healing in the
crucifixion of Jesus.

Tomorrow is Palm Sunday, the beginning of Holy Week. The conflict that has been smoldering over the question of Jesus' mission is about to flare up. It is a week full of contrasts. Crowds of people already believe in Jesus, at least to some degree, and they line the streets to welcome him to Jerusalem. Others oppose him, especially the jealous and defensive chief priests and the Pharisees, who have already determined that Jesus must be killed. We see hatred and we see Love's response. We see Jerusalem, a city confused and divided, a picture of humanity today, a humanity in desperate need of salvation in Christ and yet not convinced of his goodness.

The division of the people stands in contrast to the prophecies in the Old Testament which speak of the Lord's desire to unite his people as one flock under one shepherd. In today's first reading the Lord tells Ezekiel that, although the people are filthy and defiled, scattered like stray sheep among many nations, he will rescue them and cleanse them of their sins. He will bring them back to unity under one holy king, a descendant of David.

It is sin which defiles, divides, and scatters us. Sin deeply damages our relationship with God and cuts us off from one another. In order for us to be re-united, the devastating effects of sin must be overcome. This is the mission of Jesus Christ. "The Word became flesh for us *in order to save us by reconciling us with God"* (*CCC* 457). As the Jewish Passover draws near, so does the hour for the accomplishment of this mission of Jesus.

In the Gospel, the Pharisees are gripped with fear that if Jesus keeps on attracting followers the results will certainly be bad: the Romans will come and destroy their nation. They are not thinking logically, for though they can see that the everyone is coming to believe in Jesus, they exclude the possibility that the Romans too may believe. Responding to Caiaphas' unwitting prophecy, they come up with a plan to kill Jesus in order to save their nation. God's plan, as always, is far greater than man's. Jesus' Death will save not only the Jews but all people. He has come, not to prevent a foreign military invasion, but a much more devastating disaster, eternal damnation. His mission – which includes his Death – is "to gather into one the dispersed children of God" – in perfect fulfillment of Ezekiel's prophecy.

Caiaphas is gravely wrong in proposing the death of an innocent man, even if his intention is to save the nation. "The condemnation of an innocent person cannot be justified as a legitimate means of saving the nation" (*CCC* 1753). The end never justifies the means. This basic moral principal is often violated when those in authority try to justify whatever they do by claiming that "it is for the good of the nation." Once the suggestion to do evil is raised, the action must be immediately rejected, no matter how beneficial the desired outcome or how convincing the arguments. Promoters of so-called abortion rights think like Caiaphas, and use similar arguments. We can never accept any proposal to do evil for the sake of good. Whenever we deliberately choose an evil act, our intention is already not good.

What we will see this coming week is that God is not defeated, even when we do choose evil. God brings good out of evil in a wondrous way. The sin of Caiaphas becomes part of God's great plan for our salvation. As we follow in Christ's footsteps, we anticipate his victory even while he looks defeated on the Cross. As we suffer in this life, we do not lose hope because we know he has power to overcome death itself.

> *Have I ever experienced that the end never justifies the means? When has sin damaged my relationship with God and cut me off from others? As I ponder on God's plan for my life, when has good came out of an evil situation?*

Mary, guide me to be as steadfast as Jesus was to the will of God.

Notes

Holy Week:
Palm Sunday to Holy Thursday

The Lord God is my help,
therefore I am not disgraced;
I have set my face like flint,
knowing that I shall not be put to shame.

Isaiah 50:7

Theme for the Week

In perfect obedience to the will of his Father, the Lord Jesus enters Jerusalem to complete his mission of bringing salvation to a sinful world. He brings our sins to the Cross, and our sins bring him to the Cross. Let us walk with Jesus through the holy days ahead leading to his Passion and Death in order to share in his Resurrection.

CALLED TO BE SERVANTS OF CHRIST
IN HUMILITY AND SELF-ABANDONMENT
A Spiritual Reflection by Pope Francis

Jesus "emptied himself, taking the form of a servant" (*Phil* 2:7). Let us allow these words of the Apostle Paul to lead us into these holy days, when the word of God, like a refrain, presents Jesus as *servant*: on Holy Thursday, he is portrayed as the servant who washes the feet of his disciples; on Good Friday, he is presented as the suffering and victorious servant (cf. *Is* 52:13); and tomorrow we will hear the prophecy of Isaiah about him: "Behold my servant, whom I uphold" (*Is* 42:1). God saved us *by serving us*. We often think we are the ones who serve God. No, he is the one who freely chose to serve us, for he loved us first. It is difficult to love and not be loved in return. And it is even more difficult to serve if we do not let ourselves be served by God.

But – just one question – how did the Lord serve us? By giving his life for us. We are dear to him; we cost him dearly. Saint Angela of Foligno said she once heard Jesus say: "My love for you is no joke." His love for us led him to sacrifice himself and to take upon himself our sins. This astonishes us: God saved us by taking upon himself all the punishment of our sins. Without complaining, but with the humility, patience, and obedience of a servant, and purely out of love. And the Father *upheld* Jesus in his service. He did not take away the evil that crushed him, but rather strengthened him in his suffering so that our evil could be overcome by good, by a love that loves to the very end.

The Lord served us to the point of experiencing the most painful situations of those who love: *betrayal* and *abandonment*.

Betrayal. Jesus suffered betrayal by the disciple who sold him and by the disciple who denied him. He was betrayed by the people who sang hosanna to him and then shouted: "Crucify him!" (*Mt* 27:22). He was betrayed by the religious institution that unjustly condemned him and by the political institution that washed its hands of him. We can think of all the small or great betrayals that we have suffered in life. It is terrible to discover that a firmly placed trust has been betrayed. From deep within our heart a disappointment surges up that can even make life seem meaningless. This happens because we were born to be loved and to love, and the most painful thing is to be betrayed by someone who promised to be loyal and close to us. We cannot even imagine how painful it was for God who *is* love.

Let us look within. If we are honest with ourselves, we will see our infidelities. How many falsehoods, hypocrisies, and duplicities! How many good intentions betrayed! How many broken promises! How many resolutions left unfulfilled! The Lord knows our hearts better than we do. He knows how weak and irresolute we are, how many times we fall, how hard it is for us to get up and how difficult it is to heal certain wounds. And what did he do in order to come to our aid and serve us? He told us through the Prophet: "I will heal their faithlessness; I will love them deeply" (*Hos* 14:5). He healed us by taking upon himself our infidelity and by taking from us our betrayals. Instead of being discouraged by the fear of failing, we can now look upon the crucifix, feel his embrace, and say: "Behold, there is my infidelity, you took it, Jesus, upon yourself. You open your arms to me, you serve me with your love, you continue to support me… And so I will keep pressing on."

Abandonment. In today's Gospel, Jesus says one thing from the Cross, one thing alone: "My God, my God, why have you forsaken me?" (*Mt* 27:46). These are powerful words. Jesus had suffered the abandonment of his own, who had fled. But the Father remained for him. Now, in the abyss of solitude, for the first time he calls him by the generic name "God." And "in a loud voice" he asks the question "why?", the most excruciating "why?": "Why did you too abandon me?" These words are in fact those of a Psalm (cf. 22:2); they tell us that Jesus also brought the experience of extreme desolation to his prayer. But the fact remains that he himself experienced that desolation: he experienced the utmost abandonment, which the Gospels testify to by quoting his very words.

Why did all this take place? Once again, it was done for our sake, to *serve* us. So that when we have our back to the wall, when we find ourselves at a dead end, with no light and no way of escape, when it seems that God himself is not responding, we should remember that we are not alone. Jesus experienced total abandonment in a situation he had never before experienced in order to be one with us in everything. He did it for me, for you, for all of us; he did it to say to us: "Do not be afraid, you are not alone. I experienced all your desolation in order to be ever close to you." That is the extent to which Jesus served us: he descended into the abyss of our most bitter sufferings, culminating in betrayal and abandonment. Today, in the tragedy of a pandemic, in the face of the many false securities that have now crumbled, in the face of so many hopes betrayed, in the sense of abandonment that weighs upon our hearts, Jesus says to each one of us: "Courage, open your heart to my love. You will feel the consolation of God who sustains you."

Dear brothers and sisters, what can we do in comparison with God, who served us even to the point of being betrayed and abandoned? We can refuse to betray him for whom we were created, and not abandon what really matters in our lives. We were put in this world to love him and our neighbors. Everything else passes away, only this remains. The tragedy we are experiencing at this time summons us to take seriously the things that are serious, and not to be caught up in those that matter less; to rediscover that *life is of no use if not used to serve others*. For life is measured by love. So, in these holy days, in our homes, let us stand before the Crucified One – look upon the Crucified One! – the fullest measure of God's love for us, and before the God who serves us to the point of giving his life, and – fixing our gaze on the Crucified One – let us ask for the grace to *live in order to serve*. May we reach out to those who are suffering and those most in need. May we not be concerned about what we lack, but what good we can do for others.

Behold my servant, whom I uphold. The Father, who sustained Jesus in his Passion also supports us in our efforts to serve. Loving, praying, forgiving, caring for others, in the family and in society: all this can certainly be difficult. It can feel like a *via crucis* [way of the Cross]. But the path of service is the victorious and life-giving path by which we were saved. I would like to say this especially to young people, on this Day which has been dedicated to them for thirty-five years now. Dear friends, look at the *real heroes* who come to light in these days: they are not famous, rich and successful people; rather, they are those who are giving themselves in order to serve others. Feel called yourselves to put your lives on the line. Do not be afraid to devote your life to God and to others; it pays! For life is a gift we receive only when we give ourselves away, and our deepest joy comes from saying yes to love, without ifs and buts. To truly say yes to love, without ifs and buts. As Jesus did for us.

Pope Francis, Homily, Palm Sunday, April 5, 2020
35th World Youth Day, St. Peter's Basilica, Rome
© Copyright 2020 - Libreria Editrice Vaticana

Procession with Palms:

✝ *Gospel: Matthew 21:1-11*

When Jesus and the disciples drew near Jerusalem and came to Bethphage on the Mount of Olives, Jesus sent two disciples, saying to them, "Go into the village opposite you, and immediately you will find an ass tethered, and a colt with her. Untie them and bring them here to me. And if anyone should say anything to you, reply, 'The master has need of them.' Then he will send them at once." This happened so that what had been spoken through the prophet might be fulfilled:

> *Say to daughter Zion,*
> *"Behold, your king comes to you,*
> *meek and riding on an ass,*
> *and on a colt, the foal of a beast of burden."*

The disciples went and did as Jesus had ordered them. They brought the ass and the colt and laid their cloaks over them, and he sat upon them. The very large crowd spread their cloaks on the road, while others cut branches from the trees and strewed them on the road. The crowds preceding him and those following kept crying out and saying:

> "Hosanna to the Son of David;
> blessed is he who comes in the name of the Lord;
> hosanna in the highest."

And when he entered Jerusalem the whole city was shaken and asked, "Who is this?" And the crowds replied, "This is Jesus the prophet, from Nazareth in Galilee."

First Reading: Isaiah 50:4-7

The Lord GOD has given me
    a well-trained tongue,
that I might know how to speak to the weary
    a word that will rouse them.
Morning after morning
    he opens my ear that I may hear;
and I have not rebelled,
    have not turned back.
    I gave my back to those who beat me,
    my cheeks to those who plucked my beard;
my face I did not shield
    from buffets and spitting.

The Lord GOD is my help,
   therefore I am not disgraced;
I have set my face like flint,
   knowing that I shall not be put to shame.

Responsorial Psalm: Psalm 22:8-9, 17-18, 19-20, 23-24
My God, my God, why have you abandoned me?

All who see me scoff at me;
   they mock me with parted lips, they wag their heads:
"He relied on the LORD; let him deliver him,
   . let him rescue him, if he loves him."
R. My God, my God, why have you abandoned me?
Indeed, many dogs surround me,
   a pack of evildoers closes in upon me;
they have pierced my hands and my feet;
   I can count all my bones.
R. My God, my God, why have you abandoned me?
They divide my garments among them,
   and for my vesture they cast lots.
But you, O LORD, be not far from me;
   O my help, hasten to aid me.
R. My God, my God, why have you abandoned me?
I will proclaim your name to my brethren;
   in the midst of the assembly I will praise you:
"You who fear the LORD, praise him;
   all you descendants of Jacob, give glory to him;
   revere him, all you descendants of Israel!"
R. My God, my God, why have you abandoned me?

Second Reading: Philippians 2:6-11
Christ Jesus, though he was in the form of God,
   did not regard equality with God
   something to be grasped.
Rather, he emptied himself,
   taking the form of a slave,
   coming in human likeness;
   and found human in appearance,
   he humbled himself,
   becoming obedient to the point of death,
   even death on a cross.

Because of this, God greatly exalted him
    and bestowed on him the name
    which is above every name,
    that at the name of Jesus
    every knee should bend,
    of those in heaven and on earth and under the earth,
    and every tongue confess that
    Jesus Christ is Lord,
       to the glory of God the Father.

Gospel Acclamation: Philippians 2:8-9

Christ became obedient to the point of death, even death on a cross. Because of this, God greatly exalted him and bestowed on him the name which is above every name.

 ### *Gospel: Matthew 26:14–27:66*
(Short Form: Matthew 27:11-54)

One of the Twelve, who was called Judas Iscariot, went to the chief priests and said, "What are you willing to give me if I hand him over to you?" They paid him thirty pieces of silver, and from that time on he looked for an opportunity to hand him over.

On the first day of the Feast of Unleavened Bread, the disciples approached Jesus and said, "Where do you want us to prepare for you to eat the Passover?" He said, "Go into the city to a certain man and tell him, 'The teacher says, "My appointed time draws near; in your house I shall celebrate the Passover with my disciples."'" The disciples then did as Jesus had ordered, and prepared the Passover.

When it was evening, he reclined at table with the Twelve. And while they were eating, he said, "Amen, I say to you, one of you will betray me." Deeply distressed at this, they began to say to him one after another, "Surely it is not I, Lord?" He said in reply, "He who has dipped his hand into the dish with me is the one who will betray me. The Son of Man indeed goes, as it is written of him, but woe to that man by whom the Son of Man is betrayed. It would be better for that man if he had never been born." Then Judas, his betrayer, said in reply, "Surely it is not I, Rabbi?" He answered, "You have said so."

While they were eating, Jesus took bread, said the blessing, broke it, and giving it to his disciples said, "Take and eat; this is my body." Then he took a cup, gave thanks, and gave it to them, saying, "Drink from it, all of you, for this is my blood of the covenant, which will be shed on behalf of many for the forgiveness of sins. I tell you, from now on I shall not drink this fruit of the vine until the day when I drink it with you new in the kingdom of my Father." Then, after singing a hymn, they went out to the Mount of Olives.

Then Jesus said to them, "This night all of you will have your faith in me shaken, for it is written:

I will strike the shepherd,

    and the sheep of the flock will be dispersed;

but after I have been raised up, I shall go before you to Galilee." Peter said to him in reply, "Though all may have their faith in you shaken, mine will never be." Jesus said to him, "Amen, I say to you, this very night before the cock crows, you will deny me three times." Peter said to him, "Even though I should have to die with you, I will not deny you." And all the disciples spoke likewise.

Then Jesus came with them to a place called Gethsemane, and he said to his disciples, "Sit here while I go over there and pray." He took along Peter and the two sons of Zebedee, and began to feel sorrow and distress. Then he said to them, "My soul is sorrowful even to death. Remain here and keep watch with me." He advanced a little and fell prostrate in prayer, saying, "My Father, if it is possible, let this cup pass from me; yet, not as I will, but as you will." When he returned to his disciples he found them asleep. He said to Peter, "So you could not keep watch with me for one hour? Watch and pray that you may not undergo the test. The spirit is willing, but the flesh is weak." Withdrawing a second time, he prayed again, "My Father, if it is not possible that this cup pass without my drinking it, your will be done!" Then he returned once more and found them asleep, for they could not keep their eyes open. He left them and withdrew again and prayed a third time, saying the same thing again. Then he returned to his disciples and said to them, "Are you still sleeping and taking your rest? Behold, the hour is at hand when the Son of Man is to be handed over to sinners. Get up, let us go. Look, my betrayer is at hand."

While he was still speaking, Judas, one of the Twelve, arrived, accompanied by a large crowd, with swords and clubs, who had come from the chief priests and the elders of the people. His betrayer had arranged a sign with them, saying, "The man I shall kiss is the one; arrest him." Immediately he went over to Jesus and said, "Hail, Rabbi!" and he kissed him. Jesus answered him, "Friend, do what you have come for." Then stepping forward they laid hands on Jesus and arrested him. And behold, one of those who accompanied Jesus put his hand to his sword, drew it, and struck the high priest's servant, cutting off his ear. Then Jesus said to him, "Put your sword back into its sheath, for all who take the sword will perish by the sword. Do you think that I cannot call upon my

Father and he will not provide me at this moment with more than twelve legions of angels? But then how would the Scriptures be fulfilled which say that it must come to pass in this way?" At that hour Jesus said to the crowds, "Have you come out as against a robber, with swords and clubs to seize me? Day after day I sat teaching in the temple area, yet you did not arrest me. But all this has come to pass that the writings of the prophets may be fulfilled." Then all the disciples left him and fled.

Those who had arrested Jesus led him away to Caiaphas the high priest, where the scribes and the elders were assembled. Peter was following him at a distance as far as the high priest's courtyard, and going inside he sat down with the servants to see the outcome. The chief priests and the entire Sanhedrin kept trying to obtain false testimony against Jesus in order to put him to death, but they found none, though many false witnesses came forward. Finally two came forward who stated, "This man said, 'I can destroy the temple of God and within three days rebuild it.'" The high priest rose and addressed him, "Have you no answer? What are these men testifying against you?" But Jesus was silent. Then the high priest said to him, "I order you to tell us under oath before the living God whether you are the Christ, the Son of God." Jesus said to him in reply, "You have said so. But I tell you:

From now on you will see the 'Son of Man
seated at the right hand of the Power'
and 'coming on the clouds of heaven.'"

Then the high priest tore his robes and said, "He has blasphemed! What further need have we of witnesses? You have now heard the blasphemy; what is your opinion?" They said in reply, "He deserves to die!" Then they spat in his face and struck him, while some slapped him, saying, "Prophesy for us, Christ: who is it that struck you?"

Now Peter was sitting outside in the courtyard. One of the maids came over to him and said, "You too were with Jesus the Galilean." But he denied it in front of everyone, saying, "I do not know what you are talking about!" As he went out to the gate, another girl saw him and said to those who were there, "This man was with Jesus the Nazorean." Again he denied it with an oath, "I do not know the man!" A little later the bystanders came over and said to Peter, "Surely you too are one of them; even your speech gives you away." At that he began to curse and to swear, "I do not know the man." And immediately a cock crowed. Then Peter remembered the words that Jesus had spoken: "Before the cock crows you will deny me three times." He went out and began to weep bitterly.

When it was morning, all the chief priests and the elders of the people took counsel against Jesus to put him to death. They bound him, led him away, and handed him over to Pilate, the governor.

Then Judas, his betrayer, seeing that Jesus had been condemned, deeply regretted what he had done. He returned the thirty pieces of silver to the chief priests and elders, saying, "I have sinned in betraying innocent blood." They said, "What is that to us? Look to it yourself." Flinging the money into the temple, he departed and went off and hanged himself. The chief priests gathered up the money, but said, "It is not lawful to deposit this in the temple treasury, for it is the price of blood." After consultation, they used it to buy the potter's field as a burial place for foreigners. That is why that field even today is called the Field of Blood. Then was fulfilled what had been said through Jeremiah the prophet,

And they took the thirty pieces of silver,
the value of a man with a price on his head,
a price set by some of the Israelites,
and they paid it out for the potter's field
just as the Lord had commanded me.

Now Jesus stood before the governor, and he questioned him, "Are you the king of the Jews?" Jesus said, "You say so." And when he was accused by the chief priests and elders, he made no answer. Then Pilate said to him, "Do you not hear how many things they are testifying against you?" But he did not answer him one word, so that the governor was greatly amazed.

Now on the occasion of the feast the governor was accustomed to release to the crowd one prisoner whom they wished. And at that time they had a notorious prisoner called Barabbas. So when they had assembled, Pilate said to them, "Which one do you want me to release to you, Barabbas, or Jesus called Christ?" For he knew that it was out of envy that they had handed him over. While he was still seated on the bench, his wife sent him a message, "Have nothing to do with that righteous man. I suffered much in a dream today because of him." The chief priests and the elders persuaded the crowds to ask for Barabbas but to destroy Jesus. The governor said to them in reply, "Which of the two do you want me to release to you?" They answered, "Barabbas!" Pilate said to them, "Then what shall I do with Jesus called Christ?" They all said, "Let him be crucified!" But he said, "Why? What evil has he done?" They only shouted the louder, "Let him be crucified!" When Pilate saw that he was not succeeding at all, but that a riot was breaking out instead, he took water and washed his hands in the sight of the crowd, saying, "I am innocent of this man's blood. Look to it yourselves." And the whole people said in reply, "His blood be upon us and upon our children." Then he released Barabbas to them, but after he had Jesus scourged, he handed him over to be crucified.

Then the soldiers of the governor took Jesus inside the praetorium and gathered the whole cohort around him. They stripped off his clothes and threw a scarlet military cloak about him. Weaving a crown out of thorns, they placed it on his head, and a reed in his right hand. And kneeling before him, they mocked him, saying, "Hail, King of the Jews!" They spat upon him and took the reed and kept striking him on the head. And when they had mocked him, they stripped him of the cloak, dressed him in his own clothes, and led him off to crucify him.

As they were going out, they met a Cyrenian named Simon; this man they pressed into service to carry his cross.

And when they came to a place called Golgotha – which means Place of the Skull –, they gave Jesus wine to drink mixed with gall. But when he had tasted it, he refused to drink. After they had crucified him, they divided his garments by casting lots; then they sat down and kept watch over him there. And they placed over his head the written charge against him: This is Jesus, the King of the Jews. Two revolutionaries were crucified with him, one on his right and the other on his left. Those passing by reviled him, shaking their heads and saying, "You who would destroy the temple and rebuild it in three days, save yourself, if you are the Son of God, and come down from the cross!" Likewise the chief priests with the scribes and elders mocked him and said, "He saved others; he cannot save himself. So he is the king of Israel! Let him come down from the cross now, and we will believe in him. He trusted in God; let him deliver him now if he wants him. For he said, 'I am the Son of God.'" The revolutionaries who were crucified with him also kept abusing him in the same way.

From noon onward, darkness came over the whole land until three in the afternoon. And about three o'clock Jesus cried out in a loud voice, *"Eli, Eli, lema sabachthani?"* which means, "My God, my God, why have you forsaken me?" Some of the bystanders who heard it said, "This one is calling for Elijah." Immediately one of them ran to get a sponge; he soaked it in wine, and putting it on a reed, gave it to him to drink. But the rest said, "Wait, let us see if Elijah comes to save him." But Jesus cried out again in a loud voice, and gave up his spirit.

[Here all kneel and pause for a short time.]

And behold, the veil of the sanctuary was torn in two from top to bottom. The earth quaked, rocks were split, tombs were opened, and the bodies of many saints who had fallen asleep were raised. And coming forth from their tombs after his resurrection, they entered the holy city and appeared to many. The centurion and the men with him who were keeping watch over Jesus feared greatly when they saw the earthquake and all that was happening, and they said, "Truly, this was the Son of God!" There were many women there, looking on from a distance, who had followed Jesus from Galilee, ministering to him. Among them were Mary Magdalene and Mary the mother of James and Joseph, and the mother of the sons of Zebedee.

When it was evening, there came a rich man from Arimathea named Joseph, who was himself a disciple of Jesus. He went to Pilate and asked for the body of Jesus; then Pilate ordered it to be handed over. Taking the body, Joseph wrapped it in clean linen and laid it in his new tomb that he had hewn in the rock. Then he rolled a huge stone across the entrance to the tomb and departed. But Mary Magdalene and the other Mary remained sitting there, facing the tomb.

The next day, the one following the day of preparation, the chief priests and the Pharisees gathered before Pilate and said, "Sir, we remember that this impostor while still alive said, 'After three days I will be raised up.' Give orders, then, that the grave be secured until the third day, lest his disciples come and steal him and say to the people, 'He has been raised from the dead.' This last imposture would be worse than the first." Pilate said to them, "The guard is yours; go, secure it as best you can." So they went and secured the tomb by fixing a seal to the stone and setting the guard.

Meditation:

On this Holy Day, "Palm Sunday of the Passion of the Lord," we celebrate the triumphal entry of Christ the Lord into Jerusalem, where he will accomplish the saving work of our redemption and then enter into his glory.

Jesus enters the Royal and Holy City of Jerusalem because he is truly its King – indeed, the true King who gives eternal life. Because he is the King, he rides on a donkey, thus fulfilling the prophecy of Zechariah 9:9 that St. Matthew quotes in today's processional Gospel: *"Behold, your king comes to you, / meek and riding on an ass."* Yes, by riding on a donkey, Jesus makes a royal claim, but in a unique way. Unlike earthly kings, he is a King who is humble and meek. He tells us: "Come to me, all you who labor and are overburdened, and I will give you rest. Shoulder my yoke and learn from me, for I am gentle and humble in heart, and you will find rest for your souls" (Mt 11:28-30). Through his meekness, as a lamb who is obedient unto death on the Cross, he obtains life, peace, and victory for the whole world.

Today's readings help us enter deeply into the mystery we celebrate throughout Holy Week. As Jesus made his way on the donkey into Jerusalem, pilgrims who were also going to Jerusalem were caught up in the enthusiasm of his disciples. Some of them spread their garments on the road for Jesus. Others cut branches from the trees and spread them on his path, singing loudly, "Hosanna to the Son of David; / blessed is he who comes in the name of the Lord; / hosanna in the highest!" It is profoundly significant that included in the acclamation of the crowds is this verse from Psalm 118: "Blessed is he who comes in the name of the LORD" (v. 26.) By the time of Jesus, this Psalm formed part of Israel's pilgrim liturgy, and had already acquired messianic overtones. It was seen as a prophetic description of the awaited King, the Messiah who would come to Jerusalem. Psalm 118 also indicates that the awaited King-Messiah was expected to be a priest who would ascend to the altar to offer sacrifice (cf. Ps 118:27). The large crowds welcomed Jesus as King, Messiah, and Priest – even though their expectations of how he would fulfill his mission were quite incorrect.

Jesus fulfills the prophetic nature of Psalm 118. He is the true King; he is the Messiah who comes in the name of the Lord; he is the one who goes to the altar to offer sacrifice. However, he will act as King, Messiah, and Priest in a manner that will disappoint many. He is not headed to the Jerusalem temple to sacrifice on the altar there. Rather, he is going to the altar of the Cross on which he will offer himself for the glory of God and for the salvation of the world. In the light of Easter, the early Christians took the acclamation with which the crowds welcomed Jesus on Palm Sunday and adopted it to welcome the One who comes to us in the Holy Eucharistic Sacrifice. We still sing this very acclamation at every Mass, at the beginning of the Liturgy of the Eucharist, with the *Sanctus*: "Hosanna in the highest. Blessed is he who comes in the name of the Lord. Hosanna in the highest."

We can now see that, while Jesus was entering Jerusalem, the earthly holy city, for the ancient Jewish Passover, his ultimate goal was the Heavenly Jerusalem. He had come to offer the Sacrifice of himself on the Cross as the New and True Passover Lamb which fulfills and supersedes the Passover of the Old Testament. He establishes the New Passover, the New Covenant with his Blood (cf. Mt 26:28). As our true and eternal High Priest, Christ is heading not to a man-made sanctuary in Jerusalem which is merely a shadow of the real one, but he is entering the real sanctuary, Heaven, in the presence of God (cf. Heb 9:24), where he will reign in glory as God with the Father. Hence, today's second reading describes how his humble descent through self-emptying led to his exaltation in glory. Jesus has come to take us along with him to the glory of Heaven, our true homeland (cf. Phil 3:20). At Holy Mass, he makes present to us the merits of his Passion, Death, and Resurrection, and he opens for us the gates of Heaven.

His Passion started in the garden of Gethsemane where he was overwhelmed by the burden of the sufferings and sins of the whole world, which he took upon himself. We meditate on this in the First Sorrowful Mystery of the Rosary: the prayer and agony of Jesus in the garden. His human nature recoiled from the unspeakable suffering that awaited him, and so he prayed: "My Father, if it is possible let this cup pass from me; yet, not as I will, but as you will." With this prayer, he submitted our reluctant and recalcitrant human will to the divine will and made it possible for us to obey God.

It is not by chance that Jesus endures his agony in a garden, and that he was crucified in a garden. This is where he chose to undo the sin that was committed in the original garden by Adam. Through his Passion, Death, and Resurrection in a garden, Jesus Christ the New Adam ushers in a restoration – a total renewal. His Death in the garden overcomes the curse of death and brings us life and every heavenly blessing. On our journey through Holy Week, we follow in the footsteps of the Lord, so that we may share in his Passover from death to new life.

During Lent, how has Jesus' meekness and obedience unto death on the Cross instilled in me a greater love for him? How often in my daily trials and sufferings do I utter the words of Jesus, "Father, not my will but your will be done"? How has my Lenten observances prepared me to follow Jesus on his journey to Calvary?

Mary, walk beside me as I journey with Jesus to his Death on the Cross.

Pastoral Note: The Chrism Mass

The Chrism Mass is normally celebrated on the morning of Holy Thursday. However, in some dioceses, where it is difficult for the priests to gather with their bishop at the cathedral on that day, the Chrism Mass may be transferred to an earlier day in Holy Week. The readings and meditation for this Mass can be found on pages 214-220.

First Reading: Isaiah 42:1-7

Here is my servant whom I uphold,
    my chosen one with whom I am pleased,
Upon whom I have put my Spirit;
    he shall bring forth justice to the nations,
Not crying out, not shouting,
    not making his voice heard in the street.
A bruised reed he shall not break,
    and a smoldering wick he shall not quench,
Until he establishes justice on the earth;
    the coastlands will wait for his teaching.

Thus says God, the LORD,
    who created the heavens and stretched them out,
    who spreads out the earth with its crops,
Who gives breath to its people
    and spirit to those who walk on it:
I, the LORD, have called you for the victory of justice,
    I have grasped you by the hand;
I formed you, and set you
    as a covenant of the people,
    a light for the nations,
To open the eyes of the blind,
    to bring out prisoners from confinement,
    and from the dungeon, those who live in darkness.

Responsorial Psalm: Psalm 27:1, 2, 3, 13-14
The Lord is my light and my salvation.

The LORD is my light and my salvation;
    whom should I fear?
The LORD is my life's refuge;
    of whom should I be afraid?
R. The Lord is my light and my salvation.
When evildoers come at me
    to devour my flesh,
My foes and my enemies
    themselves stumble and fall.
R. The Lord is my light and my salvation.

Though an army encamp against me,
my heart will not fear;
Though war be waged upon me,
even then will I trust.
R. The Lord is my light and my salvation.
I believe that I shall see the bounty of the LORD
in the land of the living.
Wait for the LORD with courage;
be stouthearted, and wait for the LORD.
R. The Lord is my light and my salvation.

Gospel Acclamation:
Hail to you, our King; you alone are compassionate with our faults.

✠ *Gospel: John 12:1-11*
Six days before Passover Jesus came to Bethany, where Lazarus was, whom Jesus had raised from the dead. They gave a dinner for him there, and Martha served, while Lazarus was one of those reclining at table with him. Mary took a liter of costly perfumed oil made from genuine aromatic nard and anointed the feet of Jesus and dried them with her hair; the house was filled with the fragrance of the oil. Then Judas the Iscariot, one of his disciples, and the one who would betray him, said, "Why was this oil not sold for three hundred days' wages and given to the poor?" He said this not because he cared about the poor but because he was a thief and held the money bag and used to steal the contributions. So Jesus said, "Leave her alone. Let her keep this for the day of my burial. You always have the poor with you, but you do not always have me."

The large crowd of the Jews found out that he was there and came, not only because of him, but also to see Lazarus, whom he had raised from the dead. And the chief priests plotted to kill Lazarus too, because many of the Jews were turning away and believing in Jesus because of him.

Meditation:
Yesterday we celebrated Jesus' triumphal entry into the city of Jerusalem. Great crowds were there to welcome him! They waved their palm branches in acclamation, and then laid their palms and cloaks on the ground for him to walk on. Those who did not welcome him were nevertheless affected by his presence. No one can simply sit

and watch Jesus walk by – because Jesus does not simply walk by. He approaches us personally; he disturbs us; he enters into our hearts and our lives. We must make some kind of response. If we do not welcome him, we hide from him, or defend ourselves against his presence, or reject him. The interior place where we make our response to Jesus is the *conscience*, the seat of our deepest convictions. Holy Week is conscience week.

In today's Gospel Mary of Bethany reveals how she responds to the presence of Jesus, with a spirit of welcome and great devotion. She does so, not with palm branches, but with the extravagant gift of expensive perfumed oil. This Mary is the same woman who, earlier in Jesus' ministry, sat at his feet while her sister Martha was doing all the housework. At that time, Jesus said that she had chosen the better part and she would not be deprived of it (cf. Lk 10:42). Her actions in today's Gospel reveal the beauty hidden in the inner life of this woman. After anointing Jesus' feet, she stoops to the ground to wipe them with her hair. This is how she pours herself out at the feet of the Lord.

Mary's actions bring to mind yesterday's reading from Philippians 2, where it says that Jesus did not cling to the glory he had as the equal of the Father. Instead he emptied himself and humbled himself unto death. This inner movement of profound self-emptying is what he taught Mary – and she learned it very well. Mary is not just emptying a jar of perfume; she is emptying herself. She is modeling her life on what Jesus has taught and on what he himself is doing.

Judas is a disciple of Jesus, but he does not have a clue about what is really going on. He is so full of himself that he cannot even imagine emptying himself. He is fascinated by worldly glory, especially the glory of money; he is blind to the glory of God which shines forth in humility. When Judas protests that Mary's beautiful act is a wasteful act, Jesus immediately responds with a correction and an insightful instruction. He honors Mary for preparing him for burial and he proclaims that her gift to him is no offense to the poor. The first commandment is to love the Lord with all our soul, with all our mind, and with all our strength. Mary is a living witness of this first love, an example of how we are to love. If we give ourselves totally to the Lord, then he can serve the poor through us.

Mary's gift of herself to the Lord fills the whole house with the fragrance of her perfume. Whenever anyone gives himself or herself to the Lord, whether in the sacrifices of love hidden in the heart or in service to a neighbor in need, the whole "house," the whole world, is filled with the fragrance of holiness. Everyone experiences it as it permeates the atmosphere, though they may not know its origin. The Marys of the world – the ones who are not noticed or who seem to be wasting their time, the ones who pray and give themselves in humble service – are the ones who are filling the world with love, with hope, and with faith. Let us fill the world by giving it our selfless witness of dedication to love in truth. Let us be Marys in today's world.

> *In what ways do I resemble Mary of Bethany and Judas? What have I learned from the humble attitude of Mary as she washed the feet of Jesus? How does my life relate to the hypocrisy and false piety of Judas?*

Mary, stay close to me as I spend this week of Christ's passion in devotion and courage.

Notes

First Reading: Isaiah 49:1-6

Hear me, O islands,
　　listen, O distant peoples.
The LORD called me from birth,
　　from my mother's womb he gave me my name.
He made of me a sharp-edged sword
　　and concealed me in the shadow of his arm.
He made me a polished arrow,
　　in his quiver he hid me.
You are my servant, he said to me,
　　Israel, through whom I show my glory.

Though I thought I had toiled in vain,
　　and for nothing, uselessly, spent my strength,
Yet my reward is with the LORD,
　　my recompense is with my God.
For now the LORD has spoken
　　who formed me as his servant from the womb,
That Jacob may be brought back to him
　　and Israel gathered to him;
And I am made glorious in the sight of the LORD,
　　and my God is now my strength!
It is too little, he says, for you to be my servant,
　　to raise up the tribes of Jacob,
　　and restore the survivors of Israel;
I will make you a light to the nations,
　　that my salvation may reach to the ends of the earth.

Responsorial Psalm: Psalm 71:1-2, 3-4a, 5ab-6ab, 15 and 17
I will sing of your salvation.

In you, O LORD, I take refuge;
　　let me never be put to shame.
In your justice rescue me, and deliver me;
　　incline your ear to me, and save me.
R. *I will sing of your salvation.*
Be my rock of refuge,
　　a stronghold to give me safety,
　　for you are my rock and my fortress.
O my God, rescue me from the hand of the wicked.
R. *I will sing of your salvation.*

For you are my hope, O Lord;
    my trust, O God, from my youth.
On you I depend from birth;
    from my mother's womb you are my strength.
R. *I will sing of your salvation.*
My mouth shall declare your justice,
    day by day your salvation.
O God, you have taught me from my youth,
    and till the present I proclaim your wondrous deeds.
R. *I will sing of your salvation.*

Gospel Acclamation:
Hail to you, our King, obedient to the Father; you were led to your crucifixion like a gentle lamb to the slaughter.

✝ *Gospel: John 13:21-33, 36-38*
    Reclining at table with his disciples, Jesus was deeply troubled and testified, "Amen, amen, I say to you, one of you will betray me." The disciples looked at one another, at a loss as to whom he meant. One of his disciples, the one whom Jesus loved, was reclining at Jesus' side. So Simon Peter nodded to him to find out whom he meant. He leaned back against Jesus' chest and said to him, "Master, who is it?" Jesus answered, "It is the one to whom I hand the morsel after I have dipped it." So he dipped the morsel and took it and handed it to Judas, son of Simon the Iscariot. After Judas took the morsel, Satan entered him. So Jesus said to him, "What you are going to do, do quickly." Now none of those reclining at table realized why he said this to him. Some thought that since Judas kept the money bag, Jesus had told him, "Buy what we need for the feast," or to give something to the poor. So Judas took the morsel and left at once. And it was night.

    When he had left, Jesus said, "Now is the Son of Man glorified, and God is glorified in him. If God is glorified in him, God will also glorify him in himself, and he will glorify him at once. My children, I will be with you only a little while longer. You will look for me, and as I told the Jews, 'Where I go you cannot come,' so now I say it to you."

    Simon Peter said to him, "Master, where are you going?" Jesus answered him, "Where I am going, you cannot follow me now, though you will follow later." Peter said to him, "Master, why can I not follow you now? I will lay down my life for you." Jesus answered, "Will you lay down your life for me? Amen, amen, I say to you, the cock will not crow before you deny me three times."

Meditation:

As we enter into the holiest days of the year, the Liturgy of the Church leads us to a deeper level of reflection. Today's Gospel takes us to the night of the Passover and seats us at the table with Jesus and his disciples. It is the Last Supper of the Lord. This is "the hour" about which Jesus so often spoke.

Jesus grows "deeply troubled"; he knows that he is about to be betrayed. He even knows who his betrayer is, Judas. But Jesus also knows that this is the hour of his glorification. Immediately after Judas goes out, Jesus says, "Now is the Son of Man glorified and God is glorified in him." He reveals to us that even in the hour of his suffering, he is perfectly one with the Father. The Cross is a vehicle of his glorification.

However, Judas knows none of this. Disguised as a friend, Judas has the heart of an enemy. In regard to Judas, Jesus will put into full effect the instruction he gave in his Sermon on the Mount, "Love your enemies"; for he loves Judas, even enough to die for him. Judas is going to kiss Jesus – not out of love, but out of betrayal – a kiss of death. This is the epitome of hypocrisy, to use a sign of love as a means of betraying. It is hard to find a worse example of misusing our freedom. It is one thing to fall into sin out of human weakness; it is worse to freely choose an evil course of action; and it is even worse to do evil while pretending that what we do is good.

Jesus does not give up on Judas. He is the only one who knows fully the evil plot that is unfolding, and still he shares a meal with his betrayer. He is still willing to give Judas the privileged morsel of food from the Passover supper. His gesture is a tender way of saying: *You are my beloved disciple. You are my brother. I have nothing against you.* Jesus is still trying to reach Judas's conscience, appealing to him with the power of self-emptying love.

There is another character present in the room but hidden from their eyes – Satan. He is mentioned by name immediately after Judas receives the morsel. Exteriorly Judas welcomes the sign of unity and love, but interiorly he rejects it. By hardening his heart to love, he opens the door to evil. The Gospel puts it bluntly: "Satan entered him." Satan lurks at the threshold of every heart, at the edge of every moral decision.

Satan cannot enter our hearts unless we give him some space. We cannot blame him for our sins, because he cannot make us do anything. He tempts us, he deceives us, but from the outside, so to speak. Only when we choose to sin does Satan have permission to enter in. This is what happened to Judas. He is not thinking about Satan, but about the thirty pieces of silver he already has in his pocket. Judas' decision perverts the normal dynamic of love from self-giving to self-taking. This change in Judas excludes God, for God is love. Any deliberate act against love, that is, against God, gives Satan room to operate. On this night of the Passover, Satan mistakenly thinks that the hour has come for him to achieve his greatest victory.

Peter is also highlighted in this Gospel. The decision in his heart is opposite that of Judas. Peter is firmly committed to following the Lord: "I will lay down my life for you!" He is sincere in saying this. He is not being hypocritical, pretending to be good. Peter's problem is that he is unaware of himself, unaware that he is relying on his own strength. He is making a human determination, without realizing that by himself he is too weak to follow Jesus in the moment of temptation. Peter reminds us that we are not as strong as we may think we are in a moment of fervor. Only when we humble ourselves and rely on the strength that comes from God can we persevere in our desire to "lay down our life." With the power of the Holy Spirit we can indeed make an offering of ourselves in love for God.

Holy Week is a time for us to see ourselves in Judas and in Peter. It is not a time to grow discouraged about our weakness and sin, but to witness the extent of Jesus' love for his disciples and to rely on that gift of divine love. Jesus not only loves us before we sin, he also loves us even after we sin. In the most excellent "morsel" which he personally hands to us, the Eucharist, Jesus gives us himself. We pray for the strength to persevere in his love, so that Satan will find no way to enter. This is no time to let darkness triumph; it is the time for the triumph of divine mercy. This is the hour of the glorification of Jesus in our own lives.

> *What are my interior responses to the crosses that God sends me? When have I freely chosen an evil course of action while justifying that what I did was good? Like Peter, how do I rely on my own strength and not on God's?*

Mary, teach me to rely more on the Lord in the midst of temptations.

First Reading: Isaiah 50:4-9a

The Lord GOD has given me
a well-tràined tongue,
That I might know how to speak to the weary
a word that will rouse them.
Morning after morning
he opens my ear that I may hear;
And I have not rebelled,
have not turned back.
I gave my back to those who beat me,
my cheeks to those who plucked my beard;
My face I did not shield
from buffets and spitting.

The Lord GOD is my help,
therefore I am not disgraced;
I have set my face like flint,
knowing that I shall not be put to shame.
He is near who upholds my right;
if anyone wishes to oppose me,
let us appear together.
Who disputes my right?
Let him confront me.
See, the Lord GOD is my help;
who will prove me wrong?

Responsorial Psalm: Psalm 69:8-10, 21-22, 31 and 33-34
Lord, in your great love, answer me.

For your sake I bear insult,
and shame covers my face.
I have become an outcast to my brothers,
a stranger to my mother's sons,
because zeal for your house consumes me,
and the insults of those who blaspheme you fall upon me.
R. Lord, in your great love, answer me.
Insult has broken my heart, and I am weak,
I looked for sympathy, but there was none;
for consolers, not one could I find.
Rather they put gall in my food,
and in my thirst they gave me vinegar to drink.
R. Lord, in your great love, answer me.

I will praise the name of God in song,
    and I will glorify him with thanksgiving:
"See, you lowly ones, and be glad;
    you who seek God, may your hearts revive!
For the LORD hears the poor,
    and his own who are in bonds he spurns not."
R. *Lord, in your great love, answer me.*

Gospel Acclamation:
Hail to you, our King; you alone are compassionate with our errors.
or
Hail to you, our King, obedient to the Father; you were led to your
crucifixion like a gentle lamb to the slaughter.

Gospel: Matthew 26:14-25
One of the Twelve, who was called Judas Iscariot, went to the
chief priests and said, "What are you willing to give me if I hand him
over to you?" They paid him thirty pieces of silver, and from that time
on he looked for an opportunity to hand him over.

On the first day of the Feast of Unleavened Bread, the disciples
approached Jesus and said, "Where do you want us to prepare for you
to eat the Passover?" He said, "Go into the city to a certain man and tell
him, 'The teacher says, "My appointed time draws near; in your house
I shall celebrate the Passover with my disciples."'" The disciples then
did as Jesus had ordered, and prepared the Passover.

When it was evening, he reclined at table with the Twelve. And
while they were eating, he said, "Amen, I say to you, one of you will
betray me." Deeply distressed at this, they began to say to him one after
another, "Surely it is not I, Lord?" He said in reply, "He who has dipped
his hand into the dish with me is the one who will betray me. The Son
of Man indeed goes, as it is written of him, but woe to that man by whom
the Son of Man is betrayed. It would be better for that man if he had
never been born." Then Judas, his betrayer, said in reply, "Surely it is
not I, Rabbi?" He answered, "You have said so."

Meditation:
In today's Gospel, Jesus and Judas, by their free and conscious
decisions, are going in opposite directions. We can see them as
examples of how to use or abuse our human freedom. Jesus, fully aware
of the risks involved, is determined to be in Jerusalem for the Passover.
As his appointed time draws near, he "sets his face like flint" and makes
all the necessary preparations: "Go into the city to a certain man and tell

211

him… in your house I shall celebrate the Passover with my disciples." Jesus, in perfect union with the will of his Father, has been waiting for this hour to complete his mission. He is fulfilling the prophecy of Isaiah about the *suffering servant of the Lord*. He fulfills it through the decisions he makes with his human will.

Judas gives us a very different picture of the use – or rather, misuse – of human freedom. This is the third time this week that we are being reminded of his terrible act of betrayal. After Jesus reveals that someone will betray him, Judas says: "Surely it is not I, Rabbi?" He knows very well that he is going to betray Jesus, so this is a shameless lie. In fact, he has already betrayed him, for he has already made a secret deal with the chief priests: "What are you willing to give me if I hand him over to you?" Judas is not acting out of weakness or because of social pressure. He freely initiates the betrayal. This makes his lie more serious and his moral condition very grave.

Judas betrays Jesus to death, yet the harm he does to himself is even worse than what he does to the Lord. He betrays himself. Spiritually, he destroys himself. The act of suicide that he commits later the next day is a manifestation of the spiritually self-destructive deed he does for the sake of gaining thirty pieces of silver. Jesus, for his part, even though he is deeply burdened with the task he is about to undertake, is genuinely more concerned about Judas than about himself. He says that Judas is doing something so morally evil that it would be better for him if he had never been born. Mortal sin is the worst kind of self-destruction. It would be better to die than to commit a mortal sin.

It is important for us to make a study of sin, especially in these days which reveal to us how much our redemption costs. Judas is not the only sinner in Holy Week. Jesus is surrounded by sinners, and each of us is among them. Through the Scriptures of the Liturgy, the Lord is probing our conscience, inviting us to identify our own sin, and to repent.

How many times have we betrayed Jesus, as Judas did? Honest acknowledgment that we are sinners is half the battle in the fight against sin. Humbly asking for God's forgiveness and help is the other half. The good news is that, however we may have used our freedom in the past, however we may have sinned, Jesus is always determined to save us, now and always. Let us open our hearts to the great power of redemption as we prepare to enter into the sacred Easter Triduum.

How is my conscience being probed during this Holy Week? In what ways is sin a manifestation of a spiritually self-destructive deed? Why is it difficult for me to acknowledge in humility that I am a sinner?

Mary, renew my mind and heart as I prepare to celebrate the Paschal festivities.

Notes

April 6, Holy Thursday
The Chrism Mass

Note: *Holy Thursday is the sacred day on which two Sacraments were instituted, the Eucharist and Holy Orders. The evening **Mass of the Lord's Supper** focuses more on the Eucharist, while the morning Mass, the **Chrism Mass**, celebrates the precious gift of the ordained priesthood.*

At the Chrism Mass, all the priests gather in unity with their Bishop in the diocesan cathedral. The rubrics indicate that the Bishop is to give a homily: "Taking as a starting point the texts of the readings which were proclaimed in the Liturgy of the Word, he speaks to the people and to the priests about the priestly anointing, urging the priests to be faithful in fulfilling their office and inviting them to renew publicly their priestly promises." Afterward the priests profess together a solemn "Renewal of Commitment to Priestly Service."

*Another highlight of the Chrism Mass – and the origin of its name – is the blessing of the Church's sacred oils and the consecration of Chrism for use throughout the year. The **Oil of Catechumens** will be used in the preparation for Baptism. The **Oil of the Infirm** will be used in the Sacrament of the Anointing of the Sick. The **Sacred Chrism** (oil mixed with fragrant balsam) will be used in the Sacraments of Baptism, Confirmation and Holy Orders. It is a great blessing and privilege to be able to participate in the annual Chrism Mass. This day is also a day to give thanks to God for our priests and to pray for them.*

 First Reading: Isaiah 61:1-3a, 6a, 8b-9
The spirit of the Lord GOD is upon me,
    because the LORD has anointed me;
He has sent me to bring glad tidings to the lowly,
    to heal the brokenhearted,
To proclaim liberty to the captives
    and release to the prisoners,
To announce a year of favor from the LORD
    and a day of vindication by our God,
    to comfort all who mourn;
To place on those who mourn in Zion
    a diadem instead of ashes,
To give them oil of gladness in place of mourning,
    a glorious mantle instead of a listless spirit.

You yourselves shall be named priests of the LORD,
    ministers of our God you shall be called.

I will give them their recompense faithfully,
    a lasting covenant I will make with them.
Their descendants shall be renowned among the nations,
    and their offspring among the peoples;
All who see them shall acknowledge them
    as a race the LORD has blessed.

Responsorial Psalm: Psalm 89:21-22, 25 and 27
For ever I will sing the goodness of the Lord.

"I have found David, my servant;
    with my holy oil I have anointed him.
That my hand may always be with him;
    and that my arm may make him strong."

R. For ever I will sing the goodness of the Lord.

"My faithfulness and my mercy shall be with him;
    and through my name shall his horn be exalted.
He shall say of me, 'You are my father,
    my God, the Rock, my savior!'"

R. For ever I will sing the goodness of the Lord.

Second reading: Revelation 1:5-8

[Grace to you and peace] from Jesus Christ, who is the faithful witness, the firstborn of the dead and ruler of the kings of the earth. To him who loves us and has freed us from our sins by his Blood, who has made us into a Kingdom, priests for his God and Father, to him be glory and power forever and ever. Amen.

Behold, he is coming amid the clouds,
    and every eye will see him,
    even those who pierced him.
All the peoples of the earth will lament him.
    Yes. Amen.

"I am the Alpha and the Omega," says the Lord God, "the one who is and who was and who is to come, the Almighty."

Gospel Acclamation: Isaiah 61:1 (cited in Luke 4:18)

The Spirit of the LORD is upon me; for he has sent me to bring glad tidings to the poor.

Gospel: Luke 4:16-21

Jesus came to Nazareth, where he had grown up, and went according to his custom into the synagogue on the sabbath day. He stood up to read and was handed a scroll of the prophet Isaiah. He unrolled the scroll and found the passage where it was written:

The Spirit of the Lord is upon me,
    because he has anointed me
      to bring glad tidings to the poor.

He has sent me to proclaim liberty to captives
and recovery of sight to the blind,
to let the oppressed go free,
and to proclaim a year acceptable to the Lord.

Rolling up the scroll, he handed it back to the attendant and sat down, and the eyes of all in the synagogue looked intently at him. He said to them, "Today this Scripture passage is fulfilled in your hearing."

Meditation:

To enrich our reflection on the gift of the priesthood and to move us to pray for our priests, we may turn to the words of Pope Francis, from the homily he gave at the Chrism Mass at St. Peter's Basilica in Rome on Holy Thursday, April 18, 2019:

The Gospel of Luke, which we just heard, makes us relive the excitement of that moment when the Lord made his own the prophecy of Isaiah, as he read it solemnly in the midst of his people. The synagogue in Nazareth was filled with his relatives, neighbors, acquaintances, friends... and not only friends. All had their eyes fixed on him. The Church always has her eyes fixed on Jesus Christ, the Anointed One, whom the Spirit sends to anoint God's people.

The Gospels frequently present us with this image of the Lord in the midst of a crowd, surrounded and pressed by people who approach him with their sick ones, who ask him to cast out evil spirits, who hear his teachings and accompany him on the way. "My sheep hear my voice. I know them and they follow me" (*Jn* 10:27-28).

The Lord never lost that direct contact with people. Amid those crowds, he always kept the grace of closeness with the people as a whole, and with each individual. We see this throughout his public life, and so it was from the beginning: the radiance of the Child gently attracted shepherds, kings, and elderly dreamers like Simeon and Anna. So it was on the Cross: his Heart draws all people to himself (*Jn* 12:32): Veronicas, Cyreneans, thieves, centurions...

The term "crowd" is not disparaging. Perhaps to some people's ears, it can evoke a faceless, nameless throng... But in the Gospel we see that when the crowd interacts with the Lord – who stands in their midst like a shepherd among his flock – something happens. Deep within, people feel the desire to *follow* Jesus, *amazement* wells up, *discernment* grows apace.

I would like to reflect with you on these three graces that characterize the relationship between Jesus and the crowd.

The grace of following

Saint Luke says that the crowds "looked for Jesus" (4:42) and "travelled with him" (14:25). They "pressed in on him" and "surrounded him" (8:42-45); they "gathered to hear him" (5:15). Their "following" is something completely unexpected, unconditional, and full of affection. It contrasts with the small-mindedness of the disciples, whose attitude towards people verges on cruelty when they suggest to the Lord that he send them away, so that they can get something to eat. Here, I believe, was the beginning of clericalism: in this desire to be assured of a meal and personal comfort without any concern for the people. The Lord cut short that temptation: "You give them something to eat!" was Jesus' response. "Take care of the people!"

The grace of amazement

The second grace that the crowd receives when it follows Jesus is that of joy-filled amazement. People were amazed by Jesus (*Lk* 11:14), by his miracles, but above all by his very person. People loved to meet him along the way, to receive his blessing and to bless him, like the woman in the midst of the crowd who blessed his Mother. The Lord himself was amazed by people's faith; he rejoiced, and he lost no opportunity to speak about it.

The grace of discernment

The third grace that people receive is that of discernment. "The crowds found out [where Jesus had gone] and followed him" (*Lk* 9:11). They "were astounded by his teaching, for he taught them as one having authority" (*Mt* 7:28-29; cf. *Lk* 5:26). Christ, the Word of God come in the flesh, awakens in people this charism of discernment, which is certainly not the discernment of those who specialize in disputed questions. When the Pharisees and the teachers of the law debated with him, what people discerned was Jesus' authority, the power of his teaching to touch their hearts, and the fact that evil spirits obeyed him (leaving momentarily speechless those who tried to trap him by their questions; the people liked that; they were able to distinguish this, and they liked it).

Let us take a closer look at the way the Gospel views the crowd. Luke points out four large groups who are the preferred beneficiaries of the Lord's anointing: the poor, the blind, the oppressed and captives. He speaks of them in general terms, but then we are glad to see that, in the course of the Lord's life, these anointed ones gradually take on real names and faces. When oil is applied to one part of the body, its beneficial effect is felt throughout the entire body. So too, the Lord, taking up the prophecy of Isaiah, names various "crowds" to whom the Spirit sends him, according to what we may call an "inclusive preferentiality": the grace and the charism given to one individual person or a particular group then redounds, like every action of the Spirit, to the good of all.

The poor (in Greek, *ptochoi*) are those who are bent over, like beggars who bow down and ask for alms. But poor too (*ptochè*) was that widow who anointed with her fingers the two small coins which were all she had to live on that day. *The anointing by the widow to give alms* went unnoticed by the eyes of all except Jesus, who looks kindly on her lowliness. Through her, the Lord can accomplish fully his mission of proclaiming the Gospel to the poor. Paradoxically, the disciples heard the good news that people like her exist. She – the generous woman – could not imagine that she would "make it to the Gospel," that her simple gesture would be recorded in the Gospel. Like all those men and women who are the "saints next door," she lives interiorly the joyful fact that her actions "carry weight" in the Kingdom, and are worth more than all the riches of the world.

The blind are represented by one of the most likable figures in the Gospel: Bartimaeus (cf. *Mt* 10:46-52), the blind beggar who regained his sight and, from that moment on, only had eyes to follow Jesus on his journey. *The anointing of the gaze!* Our gaze, to which the eyes of Jesus can restore the brightness which only gratuitous love can give, the brightness daily stolen from us by the manipulative and banal images with which the world overwhelms us.

To refer to *the oppressed* (in Greek, *tethrausmenoi*), Luke uses a word that contains the idea of "trauma." It is enough to evoke the parable – perhaps Luke's favourite – of the Good Samaritan, who anoints with oil and binds the wounds (*traumata*: *Lk* 10:34) of the man who had been beaten by robbers and left lying at the side of the road. *The anointing of the wounded flesh of Christ!* In that anointing we find the remedy for all those traumas that leave individuals, families, and entire peoples ignored, excluded, and unwanted, on the sidelines of history.

The captives are prisoners of war (in Greek, *aichmalotoi*), those who had been led at the point of a spear (*aichmé*). Jesus would use the same word in speaking of the taking of Jerusalem, his beloved city, and the deportation of its people (*Lk* 21:24). Our cities today are taken prisoner not so much at spear point, but by more subtle means of ideological colonization.

Only *the anointing of culture,* built up by the labor and the art of our forebears, can free our cities from these new forms of slavery.

As for us, dear brother priests, we must not forget that our evangelical models are those "people," the "crowd," with its real faces, which the anointing of the Lord raises up and revives. They are the ones who complete and make real the anointing of the Spirit in ourselves; they are the ones whom we have been anointed to anoint. We have been taken from their midst, and we can fearlessly identify with these ordinary people. Each of us has our own story. A little bit of memory will do us much good. They are an image of our soul and an image of the Church. Each of them incarnates the one heart of our people.

We priests are the poor man, and we would like to have the heart of the poor widow whenever we give alms, touching the hand of the beggar and looking him or her in the eye. We priests are Bartimaeus, and each morning we get up and pray: "Lord, that I may see." We priests are, at some point of our sinfulness, the man beaten by the robbers. And we want first to be in the compassionate hands of the good Samaritan, in order then to be able to show compassion to others with our own hands.

I confess to you that whenever I confirm and ordain, I like to smear with chrism the foreheads and the hands of those I anoint. In that generous anointing, we can sense that our own anointing is being renewed. I would say this: We are not distributors of bottled oil. We have been anointed to anoint. We anoint by distributing ourselves, distributing our vocation and our heart. When we anoint others, we ourselves are anointed anew by the faith and the affection of our people. We anoint by dirtying our hands in touching the wounds, the sins, and the worries of the people. We anoint by perfuming our hands in touching their faith, their hopes, their fidelity, and the unconditional generosity of their self-giving, which many significant figures describe as superstition.

The one who learns how to anoint and to bless is thus healed of meanness, abuse, and cruelty.

Let us pray, dear brothers; being with Jesus in the midst of our people is the most beautiful place to be. May the Father *renew deep within us the Spirit of holiness*; may he grant that we be one *in imploring his mercy for the people entrusted to our care and for all the world*. In this way, the multitude of the peoples, gathered in Christ, may become the one faithful people of God, which will attain its fullness in the Kingdom (cf. *Prayer of Priestly Ordination*).

What events in my life fill me with amazement of the Lord? How have the teachings of Jesus touched and changed my heart? Who are the "saints next door" who touch me interiorly and draw me closer to the Lord?

Mary, grant me the grace to pray daily for priests who have been especially anointed by Jesus.

Notes

The Anawim Way is available in the ff. outlets:

1. Bookstores (Philippines)

St. Pauls
- Main Branch, Makati City: 8895-6861
- Fairview Terraces: 8426-5491 • Gateway Mall, Cubao: 8911-3380, 3376-6536
- Marque Mall, Angeles City: (045) 304-1011
- Ayala Center, Cebu: (032) 231-7486 • Alimall, Cubao: 8912-7841, 3441-2137
- Marymart Center III, Iloilo City: (033) 335-0636
- Limketkai Mall, Cagayan de Oro City: (088) 856-1904
- SM Malls:
  - North Edsa: 8929-4925, 8441-4263 - Manila: 8522-8233
  - Sta. Mesa: 8716-1559, 8353-0794 - Bicutan: 8836-9758, 8511-1762
  - South Mall: 8806-6867, 8511-0941 - San Lazaro: 8353-4823, 8353-1238
  - Mega Mall: 7634-1295, 7631-0536 - Mall of Asia: 8556-0251, 8823-1373
  - Bacoor: (046) 417-2346, 417-1529 - Dasmariñas: (046) 416-1278
  - Pampanga: (045) 455-3380 - Iloilo: (033) 320-8251
  - Davao: (082) 282-2881 - Cebu: (032) 232-0760, (032) 232-1407

Pauline's Media Center
Metro Manila
- 2655 FB Harrison St., Pasay City: 8831-6420, 8831-6928 loc 115

Luzon (Daughters of St. Paul)
- Rizal St., Legazpi City: (052) 742-1950 • M.K. Lina St., Lipa City: (043) 756-2212
- 47 Upper Gen. Luna Rd., Baguio City: (074) 442-2559
- Elias Angeles St., Naga City: (054) 881-2553
- 41 Arellano St., Tuguegarao City: (078) 844-0001

Visayas (Daughters of St. Paul)
- 29 Cor. Henares-Hernaez Sts., Bacolod City: (034) 433-1648
- 34 Osmeña Blvd., Cebu City: (032) 253-4061• Real St., Tacloban City: (053) 832-0482
- 425 E. Lopez St., Jaro, Iloilo City: (033) 320-9487

Mindanao (Daughters of St. Paul)
- Fatima Chapel, A. Velez St., Cagayan de Oro City: (088) 850-1524
- Bolton St., P.O. Box 80404, Davao City: (082) 221-4149/9490
- Natividad St., Tetuan, Zamboanga City: (062) 991-2450/4467

Catholic Book Center
- 121 Arzobispo St., Intramuros, Manila: 8634-4148
- Diocese of Cubao Chancery, 41 Lantana St., Cubao, Quezon City: 723-5116 to 17
- Pope Pius XII Catholic Center, 1175 U.N. Ave., Paco, Manila: 400-1850

PDDM– Ermita, Manila: 536-0691; Sta. Mesa, Manila: 715-6344

Rogate– Km. 51.B Aguinaldo Highway, Lalaan 2, Silang, Cavite: (046) 686-3299, (02) 359-7801, 0917-554-5564

Word and Life Publications– Don Bosco Compound, Amaiz Ave. cor. Chino Roces Ave., Makati City: 894-5401 to 02

 Lazada online store:
https://www.lazada.com.ph/shop/ anawim-community/

Shopee online store:
https://shopee.ph/anawim75?

2. Parishes

Casa Benedicto Rel. Items – Manila Cathedral: 0917-637-3147 / 0947-109-9896
Presentation of the Child Jesus – Parañaque City: 8825-4151
St. Jerome Emiliani and Sta. Susana – Muntinlupa City: 8842-4947
St. John Bosco – Makati City: 8894-5932 to 34

3. Anawim Centers

Philippines: 4217 Marcus Aurelius St., Italia 500, BF Resort Vill., Las Piñas City 1740
(02) 8872-2021, EMAIL: anawimway@anawim.com

USA: P.O. Box 207, 354 Jonestown Rd., Oxford, NJ 07863
(908) 453-3886, EMAIL: oxford@anawim.com

4. Distributors (Philippines)

<u>Metro Manila</u>
Muntinlupa: Sr. Myrna Villar, LGC: Mary, Mother of God Renewal Center, South Greenheights Village, Putatan, Muntinlupa– 850-0764, 0917-700-5773
Quezon City   Mt. Carmel Gift Shop c/o Josie, 5th St. cor. Broadway Ave., New Manila– 410-4786
Order of Carmelites Carmelite Mission & Development Office, Mariana., New Manila– 0961-710-1699/8289-9101

<u>Provincial</u>
Bacolod: Tess T., Colegio San Agustin, Bacolod–(034) 433-1248, 0998-537-3011
Baguio: Lizelle, 304 VJV La Azotea Bldg., Session Rd.– 0922-790-0898
Batangas: Marlo– 0918-571-9934; Dr. Joy– 0998-571-1527
Bohol: St. Isidore Parish c/o Grace– (038) 535-9021, 0921-373-2582
Butuan: St. Benedict Rel. Store c/o Babylyn– 09079418506
Cagayan de Oro: Missionary Sisters of the Holy Family, 12th st. Nazareth, CDO– (0882) 728-496
Catarman: Greatbuys Gen. Merch., G. H. Del Pilar St., Brgy. Mabolo, Catarman 6400 No. Samar– (055) 500-9120 / 0929-626-0036
Cebu: Archdiocesan Book Center, Patria de Cebu Bldg., P. Burgos cor. Legaspi St., Cebu City– (032) 253-3642
Davao: Acasia St., Juna Subd., Brgy. Bucana 76-A, Matina, Davao City 0917-705-4617
Masbate: Lilian– (056) 333-2302, 0918-965-8123
Tacloban: Godsend Grocery, Real cor. Sampaguita St., Tacloban– (053) 325-7265
Tagaytay: Don & Rose– 0933-856-8661, 0977-853-8269
Tarlac: Teresita– 0922-888-4109
Tuguegarao: Elmer– 0917-564-3357
Zamboanga: Our Lady of Pilar Retreat & Lay Formation Center, View Island, Mercedes, Zamboanga City– 0906-780-4787

5. Distributors (International)

Hong Kong: Gigi Tse– 9318-8212

If you wish to subscribe or become a distributor, kindly contact our office.

The **kindle** edition of **The Anawim Way** is also available at **amazon**.com.

THE ANAWIM WAY

SUBSCRIPTION FORM

NAME _____

MAILING ADDRESS _____

EMAIL _____

TEL. NO. _____ MOBILE NO. _____

Starting Month/Issue of Subscription: ☐ Current   ☐ Next

Please indicate how many sets you wish to receive: (1 set=8 issues/year)

☐ Annual Subscription

____ Metro Manila Philippines ₱1,200   ____ International - subject
____ Provincial Philippines ₱1,400   to current postal rates

☐ Gift Subscription

From: _____

Address: _____

Email: _____ Tel. Nos.: _____

Kindly fill up this form and send to the Philippine Anawim Center
(Email: manila@anawim.com; Viber: 0918-826-2946;
Messenger: @PonderingTheWordTheAnawimWay)

PAYMENT INSTRUCTIONS

Deposit online to **Anawim Community, Inc.**

Peso Savings Acct.   **Dollar Savings Acct.**

Banco de Oro, BF Resort Branch   PSBank, BF Resort Branch
No. 0064 6008 3079   No. 1521 3000 0802
Swift Code: BNORPHMMXXX   Swift Code: PHSBPHMMXXX

NOTE: Subscription fees do not include bank charges for Provincial and International deposits.

IMPORTANT: text/Viber deposit details to 0918-826-2946 /
0917-656-2021 or call (02) 8872-2021

THE ANAWIM WAY

SUBSCRIPTION FORM

NAME

ADDRESS

CITY   STATE   ZIP CODE

COUNTRY   EMAIL

PHONE NO.

NO. OF SUBCRIPTIONS (1 subscription = 8 issues/year)

Kindly fill up this form and mail to **P.O. Box 207, Oxford, NJ 07863**
or fax it to **(908) 453-3786**
If this is a gift, please fill in the ff. information for the recipient:

NAME

ADDRESS

CITY   STATE   ZIP CODE

COUNTRY   EMAIL

PHONE NO.

SUBSCRIPTION COST AND PAYMENT INSTRUCTIONS

NO CASH PAYMENTS ACCEPTED

USA: US$64. Send checks or money order payable to Anawim Community Inc., P.O. Box 207, Oxford, NJ 07863. Or use the credit card instructions below.

CANADA: US$76. Use the credit card instructions below.

TO PAY BY DEBIT/CREDIT CARD, please use the payments page on our website. All credit card payments are processed securely by PayPal.
http://www.anawim.com/payments